The International Politics of the New Asia Pacific

The International Politics of the New Asia Pacific

Derek McDougall

LYNNE RIENNER PUBLISHERS

ISEAS

Published in the United States of America in 1997 by
Lynne Rienner Publishers, Inc.
1800 30th Street, Boulder, Colorado 80301

and in the United Kingdom by
Lynne Rienner Publishers, Inc.
3 Henrietta Street, Covent Garden, London WC2E 8LU

Published in the Republic of Singapore by the
Institute of Southeast Asian Studies (www.iseas.ac.sg)
Heng Mui Keng Terrace, Pasir Panjang, Singapore 119596
(for distribution in the People's Republic of China, and exclusive distribution in Southeast Asia, Taiwan, and South Korea)

Library of Congress Cataloging-in-Publication Data
McDougall, Derek, 1945–
    The international politics of the new Asia Pacific / by Derek McDougall.
        p. cm.
    Includes bibliographical references and index.
    ISBN 1-55587-723-0 (hardcover : alk. paper).
    ISBN 1-55587-728-1 (pbk. : alk. paper).
    1. East Asia—Foreign relations. 2. Asia, Southeastern—Foreign relations. 3. Pacific Area—Foreign relations. I. Title.
JX1569.M38 1997
327.5'009'045—dc21   97-13573
                                                                      CIP

British Cataloguing in Publication Data
A Cataloguing in Publication record for this book
is available from the British Library.

Printed and bound in the United States of America

The paper used in this publication meets the requirements of the American National Standard for Permanence of Paper for Printed Library Materials Z39.48-1984.

5 4 3 2 1

CONTENTS

III Major Power Relationships

IV Other Regional Actors

V Conclusion

PREFACE

This book studies international politics in the new Asia Pacific—that is, Asia Pacific in the aftermath of the Cold War. The discussion of events covers the period from the late 1980s up to the end of 1996. The assumption underlying the book is that one way of coming to terms with the international politics of the new Asia Pacific is to focus on the roles of the major powers, defined here as the United States, China, and Japan. Although essentially a power in decline during this period, the USSR and post-Soviet Russia are also given attention. So much political, economic, and military power is concentrated in these states that a study of their roles and relationships can provide important insights into the dynamics of international politics in the region.

The definition of Asia Pacific used in this book covers Northeast Asia (Japan, China [including Taiwan], North and South Korea, Pacific Russia); Southeast Asia (Indonesia, Malaysia, Singapore, Brunei, the Philippines, Thailand, Vietnam, Cambodia, Laos, Burma); Australia, New Zealand, Papua New Guinea, and other South Pacific island states and territories; and the United States and Canada in their Pacific aspects. In practice the emphasis is on East Asia, but the term "Asia Pacific" does allow for a broader orientation.

The book is organized as follows: The introduction sketches the broad international context relating to the end of the Cold War and the pattern of international politics in the post–Cold War era, with particular reference to implications for Asia Pacific. Theoretical perspectives that might have a bearing on the roles of the major powers are introduced—realism, liberalism or liberal institutionalism, and a culture-based approach. Part II considers the general roles played by the United States, China, Japan, and the USSR and Russia in post–Cold War Asia Pacific, and Part III takes up the key major power relationships in the region. Part IV examines the involvement of the major powers with other actors in the region, particularly North and South Korea, Vietnam, and the ASEAN states. Issues such as Korean reunification, the North Korean nuclear issue, the Cambodian peace process, and the South China Sea are discussed in these chapters. The conclusion considers how the themes emphasized in the three main sections of the book relate to the theoretical perspectives outlined in the introductory chapter.

Inevitably, not every international issue in the new Asia Pacific can be covered in a book of this scope. The Taiwan and Hong Kong issues, for example, are examined only in the context of broader relationships. Similarly, regionalism is not dealt with as an issue in its own right, although there is some discussion of ASEAN as a regional organization and also reference to more recent developments such as APEC and the ASEAN Regional Forum. From the perspective of the roles played by the major powers, however, most of the significant issues are addressed.

In a project such as this, there are many people to acknowledge. I would like to thank Lynne Rienner Publishers for the confidence they have shown in me in publishing the book and for their assistance during the production process. Joseph Camilleri (School of Politics, La Trobe University) and Colin Campbell (Public Policy Program, Georgetown University) enabled me to have visiting status with their institutions when I first embarked on the project. Mark Considine was helpful in his role as head of the Department of Political Science at the University of Melbourne during the time I worked on this book. Other people in the department who helped me directly or indirectly were Jamie Anderson, Chris Barrett, Nick Bisley, Justin Bokor, Ann Capling, Katrina Gorjanicyn, Andrew MacDonald, Philomena Murray, Grant Parsons, and Peter Shearman. Craig Lonsdale, David Lutz, Rita De Amicis, Wendy Ruffles, and Natalie Madaffari came to my rescue on numerous occasions. I would also like to thank my students in 166-208/308, The International Politics of the Asia Pacific Region, for helping me to think about a lot of the issues discussed in this book. Last but not least, my family (Anne, Kirsty, Ros) have managed to put up with me while I worked on this book and I thank them for that.

—D. McD.

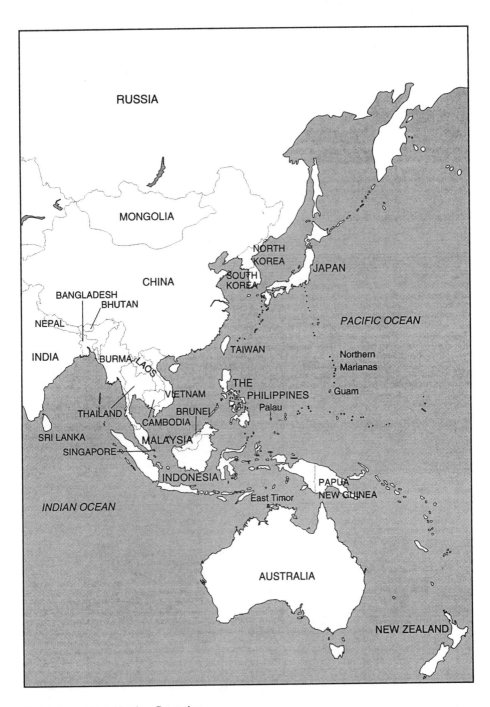

East Asia and Neighboring Countries

PART I

INTRODUCTION

1

A New World
and Asia Pacific Order

The focus of this book is the changing pattern of international politics in the Asia Pacific region in the period after the Cold War, with particular reference to the roles of the United States, China, and Japan. Attention is also given to the role of Russia and to regional situations involving Korea, Indochina, and the member states of ASEAN (Association of Southeast Asian Nations). To place the changing pattern into a broader context, this introductory chapter sketches some of the major changes at the global level that have had implications for Asia Pacific, as well as theoretical perspectives that are helpful for understanding the international politics of the region in the post–Cold War period.

The End of the Cold War

How did the end of the Cold War affect the Asia Pacific region?

The major arena at the onset of the Cold War was Europe. Although the ostensible reason for the adoption of the containment doctrine (Truman Doctrine) by the United States in March 1947 was the situation in Greece, the broader context of this development was the post–World War II situation in Europe as a whole. The USSR dominated Eastern Europe and controlled an occupation zone in eastern Germany. The countries of Western Europe were democratically ruled but were seen as vulnerable to Soviet pressure because of straitened economic circumstances and, in some instances, the political strength of local Communist parties. The containment doctrine was an indication that the United States would commit itself to resisting any extension of Soviet influence; substance was given to the doctrine by the announcement of the Marshall Plan in June 1947 and the establishment of NATO (North Atlantic Treaty Organization) in 1949.

Europe played the central role in the onset of the Cold War, but Asia Pacific was soon affected. The civil war between Communists and Nationalists in China came to be seen in a Cold War perspective. Although the United States did not intervene early or decisively in favor of the Nationalists, it came to offer overt support for Chiang Kai-shek. The punitive policy of the early occupation in Japan was superseded by a more lenient approach designed to make Japan a bastion of support for the U.S. policy of containment. Following the Communist victory on the Chinese mainland in 1949, containment in Asia was directed primarily against China. This was reinforced with the onset, in June 1950, of the Korean War, which could have been interpreted as a local conflict, but which the United States chose to see in terms of its broader Cold War strategy. South Korea was preserved as one of the mainstays of the U.S. military presence in Asia Pacific.

In Southeast Asia, the Philippines had historically been the linchpin of U.S. involvement, and this involvement was broadened considerably during the Cold War period. In Vietnam, containment led to U.S. support for France in its war with the Communist Vietminh, particularly after 1950. The United States was reluctant to accept the Geneva Agreement of 1954, which had provided a basis for settling the conflict, and instead took steps to establish SEATO (Southeast Asia Treaty Organization) as an anti-Communist regional organization. In the 1960s and early 1970s, the United States undertook a major war in support of the embattled Saigon government in South Vietnam.

When the United States failed to achieve its objectives in Vietnam, the Nixon administration in particular became more open to attempts to provide a new basis for U.S. strategy in Asia Pacific. The Guam doctrine of 1969 was an indication that the United States would avoid direct involvement in major ground wars in the future, and at the same time there was an attempt to come to an accommodation with China, which had previously been viewed as the most important adversary of the United States in Asia Pacific. The Shanghai communiqué of February 1972 symbolized the new basis of that relationship.

While these changes in U.S. strategy in Asia Pacific were occurring, the Nixon administration was attempting to achieve détente on a broader level with the USSR. SALT I, in 1972, regulating U.S. and Soviet intercontinental nuclear arms, was an attempt to stabilize the nuclear relationship between the two powers, and the Helsinki Accords in 1973 and West Germany's Ostpolitik in the early 1970s also contributed to a reduction of tensions in Europe. But by the late 1970s, the attempt at détente had been superseded by a return to Cold War tensions. The Soviet intervention in Afghanistan in late 1979 was perhaps the clearest evidence of the deteriorating Soviet-U.S. relationship at this time. Ronald Reagan assumed office in early 1981 intent on standing firm against the "evil empire."

In the Asia Pacific region, the "new" Cold War reinforced the Sino-U.S. accommodation: A concern about Soviet expansionism gave China and the United States an additional interest in common. Vietnamese intervention in Cambodia in late 1978 was the main manifestation of the new Cold War. Although Vietnam instigated the intervention to overthrow the Pol Pot regime, China in particular saw Vietnam as an ally of the USSR. Over the next decade, China, the United States, and the ASEAN countries acted together to oppose Vietnamese intervention.

The end of the Cold War is often associated with the emergence in 1985 of Soviet leader Mikhail Gorbachev. Gorbachev's commitment to democratization made it untenable for the USSR to continue its domination of Eastern Europe. Released from their obligation to maintain Communist governments, the various countries of Eastern Europe underwent a transition to post-Communist governments throughout 1989. November 1989 saw the fall of the Berlin Wall, the most powerful symbol of the Cold War division of Europe. By October 1990, German unification had been achieved. Democratization in the USSR did not bring the economic renewal Gorbachev had hoped for; instead, it released pent-up forces of ethnic nationalism. By December 1991, the USSR had collapsed and was replaced by a number of independent states, the most important of which was Russia.

In Asia Pacific, the end of the Cold War was less dramatic. The Soviet-U.S. confrontation—a particular source of tension—was no longer relevant, and the nature of Soviet (and subsequently Russian) involvement in the region changed. Gorbachev began to give more attention to relationships that might bring economic benefits to the USSR. The Soviet Union continued its attempts from the early 1980s to improve relations with China, but its dispute with Japan over the Northern Territories remained an obstacle to improved Soviet-Japanese relations. South Korea was able to develop a better relationship with the USSR, but Vietnam, previously aligned to the USSR, became less important to Moscow in the new scheme of things.

The end of the Cold War also had an effect on various multilateral situations in which the USSR was involved. It was a significant factor, for example, in facilitating a settlement of the Indochina conflict, and on the Korean peninsula, North Korea could no longer look to Moscow as a possible source of support. In terms of the broader strategic patterns in the region, the United States assumed a stronger position vis-à-vis the USSR, as did Japan and China. With its various economic and political problems, post-Soviet Russia could not be regarded as a major power in Asia Pacific in the way that the USSR had been.

After the Cold War

With the end of the Cold War, new patterns have emerged in international relations at the global level. One feature particularly relevant to international politics in Asia Pacific is the diminished significance of Russia as the major successor state to the USSR, and more broadly, the nature of great power relationships in the post–Cold War world. The collapse of the USSR has not necessarily meant that the United States has become the dominant power in a unipolar world. Although the United States is clearly the single most important power, other powers play a major role both at a regional level and on the broader international stage. Most important among the Asian countries are China, Japan, and India; Germany, France, Britain, and Russia (which is primarily European) are the most important European powers.

To say that the relationships among these powers are characterized by multipolarity would be an oversimplification. "Multipolarity" implies the existence of adversarial relationships, and although these countries differ on a number of issues, they have not necessarily been engaged in long-term conflict. "Multipolarity" is only a satisfactory term if it recognizes the fluidity of many of these relationships. "Uni-multipolarity" has been suggested as a better term because it allows for both the primary role of the United States and the existence of multiple power centers.[1]

"Concert of powers"—a term that recalls the Concert of Europe, which functioned for much of the nineteenth century after the Congress of Vienna in 1815—has been suggested as another way of characterizing the relationships of the major powers in the aftermath of the Cold War. Without major long-term adversarial relationships among the great powers, it has been possible to achieve a certain level of cooperation among them in dealing with international issues. The most obvious example of such cooperation is the 1991 Gulf War. The support (or, at the very least, acquiescence) of the other great powers enabled a U.S.-led coalition to take military action against Iraq under UN auspices and to thus force Iraq's withdrawal from Kuwait.

This suggests another feature of international relations in the post–Cold War era: the much more prominent role of the UN. During the Cold War, the conflict between the superpowers meant that they were unwilling to support UN intervention in various situations if such intervention was seen as detrimental to their own interests. The fact that each superpower in the Security Council possesses a veto provided an effective means to frustrate UN intervention. UN military intervention ("peace enforcement" under Article VII) occurred in Korea in 1950 only because the USSR was boycotting Security Council meetings at the time. Peacekeeping under Article VI was usually confined to situations in which the superpowers deemed such involvement not contrary to their own interests.

The concert of powers that has emerged in the aftermath of the Cold War has opened the way for more extensive UN involvement. The Gulf War is a major example of the UN's peace enforcement, but there are many more examples of its peacekeeping efforts, among which Namibia (1989) and Cambodia (1992–1993) might be rated the most successful. UN intervention in support of humanitarian operations, as in Somalia, Bosnia, and Rwanda, has been more problematic. Whatever their outcomes, these operations would far less likely have been mounted without some consensus among the major powers. Nevertheless, it remains to be seen whether the faith placed in the UN during the early years of the post–Cold War era will continue.

Another dimension of the changing relationships among the major powers is the increased emphasis on the role of economics. Some commentators speak of geopolitics being superseded by geoeconomics. Traditional military power appears less important as economic factors loom increasingly large. Whereas the United States is the leading power in both fields, the rising importance of geoeconomics has enhanced the roles of both Japan and Germany. The importance of geoeconomics is also reflected in a shift toward regional economic groupings. The European Union is the most integrated of the regional economic blocs, but APEC (Asia-Pacific Economic Cooperation) and NAFTA (North American Free Trade Agreement) also have the potential to emerge as blocs should the liberal international trading system come under threat.

The emphasis on regionalization is also relevant to the countries previously termed "the Third World." In the post–Cold War period, this term has become increasingly less appropriate as many of these countries can no longer be described as poor or developing. The most obvious indication of the regionalization process in Asia Pacific is the emergence of the NICs (newly industrializing countries). Some Latin American countries have experienced similar economic growth, but African countries have generally been less successful. Each region tends to have a range of countries at different levels of economic development, and there is less to hold the developing countries together than in the past (through such organizations as the Nonaligned Movement). Regionalization has meant that extraregional powers are far less likely to become involved in developments within particular regions than they were during the Cold War.

A major cause of conflict in the post–Cold War world has been ethnic nationalism. In many cases, the Cold War caused such conflict to be suppressed, particularly in the USSR and Communist-ruled Eastern Europe. Democratization has unleashed the ethnic conflicts that authoritarian governments could more easily control. The conflicts in the former Yugoslavia are the most obvious example of this phenomenon, but there have also been many conflicts in parts of the former USSR, such as the Caucasus, including Chechnya. A number of situations requiring UN involvement have been caused by ethnic conflict.

The extent to which Asia Pacific has been affected by these various trends in the post–Cold War world has varied. In terms of its relationships with major powers, the region is most affected by the United States, China, and Japan, the powers directly involved in Asia Pacific. The shift to geo-economics in the region is evident in the role that Japan is playing there. The nature of the emerging security relationships in Asia Pacific is one aspect of the dynamics of regionalization. The most obvious example of UN involvement in Asia Pacific in the post–Cold War period is in Cambodia, but such involvement has not been a pervasive feature of the region's post–Cold War international relations. Finally, Asia Pacific has been less affected by ethnic nationalism than has Europe.

Theoretical Perspectives

An examination of Asia Pacific's relationships with the United States, China, and Japan suggests three possible perspectives on the general character of international politics in the region: realist, liberal, and culturalistic. The first and second perspectives have developed in the context of the Western study of international relations. The third attempts to take into account the impact of particular states' cultures on the conduct of international relations. I will elaborate briefly on each approach before considering its application to the Asia Pacific region.

Realism

One version of realism can be traced back to the writings of people such as Thucydides, Machiavelli, and Hobbes. A leading exponent of its modern version was Hans Morgenthau.[2] Realists focus on power and conflict as the dynamic elements of international politics and pay particular attention to the military dimensions of power. States are seen as motivated by the pursuit of their national interests; in pursuing those interests, states are influenced by the prevailing "balance of power." Although the concept of "balance of power" can be interpreted in various ways, it may be defined as the way in which power is distributed within international politics, particularly among the major states. The concept also has a prescriptive dimension, in that a state might try to improve its position in relation to the existing balance.[3] (The term "balance" here is clearly a misnomer.)

A more recent version of realism is "neorealism." Kenneth Waltz is often considered its leading exponent.[4] Neorealism is not so much concerned with the alleged metaphysical dimensions of power as with the logical character of state behavior in an anarchical world. This theory contends that a major influence on a state's behavior is the fact that it has to look to its survival in a state of anarchy. Neorealists believe that the structure of the system enables them to predict the likelihood of a state's actions given that particular state's location in this anarchical world.

Liberalism or Liberal Institutionalism

One can consider liberalism or liberal institutionalism as an alternative to realism and neorealism.[5] This approach puts more emphasis on the economic dimensions of power. The state remains important but less so than in the realist paradigm, and more attention is given to the ways in which states cooperate as well as compete. In this view, "anarchy" is too simplistic a term to use to characterize international politics; "complex interdependence" is suggested as an alternative. The latter term points to the way in which the various actors in the world (including states) are linked in a variety of ways. Because liberalism emphasizes the role of "low politics," liberal theorists pay more attention to the "everyday" character of these interactions and distinguish them from the more dramatic developments in the "high politics" of realism. The term "institutionalism" suggests liberals' belief that the development of international institutions will lead to new configurations in international politics. This development is seen as further evidence of the complex character of international interdependence.

A "Culturalistic" Approach

Both realism and liberalism focus primarily on the roles of various actors in international politics. Realism presents a "billiard board" model of international politics; neorealism even more so. Liberalism has a more complex view of the way in which actors interact in international politics; the state tends to be less reified than it is in realism and neorealism. At the same time, liberalism's focus is still very much on the general character of the relationships within the system. Both approaches allow little room for the role of factors that might be specific to particular actors. For this reason, a third, "culturalistic" approach might be suggested.

The culturalistic approach draws attention to the way in which factors specific to particular states exert an influence on their international behavior and thus have some bearing on the general character of international politics. Although the term "culture" suggests the general nature of the factors at work, issues concerning domestic politics and the economy may also be grouped under this heading. Lucian Pye has suggested that contrary to the view that power is "a single basic phenomenon which operate[s] according to universal principles, regardless of time, place or culture . . . people at different times and in different places have had quite different understandings of the concept of power."[6] The implication for international relations is that the interaction of states will be affected by the assumptions that the people conducting their policies bring to the task. International relations thus becomes more than working out the "logic of the system" or determining the consequences of increasing interdependence. The character of international relations will vary depending on the particular states and forces at work.[7]

Assessment in Relation to Asia Pacific

In the light of the specific relationships studied in this book, I argue that although realism and liberalism may explain some developments in post–Cold War Asia Pacific, the culturalistic dimension must also be emphasized. From the perspective of realism, one can see a certain power-balancing logic at work in the Asia Pacific region. Nevertheless, it would be difficult to speak in terms of a well-defined balance-of-power system as such. In the 1950s and 1960s, there was a "balance" between China on the one side and the United States, supported by Japan, on the other. Beginning in the 1950s, there was also an antagonistic relationship between China and the USSR. In the early 1970s, the situation changed once again when China and the United States reached a rapprochement. This did not mean that China and the United States were formally aligned, but the effect was to leave the USSR relatively more isolated than it had been previously.

In the post–Cold War era, the relationships among the major powers have been more fluid than in the past. Instead of long-term antagonisms among the major powers in the region, there tends to be a mixture of conflict and cooperation. Japan and the United States are formally aligned through a security treaty, but they still have considerable disagreements over economic issues. China and the United States have been in conflict over various issues but have also cooperated on others. A similar combination of cooperation and conflict seems to be at work in relations between China and Japan; the proximity of the two powers may be another important factor in the development of their relationship.

A power-balancing dimension may also be present in post–Cold War Sino-Russian and Japanese-Russian relations. In the latter case, the relatively difficult relationship is in some respects a continuation of a long-term antagonism. In the former case, the rapprochement of 1989 was complicated by the collapse of the USSR in 1991. Nevertheless, both China and Russia have been able to cooperate on a number of issues, and the previous antagonism has been largely superseded.

The realist perspective has some relevance in understanding the involvement of the major powers in regions of conflict. Although local factors are undoubtedly important to the dynamics of such regions, the external dimension is even more critical. Two important examples of the critical external dimension are the Korean War, which effectively developed into a Sino-U.S. war, and the way in which the United States went to war in Vietnam in the 1960s. In the post–Cold War era, the involvement of the United States, Japan, China, and Russia has had an important bearing on developments in the Korean peninsula. The improved relationship between China and the USSR was an important factor in initiating the Cambodian peace process. The positions of the United States and Japan have significantly influenced the way in which Vietnam has attempted to reorient itself in the post–Cold War world.

In comparison with realism, liberalism emphasizes the importance of the economic dimension and interdependence as keys to understanding the dynamics of post–Cold War international politics in the Asia Pacific region. Thus, from a liberal perspective, the previously noted fluidity in the relationships of the major powers in the region derives from the emphasis placed on economic issues instead of security issues. Fluctuations in both Sino-U.S. and Japanese-U.S. relations have primarily been related to differing approaches to economic issues. At the same time (and this applies to Sino-Japanese relations as well), interdependence is reflected in the importance of each of the major powers to the economies of the others. The importance of the economic dimension is also reflected in the relationships the major powers, particularly Japan, have with other states in the region, perhaps most obviously with the ASEAN region but also with South Korea. Even with Vietnam, where security issues in a broad sense seem preeminent, the economic dimension of external involvement should not be overlooked.

The institutionalism associated with the liberal perspective seems relatively underdeveloped in Asia Pacific. As the major regional organization for Southeast Asia, ASEAN does not include any of the major powers. The major institutional developments involving the major powers in Asia Pacific are APEC and the ASEAN Regional Forum. APEC is normally described as a "forum" rather than a regional organization as such. The ASEAN Regional Forum, which has a more explicit focus on security issues, is also not a regional organization but simply an annual gathering of representatives from most of the states in the region.

What realism and liberalism share is a belief that the general processes underlying international politics are the same irrespective of the part of the globe one is examining. The culturalistic perspective, in contrast, argues that there are variations in the general processes because the cultural influences at work in different regions often vary. As suggested previously, "culture" in this context includes other general factors concerning states, such as domestic politics and the economy. To assess the role played by the United States, China, and Japan in post–Cold War Asia Pacific, one needs to examine the role these general factors play in the foreign policies of each of these states and how this role in turn affects the general character of international politics in the region.

In the United States, both the realist and liberal perspectives influence U.S. behavior in the region. The emphasis varies depending on the administration in office; the Bush administration was perhaps more realist and the Clinton administration is more liberal (neither being exclusively one or the other).

China's preoccupation historically as well as in the post–Cold War period has been with status. The nation's assertive stance on various issues is not necessarily realism at work, but may derive from the particular view of its place in the world that Chinese culture emphasizes. The influence of culture is also a key to understanding Japan's role. Whereas on one level the emphasis on the economic dimension and interdependence in Japanese foreign policy might be seen as substantiating the liberal perspective, Japan's failure to re-create itself as another great power along traditional lines could be viewed as the outcome of its own particular historical experience. World War II (including the use of atomic weapons against Japan), the impact of that war on other countries in the region, and the success of "economism" in providing high living standards for the Japanese people all helped Japan develop a role in the region that emphasizes the economic dimension, a relatively "quiet" diplomacy, and the nonuse of force.

Insofar as these cultural perspectives do play a key role in determining the behavior of the major powers, they should be emphasized when one is attempting to characterize the nature of international politics in post–Cold War Asia Pacific. One might begin by examining the impact of cultural factors on key bilateral relationships and from there move to generalizations about the significance of the cultural dimension for the international politics of the region as a whole. In developing this approach, one need not agree with Samuel Huntington's argument that the "clash of civilizations" provides the underlying dynamic of post–Cold War international politics.[8] Asia Pacific is not simply a region where the fault lines are based on categories such as "Confucian," "Japanese," "Islamic," or "Western" civilizations. Within any one civilization there can often be significant differences, as the conflicts and tensions between China and Vietnam or between the two Koreas show only too clearly.

It would be oversimplified to attribute the political differences between China and Japan or between the United States and Japan solely to underlying civilizational differences. At the same time, one can argue that cultural factors do have some bearing on the way in which states pursue their international relations in the region. Issues such as human rights and different perceptions concerning social and economic organization illustrate this point. The fact that these kinds of issues have played an important role in the international politics of the region provides some indication of the significance of cultural factors.

This book argues that the roles played by the United States, China, and Japan provide an important insight into the dynamics of international politics in post–Cold War Asia Pacific. The relevance of the different theoretical perspectives varies according to the relationship or situation being considered. The volume also examines Russia's role in the region, even though Russia's influence in the post–Cold War period has declined. Having sketched the global context in Part I, I now turn to the role of these powers. Part II looks at the general approaches adopted by the four powers and the factors affecting those approaches. Part III focuses on relationships among the major powers in Asia Pacific, and Part IV considers the significance of some other regional situations, with particular reference to the involvement of the major powers.

Notes

1. Huntington, "America's Changing Strategic Interests," p. 6.
2. See Morgenthau and Thompson, *Politics Among Nations.*
3. The different meanings of "balance of power" have been discussed in Haas, "The Balance of Power."
4. See Waltz, *Theory of International Politics.*
5. See Keohane and Nye, *Power and Interdependence.*
6. Pye, *Asian Power and Politics,* p. 19.
7. On this point, see Solomon, "Political Culture and Diplomacy in the Twenty-first Century."
8. Huntington, "The Clash of Civilizations" and *The Clash of Civilizations and the Remaking of World Order.*

PART II

THE MAJOR POWERS IN THE REGION

2

THE UNITED STATES

Competing Perceptions

To comprehend the general approach taken by the United States toward post–Cold War Asia Pacific, it is necessary to consider relevant domestic political and economic developments. In the 1980s, U.S. policy in Asia Pacific and other regions was subject to competing domestic perceptions. On the one hand, there was "declinism," or the view that the United States was declining relative to other major powers. On the other hand, there was the belief that with the end of the Cold War and the demise of the Soviet Union the United States should be in a stronger position. The interplay of these competing perceptions has been an important influence on U.S. foreign policy in the post–Cold War era.

Paul Kennedy's thesis about "the rise and fall of great powers" focused on U.S. concern about decline.[1] Kennedy argued that great powers are subject to a process of decline because they tend to overcommit themselves in defense of their interests. The economic cost of overcommitment weakens the basis upon which the particular state has become a great power in the first place. Just as it had led to the decline of great powers in earlier eras, "imperial overstretch" was seen as weakening the position of the United States in the 1980s. The United States was also experiencing decline in relation to other great powers. As the only major power to have emerged strengthened from World War II, the United States was clearly in a dominant economic position in the early postwar period. Subsequently, it remained the single most important power in economic terms until the emergence of other powers such as Japan. Between 1960 and 1980, the U.S. share of gross world product declined from 25.9 percent to 21.5 percent, whereas Japan's share rose from 4.5 percent to 9.0 percent.[2]

Although relative economic decline appeared inevitable given the emergence of other powers, the economic problems of the United States were exacerbated by the policies of the Reagan administration during the 1980s. Elected on a platform of strengthening the defense posture of the United States in relation to the USSR, Reagan proceeded both to expand U.S. defense spending and to cut taxes. At the same time, domestic programs were not reduced significantly. Economic growth in the United States was not sufficient to support the administration's policies. Consequently, the United States had to borrow heavily to cover the gap. Instead of being the world's greatest creditor nation, the United States became the world's greatest debtor nation. Between 1980 and 1985, the U.S. federal deficit rose from U.S. $59.6 billion to U.S. $202.8 billion.[3] The need to improve economic performance and to address the issue of the federal deficit has been one of the major considerations affecting U.S. foreign policy in the post–Cold War era. In Asia Pacific, where the balance of trade has consistently been against the United States, the United States has tended to lessen its commitment to liberal trading principles in favor of "managed trade" or at least some protectionist measures.

This weakened economic situation has made it difficult for the United States to capitalize on its role as the only remaining "superpower." In addition, there has been considerable support for the view that, with the end of the Cold War, the United States should assume the role of a "normal country." Some political elements even support neoisolationism. Many are reluctant to become involved in situations that might put U.S. lives at risk. Such views have made U.S. foreign policy equivocal in a number of instances.

Impact of Domestic Politics

In the sphere of domestic politics, the post–Cold War period has covered the presidencies of George Bush (Republican) and Bill Clinton (Democrat). Bush's first year in office, 1989, coincided with the collapse of Communist power in Eastern Europe. During his tenure, Bush attempted to maintain the role of international leadership that the United States had assumed in the Cold War era. His most notable success was the U.S. victory in the Gulf War against Iraq in early 1991. Bush was able to win support from a coalition of countries and to conduct the conflict under UN auspices. Despite initial caution in the United States, the way in which Bush pursued his goals won him widespread public support. U.S. casualties were minimal, and the United States was able to take advantage of its immense superiority in technological warfare.

In spite of his success in the Gulf War, Bush could not carry through his popularity to the 1992 presidential election. Clinton's election slogan, "It's the economy, stupid," symbolized his commitment to give priority to domestic policy as opposed to foreign policy. Bush was widely perceived to have misjudged the balance between the two areas. At the very least, it was clear that Clinton would more strongly emphasize making U.S. foreign policy serve domestic ends.

Once in office, Clinton found that he had to give considerable attention to the United States' international role. Although he focused on economic issues with Western Europe and Japan in particular, he also had to face broader security questions. What long-term security role was the United States prepared to undertake in both Europe and Asia Pacific? How should the alliance structures developed during the Cold War be adapted to accommodate the changed circumstances of Russia and Eastern Europe? Under what circumstances, if any, should the United States intervene in crises relating to ethnic nationalism, "failed states," or the suppression of democracy (crises affecting the former Yugoslavia, Somalia, and Haiti, respectively)?

Clinton's general inclination seemed to be to limit the international role of the United States. In issues of international trade, he found himself caught between his own commitment to free trade and pressures for managed trade. Clinton's development of policy often appeared uncoordinated, and his own standing with the public was frequently under threat. Insofar as Clinton committed himself to particular positions, he had to fight hard to win support both within Congress and among the general public.

Asia Pacific Strategy

It is within this context that U.S. policy toward post–Cold War Asia Pacific developed. However, that policy was also shaped by the Cold War involvement of the United States in the region. The containment doctrine of 1947 had provided the original rationale for U.S. strategy in Asia Pacific. The United States aimed to prevent the expansion of the USSR and subsequently the People's Republic of China (PRC) into neighboring areas. An important basis for U.S. strategy was provided by the security agreements the United States concluded with a number of countries in the region: Japan (1951); Australia and New Zealand (ANZUS, 1951); Taiwan (the Republic of China, 1954); and South Korea (the Republic of Korea, 1954). Thailand and the Philippines were formally linked to the U.S.-dominated security system in the region by the Manila Treaty of 1954, which provided the basis for the establishment of the Southeast Asia Treaty Organization in the same year. Although SEATO disbanded in 1977, the Manila Treaty remained.

The containment doctrine was a major factor leading to U.S. involvement in the Vietnam War in the 1960s and early 1970s. Well before the end of that war in 1975, the international system in Asia Pacific had been moving increasingly in a multipolar direction; the emergence of China as a major power was perhaps the most significant development in this respect. Conflict between the USSR and China had assumed increasingly important proportions since the 1950s. Although it took much longer for the United States to respond to China's new status, the Shanghai communiqué of 1972

symbolized a new direction in U.S. policy. The United States was now prepared to develop a relationship with China as part of its general strategy in
the region. In 1979 the new relationship with the PRC led to the severing of
U.S. diplomatic relations with Taiwan and the abrogation of the 1954 security treaty. The United States' improved relations with the USSR during the
Gorbachev era in the late 1980s made the containment doctrine seem even
more a relic of an earlier age.

The military basis of U.S. involvement in Asia Pacific security derives
from the earlier containment period. Japan and South Korea have an important role in providing forward bases for U.S. forces; the Philippines had the
same role until 1991. Australia provides surveillance and communications
facilities for use by the United States. In addition, the United States is itself
a Pacific power. Apart from its military facilities on the West Coast and in
Alaska, the United States uses bases in Hawaii and Guam to project its military power in the Asia Pacific region. During the 1980s, considerable
attention was given to the "maritime strategy" as the basis of U.S. military
involvement in the region.[4] The United States' maritime superiority was
regarded as the most effective way of containing Soviet power in the
region, and it also provided a starting point for deploying U.S. military
power in other situations should this be necessary.

The extent of U.S. military deployment in Asia Pacific is indicated by
the following figures, which show personnel under U.S. Pacific Command
(with headquarters in Hawaii) as of mid-1996:[5]

Alaska
Army: 6,750
Air Force: 9,530
Total: 16,280

Hawaii
Army: 21,450
Air Force: 4,525
Navy: 19,500
Marines: 8,200
Total: 53,675

Singapore
Navy: 100 (approximate)
Air Force: 40
Total: 140

Japan
Army: 1,600
Air Force: 14,760
Navy: 7,300
Marines: 21,000
Total: 44,660

South Korea
Army: 27,250
Air Force: 8,660
Total: 35,910

Guam
Air Force: 2,100
Navy: 4,600
Total: 6,700

Australia
Navy: 100 (approximate)

Diego Garcia (Indian Ocean)
Navy: 900

Grand Total: 158,365

The Bush Administration (1989–1993)

Given the substantial U.S. military involvement in Asia Pacific, how did U.S. thinking about region-wide security concerns evolve during the period of the Bush and Clinton administrations? William Tow has argued that the United States has pursued "a 'Dominant Player' extended deterrence posture": Its goal has been "to preserve American strategic access to and influence within [the Asia Pacific] region as part of Washington's global extended deterrence strategy."[6] Based largely on a "global-realist" perspective, this strategy has been criticized on various grounds, but Tow in particular argues that it gives insufficient attention to the views of regional states on security issues: "The U.S. should instead become more sensitive to its tendency to underestimate or disregard altogether the individual security interests of individual Asia-Pacific security actors."[7] With the disappearance of the USSR as a global threat, it is interesting to consider whether U.S. strategy in Asia Pacific has moved in the direction of the "convergent deterrence" advocated by Tow by giving more attention to the views of regional states.

In an article in *Foreign Affairs* in 1991, Secretary of State James Baker characterized U.S. involvement in Asia Pacific as follows:

> To visualize the architecture of U.S. engagement in the region, imagine a fan spread wide, with its base in North America and radiating west across the Pacific. The central support is the U.S.-Japan alliance, the key connection for the security structure and the new Pacific partnership we are seeking. To the north, one spoke represents our alliance with the Republic of Korea. To the south, others extend to our treaty allies—the Association of Southeast Asian Nations (ASEAN) countries of the Philippines and Thailand. Further south a spoke extends to Australia—an important, staunch economic, political and security partner. Connecting these spokes is the fabric of shared economic interests now given form by the Asia-

Pacific Economic Cooperation (APEC) process. Within this construct, new political and economic relationships offer additional support for a system of cooperative action by groups of Pacific nations to address both residual problems and emerging challenges.[8]

Echoing Tow's convergent deterrence strategy, Baker wrote of "the multiplicity of security concerns that differ from country to country and within the subregions of this vast area."[9] In this respect, the flexibility of U.S. strategy in the region was seen as an advantage. Nevertheless, as the center of the fan, the United States was still regarded as its linchpin.

Whereas Baker's presentation outlined a general plan, the more specifically military aspects of security were examined in two studies entitled *A Strategic Framework for the Asian Pacific Rim,* produced by the U.S. Department of Defense in 1990 and 1992 in the context of its East Asia Strategy Initiative (EASI). Shifting the strategic focus away from the USSR, the 1990 study predicted that the United States, as a balancing and deterring factor, would continue to contribute to stability within the region. In light of easing tensions, U.S. forces in Japan, South Korea, and the Philippines were reduced by about 10 percent by 1993.[10]

The 1992 study continued the same line of thinking, reinforced now by the collapse of the USSR. With the demise of the Soviet threat, "the United States' regional roles, which had been secondary in our strategic calculus, have now assumed primary importance"; preventing "the rise of any hegemonic power or coalition" in the region was a major goal for the United States.[11] The planned reduction in U.S. forces in Asia by 1993 was augmented by the unanticipated loss of 8,300 military personnel resulting from the closure of U.S. bases in the Philippines. This meant that between 1990 and 1993 U.S. forces were reduced by nearly 20 percent. A further reduction of 6.5 percent was planned for the period 1993–1995.[12]

The Clinton Administration (1993–)

It is not surprising that having been elected on a platform emphasizing the centrality of U.S. economic concerns, Bill Clinton has focused on the relationship between those concerns and the involvement of the United States in political and security issues in the Asia Pacific region. On 31 March 1993, Winston Lord gave an early indication of the administration's approach in his Senate confirmation hearings to become assistant secretary of state for East Asian and Pacific Affairs. Lord spoke of the need for the United States to "integrate our economic, political and security policies" toward the Asia Pacific region. In the context of a more favorable attitude toward multilateralism, the building of "a new Pacific community" was to be encouraged.

The integration of the different facets of U.S. policy can be seen in the ten goals set out by Lord. The highest priority was to be given to the pursuit of a "comprehensive, durable partnership with Japan." The strengthening of APEC "as the cornerstone of Asian-Pacific economic cooperation" and the development of multilateral forums for security consultations "while maintaining the solid foundations of our alliances" were also important. The other goals were as follows:

> Erasing the nuclear threat and moving toward peaceful reconciliation on the Korean Peninsula;
> Restoring firm foundations for cooperation with a China where political openness catches up with economic reform;
> Deepening our ties with ASEAN as it broadens its membership and scope;
> Obtaining the fullest possible accounting of our missing in action as we normalize our relations with Vietnam;
> Securing a peaceful, independent and democratic Cambodia;
> Spurring regional cooperation on global challenges like the environment, refugees, health, narcotics, nonproliferation, and arms sales;
> Promoting democracy and human rights where freedom has yet to flower.[13]

The emphasis on democracy and human rights is another point that needs to be considered when evaluating the direction of U.S. involvement in Asia Pacific. During its first year in office, the Clinton administration articulated the goal of enlarging market democracies as an underlying rationale for its foreign policy. Winston Lord saw U.S. policy in the Asia Pacific region as being based on the "three pillars" of economic prosperity, security, and democracy:

> Economic prosperity is a powerful force for democratic change. But economies need a stable, secure environment to grow and develop. We have long worked with our allies and friends in Asia to provide that environment, to our mutual benefit. We are now reaping the fruits of that stability in the form of growing markets and flourishing trade. Likewise, we know that open, democratic societies make better trading partners and more peaceful neighbours.[14]

Clinton indicated his own priorities when he made his first official visit to Asia (to Japan and South Korea) in July 1993. He spoke of a "new Pacific Community" that would be based on "a revived partnership between the United States and Japan. . . . On progress toward more open economies and greater trade and on support for democracy. Our community must also rest on the firm and continuing commitment of the United States to maintain its treaty alliances and its forward military presence in Japan and Korea and throughout this region."[15]

By early 1994, despite the rhetoric of Clinton and Lord, U.S. policy in Asia Pacific was in serious trouble, and U.S. relationships with Japan, China, and North Korea were most at risk. The major problem appeared to be that the United States was responding in an ad hoc manner to various situations and had not sufficiently thought through its long-term objectives. In pursuing its policies in Asia Pacific, the United States was inclined to use short-term pressure tactics rather than adopting more comprehensive strategies better suited to the various milieus in which it was engaged. As Winston Lord wrote in a memorandum to Secretary of State Warren Christopher in April 1994: "A series of American measures, threatened or employed, risk corroding our positive image in the region, giving ammunition to those charging we are an international nanny, if not bully."

Many of the problems were due to the fragmented nature of the foreign policy process under Clinton and to the emphasis placed on domestic considerations. They also reflected faulty assumptions about the Asia Pacific countries where problems had arisen.[16] Among Lord's suggestions for dealing with these issues were for the United States to "temper our rhetoric and work with the US Congress to reduce expectations; . . . oppose or readjust proposals from other agencies, often pursued for domestic reasons, when we are convinced that they will prove ineffective; . . . weigh more carefully the costs/benefits of taking unilateral actions and consider multilateral alternatives."[17] As we shall see, the Clinton administration subsequently attempted to deal with the most serious conflicts, but by late 1994, it faced further difficulties with the swing to a Republican majority in the congressional elections.[18]

During 1995, the Clinton administration attempted to make clear that it foresaw long-term U.S. involvement in the security of the Asia Pacific region. Perhaps the clearest statement in this respect was *United States Security Strategy for the East Asia-Pacific Region,* issued by the Department of Defense in February 1995. Unlike the Defense Department documents of 1990 and 1992, this document did not envisage any further reductions in U.S. forces in the region; a force structure of about 100,000 was to be maintained in East Asia.[19] According to Joseph Nye, assistant secretary of defense for International Security Affairs, U.S. security strategy in East Asia was based on three elements: the strengthening of alliances, the maintenance of a forward military presence, and the development of regional institutions such as APEC and the ASEAN Regional Forum.[20]

This was essentially the policy of the Clinton administration at the time of the 1996 U.S. presidential election. Although foreign policy (including Asia Pacific) was not a major issue in the campaign, Clinton was accused by Robert Dole, his Republican challenger, of being too accommodating to China and North Korea. The appointment of Madeleine Albright as secretary of state, William Cohen as secretary of defense, and Samuel Berger as national security adviser following Clinton's reelection will have important implications for U.S. policy in Asia Pacific. Although Cohen and Berger have a strong interest in the region,[21] it remains to be seen whether the second Clinton administration will be any more successful than the first in articulating a clear conceptual basis for U.S. policy in Asia Pacific.

Notes

1. Kennedy, *The Rise and Fall of the Great Powers.*
2. Ibid., p. 436.
3. Ibid., p. 527.
4. See, for example, Langdon and Ross, *Superpower Maritime Strategy in the Pacific,* especially Part 3.
5. *The Military Balance 1996/97,* p. 29. For a detailed assessment up to the late 1980s, see McLaurin and Moon, *The United States and the Defense of the Pacific.*
6. Tow, *Encountering the Dominant Player,* p. 8.
7. Ibid., p. 21.
8. Baker, "America in Asia," pp. 4–5.
9. Ibid., p. 5.
10. See Kreisberg, "The U.S. and Asia in 1990," p. 7; Crowe and Romberg, "Rethinking Security in the Pacific," p. 125.
11. *A Strategic Framework for the Asian Pacific Rim: Report to Congress 1992,* p. 2.
12. Ibid., pp. 16, 22.
13. Lord, "A New Pacific Community," pp. 49–50. See also Susumu Awanohara, "Group Therapy," *Far Eastern Economic Review,* 15 April 1993, pp. 10–11.
14. Winston Lord, "Prosperity in the Pacific," *Far Eastern Economic Review,* 11 November 1993, p. 23.
15. Jonathan Friedland, Shim Jae Hoon, and Susumu Awanohara, "Clinton's Clarion Call," *Far Eastern Economic Review,* 22 July 1993, p. 10.
16. See Harding, "Asia Policy to the Brink."
17. Susumu Awanohara, "About Face," *Far Eastern Economic Review,* 19 May 1994, pp. 22, 23.
18. See Nigel Holloway, "New Deal," *Far Eastern Economic Review,* 24 November 1994, pp. 20–21; Nigel Holloway and Melana K. Zyla, "Collision Course," *Far Eastern Economic Review,* 19 January 1995, pp. 14–15; Nigel Holloway, "New Hands on the Wheel," *Far Eastern Economic Review,* 19 January 1995, pp. 15–16.
19. *United States Security Strategy for the East Asia-Pacific Region,* p. 24.
20. Nye, "East Asian Security," pp. 94–95.
21. Nigel Holloway, "Same Difference," *Far Eastern Economic Review,* 19 December 1996, p. 22.

3

CHINA

The Chinese approach to post–Cold War Asia Pacific has been strongly influenced by the way in which China's leaders have seen their country's place in the world. Let us consider the nature of these views before examining the way in which domestic politics has affected the course of Chinese foreign policy.

Phases in China's Worldview, 1949–1989

Chinese foreign policy has passed through various phases since the establishment of the People's Republic of China in 1949. Paralleling the oscillation in Chinese politics between revolutionary and pragmatic emphases, Chinese foreign policy also varied between revolutionary commitment and the demands of realpolitik. During the pragmatic, realist phases, China attempted to forge links with other countries on various issues; during the revolutionary phases, there was a commitment to revolutionary doctrine and relationships with revolutionary forces.

Initially, China's most significant international relationship was with the USSR, but the Sino-Soviet alliance of 1950 proved to be of limited substance. By the 1960s, the Sino-Soviet conflict was quite public, and it intensified during that decade and the 1970s. During the 1950s, particularly at the time of the Bandung Conference of Asian and African Countries in 1955, China also attempted to improve its relationships with major Afro-Asian countries such as India. When revolutionary élan was dominant, China emphasized, at least rhetorically, its support for revolutionary forces in different areas of the world, including the revolutionary struggle in Vietnam, first against France and later against the United States and the Saigon government. During the revolutionary periods, most notably during the Cultural Revolution, the Chinese government also emphasized the role of revolutionary doctrine. Perhaps the most significant doctrine was the application of Mao Tse-tung's theory of revolution to the international scene. As articulated by Lin Biao in "Long Live the Victory of People's

27

War!" the revolutionary forces of the world were to emulate the role of the countryside in the Chinese revolution and surround the reactionary forces of advanced capitalism (which paralleled the role played by the cities in the Chinese revolution).[1]

There was more scope for a revolutionary phase to assert itself during Mao's ascendancy (even though there were also significant phases when pragmatism prevailed). Following Mao's death in 1976 and the emergence of Deng Xiaoping as leader, pragmatism was the dominant theme in Chinese foreign policy. But even under Mao, foreign policy had significantly changed, evidenced by the rapprochement between China and the United States in 1972. By that time, the hostility between China and the USSR had intensified, and China sought to improve relations with the United States as a means of avoiding conflict on two fronts. By the late 1970s, China had aligned itself more openly with the United States in opposition to Soviet expansion. At this stage, the dominant Chinese foreign policy doctrine was that of the "three worlds": China, as part of the "third world," should join forces with powers from both the "second world" (capitalist, industrialized powers other than the United States) and the "first world" (the United States) against the "hegemonism" of the USSR (also regarded as part of the "first world").

During the 1980s, there was again significant change in foreign policy, though pragmatism remained the norm. Increasingly, the Chinese leadership under Deng was trying to achieve economic modernization and still retain an authoritarian political system under the auspices of the Chinese Communist Party. Sino-Soviet relations improved and China sought to maintain an equidistance between the United States and the USSR. Economically, it was important for China to maintain good relations with all of the major economic powers, particularly the United States and Japan. Strategically, equidistance between the United States and the USSR meant that China was still in an advantageous position while competition continued between those powers. Communist ideology appeared less important and there was less attention being given to developing an overarching foreign policy doctrine. China appeared essentially as a major power pursuing its national interests in a traditional manner. Multipolarity was emphasized in writings that spoke of a "new international political order in the post-hegemonic era."[2]

Although the end of the Cold War affected international relations in Asia Pacific, certain trends were evident before the end of that conflict, most significantly multipolarity and economic dynamism in a number of the region's economies. In China, the end of the Cold War was occurring at the same time as the emergence of the prodemocracy movement, which culminated in the massacre at Tiananmen Square in June 1989.

China's View of the Post–Cold War World

What, then, have been the main features of the Chinese worldview in the post–Cold War era, and how do they relate to Asia Pacific in particular? With the end of the Soviet-U.S. conflict, China has lost some of its strategic importance. While the United States remains the sole superpower, it no longer needs to win the support of China against the USSR. The marked improvement in Soviet-U.S. relations during the Gorbachev era portended the decline in China's strategic significance. Its significance has decreased even further now that the USSR no longer exists. Moreover, the stronger emphasis on geoeconomics means that countries such as Germany and Japan have acquired a new importance.

Although from this perspective China has declined in importance in international politics, a positive result has been that the country no longer believes it faces significant external threats to its security. As Bonnie S. Glaser writes: "China is more confident about its security environment than it has been at any time since the founding of the People's Republic. For the first time in its 44-year history, the PRC does not face a plausible external military threat to its heartland."[3]

The increasing emphasis on ethnic nationalism in the post–Cold War era, particularly in southeastern Europe and the former Soviet Union, has had implications for China not only regarding its own ethnic minorities in areas such as Tibet and Xinjiang but also regarding the Taiwan issue.[4] While keeping in mind these concerns, China's main preoccupation in the international environment has been to achieve its goals for economic growth. Essentially, this has meant preserving effective working relationships with Japan and the United States in particular while contributing more generally to the achievement of international stability. In China's external relations, ideology has been played down and pragmatism has prevailed. China's declining international importance in the post–Cold War era was compounded by the diplomatic isolation it experienced as a result of Tiananmen Square. In the aftermath of the massacre, China has had to work toward regaining international acceptance.[5]

China's View of the Post–Cold War Asia Pacific

With Russia (as the successor state to the USSR) of declining significance in Asia Pacific, China's main focus has been on the United States and Japan as the other major powers of the region. It has been argued that China views its relationships with Japan and the United States as part of a triad that may offer China the opportunity to play Japan and the United States against each other.[6] In the event that there is an escalation in Japanese-U.S. conflict, China might be able to play a mediating role. However, there is potential for conflict between China and Japan as the two powers actually within the region, and there have also been tensions in Sino-U.S. relations since June 1989.

Beyond the major powers, China has pursued a *zhoubian,* or good neighbor, diplomacy[7] and in general has attempted to broaden the range of its diplomatic relations. Some notable examples are its recognition of South Korea in August 1992 and the establishment of diplomatic relations with Indonesia in August 1990 and Singapore in October 1990. Through these relationships, China was attempting to secure a regional environment where it could pursue its economic goals with minimum disruption. In addition, some of these relationships (with South Korea, for example) could contribute positively to the development of the Chinese economy. At the same time, China, as a major power with an expanding economy, has taken an assertive stance on a number of issues in which its interests were at stake. One such example is its position regarding the disputed islands in the South China Sea (the Paracels and Spratlys). Relations with Vietnam did improve in the aftermath of the Cambodian settlement and the changes in the Soviet-Vietnamese relationship, but the differences over the South China Sea were one factor inhibiting further improvement.

Impact of Domestic Politics

China's general approach to the post–Cold War world and Asia Pacific in particular has also been affected by domestic politics.[8] Although it is no doubt an oversimplification to speak in terms of tension between "conservatives" and "reformers" in the leadership, these tendencies do exist.[9] The reformers, with whom Deng Xiaoping was aligned, favor a more open foreign policy and an emphasis on economic growth. The conservatives are more insistent about maintaining the primacy of the Communist Party and state involvement in the economy, and they are more cautious about foreign capital and Western cultural influence.[10]

Tiananmen Square enhanced the ability of the latter group to restrain the former, but it did not lead to a fundamental change in the direction of foreign policy. Ideology ostensibly became more important: "Leninist fundamentalism returned with a vengeance as the way of, first, reasserting control and, second, repairing the Party's shattered legitimacy."[11] Leading reformer Zhao Ziyang was purged from his position as general secretary, and people such as current premier Li Peng and Jiang Zemin (the new general secretary and also state president after 1992) gained the ascendancy. These people could be described as moderate conservatives because they support the existing authoritarian political system and also favor economic liberalization; Deng himself could have been placed in this group in the aftermath of Tiananmen. The policy of opening to the outside world as a means of promoting economic growth continued as before, but with the complication that the outside world was not necessarily as receptive to Chinese overtures as it had been previously.

The emphasis on economic growth was perhaps the key feature of Deng's leadership in China. Deng had decided that for the Communist system to survive in China, there needed to be a strong emphasis on achieving greater economic growth. Economic growth not only would make China a more powerful actor on the world stage but, by improving the standard of living for the masses, would make them more likely to accept authoritarian rule.

Deng's "four modernizations" were to reform agriculture, industry, science, and defense. The reform of agriculture involved modifying communal ownership so that peasants could also produce for their own profit, which would thereby enhance agricultural productivity. The question remains as to whether agriculture has been sufficiently improved. The reform of industry entailed opening the economy to capitalist enterprise while also allowing the state sector to continue. Foreign trade and foreign investment were to be encouraged on the assumption that the economic benefits derived from them would make political challenges less likely. As a consequence of the new strategy for economic modernization, the annual growth rates in China increased from 5.2 percent between 1970 and 1980 to 9.4 percent between 1980 and 1991.[12] The proportion of national income going to defense was to be reduced, although with an expanding economy that amount could still be greater in absolute terms than it was previously and China could become a formidable military power.

With the promotion of economic growth as the primary goal, the regions within China have assumed a greater importance that has increasingly influenced foreign policy.[13] It is not that the regions conduct their own foreign policy, but the center must now give greater attention to the needs of the regions, and the regions are more insistent about asserting their interests. This situation is particularly noticeable within regions such as Guangdong, which has experienced a very high rate of economic growth.

The role played by the military is also an important factor affecting foreign policy. The military can provide a power base for political contenders in the factionalized politics that prevails in China. The military provided such a power base for Yang Baibing, head of the People's Liberation Army's General Political Department and half-brother of PRC president Yang Shangkun. Both men were purged in 1992 in the wake of accusations that they were intent on acquiring further political power.

Although the Chinese leadership plays the key role in formulating Chinese foreign policy, it must take into account the views of a range of groups. It has thus been argued that there has been a shift in Chinese foreign policy from "vertical authoritarianism" to "horizontal authoritarianism."[14] A range of power groups exists in China, and it is the task of the center to coordinate the views of those groups rather than simply to impose its own will.

China's Military Power and Doctrines

Another consideration in China's general approach to security issues in Asia Pacific is the role of its military power and doctrines. These two elements indicate the military means China has available and the circumstances in which it would be prepared to use those means. According to *The Military Balance 1993–1994*, Chinese military spending increased from U.S. $19.85 billion in 1985 to U.S. $22.36 billion in 1992 (constant 1985 prices).[15] Thus, spending increased about 12.7 percent, though the proportion of gross domestic product/gross national product devoted to defense declined slightly in this period, from 5.1 percent to 5.0 percent. If the purchasing power parity method (PPP) of assessing defense spending is used, the value of the Chinese defense budget triples.[16] (PPP takes into account the local purchasing power of defense spending.)

Over the period 1985–1992, Chinese armed forces decreased from 3,900,000 to 3,030,000, a decrease that was in line with a stronger emphasis on technological modernization. Although this emphasis preceded the Gulf War of 1991, it was reinforced as a result of that conflict. Technological modernization is reflected in such developments as China's plans to double the size of its intercontinental ballistic missile force (to thirty) by the year 2000, the construction of a strategic submarine force, the upgrading of the air force (with Russian assistance in particular), and the acquisition of a blue-water capability for the navy.[17]

These changes in the Chinese military forces have been reflected in the development of Chinese military doctrine over the past decade.[18] Whereas previously Chinese doctrine was preoccupied with "defense in depth" against attack by a continental power (the USSR), the new emphasis is on China's role as a regional power and particularly on frontier defense. China's military capability is increasingly being designed to strengthen its ability to defend its interests within the immediate border regions.

Notes

1. Lin Piao, "Long Live the Victory of People's War!"
2. Shambaugh, "Elite Politics and Perceptions," p. 106.
3. Glaser, "China's Security Perceptions," p. 252.
4. Chen, "New Approaches in China's Foreign Policy," pp. 238–239.
5. See Hsiung, "China in the Postnuclear World," pp. 75–76.
6. Ibid., pp. 77–78.
7. Ibid., p. 87.

8. A useful recent review of approaches to the study of Chinese foreign policy is Yu, "The Study of Chinese Foreign Policy."

9. See Ross, "Succession Politics and Post-Mao Foreign Policy."

10. Ibid., p. 46.

11. Kim, "Peking's Foreign Policy in the Shadows of Tiananmen," p. 400.

12. Faust and Kornberg, *China in World Politics,* p. 74.

13. See Segal, "China Changes Shape."

14. Quansheng, "Domestic Factors of Chinese Foreign Policy."

15. *The Military Balance 1993–1994,* p. 226.

16. Shambaugh, "Growing Strong," p. 55.

17. Ibid., p. 56.

18. See Godwin, "Chinese Military Strategy Revised."

4

JAPAN

Among the factors that influenced Japan's international role during the Cold War were the external environment, the growing economy, domestic politics, and the availability of military power (including the restrictions on the use of such power). These same factors have been important in the post–Cold War period, in relation to both Japan's broader international role and its role in the Asia Pacific region. To understand the nature of Japan's involvement in the region in the post–Cold War era, it is helpful to outline the development of its international role.

Japan's International Role, 1945–1989

Following its defeat in World War II in 1945, Japan came under the occupation of the United States, an event that profoundly affected its international role in the years that followed. Although the United States had initially envisaged the imposition of a harsh peace on Japan, with the objectives of demilitarization, democratization, neutralization, and restrictions on industrialization, this soon changed with the onset of the Cold War. From about 1947, occupation policy began to emphasize the contribution that Japan could make to the Western strategy of containment. Hence, there was a shift to promoting Japan's economic recovery and to ensuring that Japan would make a vital political and strategic contribution to the Western alliance. The conclusion of a peace treaty with Japan in 1951 was also the occasion for the establishment of the U.S.-Japan Mutual Security Treaty.

Thenceforth, Japan was to look primarily to the United States for the provision of its security. This reliance on the United States was reinforced by Article 9 of the Japanese constitution, which had been drawn up when the initial antimilitaristic assumptions of the occupation still held sway. It reads as follows:

> Aspiring sincerely to an international peace based on justice and order, the Japanese people forever renounce war as a sovereign right of the nation and the threat or use of force as a means of settling international disputes.

> In order to accomplish the aim of the preceding paragraph, land, sea, and air forces, as well as other war potential, will never be maintained. The right of belligerency of the state will not be recognized.

Although the constitution was drafted by the U.S. occupation authorities, this particular clause struck a chord among the Japanese people. It was a reminder of the experience of the war and particularly the use of atomic bombs at Hiroshima and Nagasaki in August 1945. It was therefore difficult to change Article 9 to make it conform more closely to the role that Japan came to assume as part of the Western alliance. Rather than change the clause, Japanese governments interpreted it broadly to allow for "self-defense." Hence, military forces were developed but were called Self-Defense Forces (SDF). Defense spending was limited so that it did not exceed 1 percent of gross national product (GNP). U.S. military forces were stationed in Japan, and U.S. aircraft and vessels made use of military facilities in Japan. Japan's value to the United States was made clear during the Korean War, when Japan acted as a "rear base" for the United States. Japan's reliance on the United States for its security and its primary focus on economic development were enshrined in the Yoshida doctrine (named after Shigeru Yoshida, who was Japan's prime minister from 1946 to 1947 and from 1948 to 1954).

In 1960 Japan signed a revised version of the mutual security treaty with the United States. Although concessions were made to Japan, giving it equal status with the United States, the treaty was widely criticized, especially by the left wing, which resented Japan's continued role in the United States' Cold War strategy. Japan later gave passive support to the United States in the Vietnam War but did not become directly involved. The United States continued to occupy Okinawa during the war and made use of its facilities for long-range bombing missions in Vietnam. This, too, caused widespread criticism in Japan and reinforced the campaign for Okinawa to revert to Japanese sovereignty. The United States finally agreed to reversion in 1971.

By the 1970s, Japan's security environment was becoming more complex. Although the Sino-Soviet conflict continued as before, the hostility between China and the United States was replaced by the rapprochement of 1972. Japan had previously traded with China and now followed the United States in pursuing its own rapprochement with that country (Japan established diplomatic relations with the People's Republic in 1972). Japan's mutually hostile relationship with the USSR continued as before; a particular point of contention was the control of the Soviet-occupied Northern Territories (four islands immediately north of Hokkaido).

By this stage, too, Japan was emerging as one of the world's major economic powers. It has been calculated that, on the basis of purchasing power parity (PPP), Japan's per capita GNP rose from 56.2 percent of U.S.

per capita GNP in 1970, to 66.6 percent in 1980, and 73.1 percent in 1988.[1] Japan's industrial output was 29.3 percent that of the United States in 1975 and 31.9 percent in 1988.[2]

The protection of Japan's economic interests was just as important as the protection of its territorial integrity as it was traditionally understood. This issue was underscored by developments in the 1970s, particularly the oil crisis. In response to its potentially vulnerable economic situation Japan developed a new policy of "comprehensive security." A 1978 report from the National Institute for the Advancement of Research (NIRA) and the Nomura Research Institute argued in favor of comprehensive security as the basis for Japan's security policy; the concept was endorsed further in the report of a prime ministerial task force in 1980.[3]

The essence of comprehensive security was that threats to Japan could be economic, political, or military and that Japan needed to develop a multifaceted security strategy that would enable flexibility in responding to situations that might arise. Japan should endeavor to exert greater political and economic influence in an increasingly multipolar world; a greater emphasis on economic aid would be one aspect of this strategy. Militarily, Japan should concentrate on "burden sharing" and peacekeeping as a means of contributing to both the Western alliance and the international community more generally.

In the 1980s Japan was being increasingly pressured by the United States to assume a more significant defense role. Burden sharing was one way that Japan responded to this pressure. Although the limit for defense spending had been set at 1 percent of GNP in 1976, this limit was removed in 1987.[4] Japan's economic growth meant that even though defense spending remained at around 1 percent of GNP, the total Japanese defense budget was still quite large. According to NATO criteria, by 1988 Japan had the third highest defense budget in the world.[5] Prime Minister Zenko Suzuki stated in 1981 that Japan's SDF would undertake the protection of sea lanes up to 1,000 nautical miles from Japan.

Post–Cold War Role

In the post–Cold War era, we can see a continuation of the trends that had developed during the period after World War II. Let us begin with a consideration of Japan's security role in general and then focus more specifically on the Asia Pacific region. Robert Scalapino commented on the relationship between Japan's general role and its regional role:

> The nature of its development has made Japan one of the few societies of the contemporary world with truly global interests. Its future hinges partly on the emergence of a new economic internationalism among the world's

advanced nations and partly on maximal access to global resources. Exclusively or primarily regional policies would not serve either of these requirements, although this does not negate the importance of certain regional concerns and institutions.[6]

Although this observation was written in 1977, it is still relevant today. Japan's particular regional interests need to be seen in the context of the fact that it is a major power with global concerns.

The changing international power configuration seriously affected Japan's perception of its international role. Although Japan still placed great importance on its security relationship with the United States, it also had to acknowledge that the relationship was changing. Among the factors distancing the two countries were tensions over economic issues and the fact that many Japanese saw the United States as a power in decline. Japan had to come to terms with living in a "posthegemonic" world.[7]

At the same time, the end of the Cold War and the subsequent collapse of the USSR meant that an important threat to Japan had declined, if not ended. Because Japan's dispute with the USSR over the Northern Territories persisted, Japan was slower to respond to the new Soviet situation than were many other powers. Japan was also sensitive to the possibility of new economic blocs emerging to challenge its economic preeminence. These various political and economic trends ensured that the concept of comprehensive security would be of continuing relevance. Japan also moved to develop a more independent foreign policy stance, with greater emphasis on international institutions such as the UN.

UN Involvement

In the late 1980s, Japan made significant financial contributions to a number of UN peacekeeping missions, including the Good Offices Mission in Afghanistan and Pakistan (UNGOMAP), the Iran-Iraq Military Observer Group (UNIIMOG), the Interim Force in Lebanon (UNIFIL), the Disengagement Observer Force between Syria and Israel (UNDOF), and the Transition Assistance Group in Namibia (UNTAG). Japanese noncombat personnel participated in UNGOMAP, UNIIMOG, UNTAG, and the UN Observer Mission in Nicaragua (ONUVEN) during the February 1990 elections.[8]

More recently Japanese personnel played a major role in Cambodia with UNTAC (UN Transitional Authority in Cambodia) and have also been involved in Mozambique with ONUMOZ (UN Operations in Mozambique).[9] In September 1994 it was announced that the Japanese SDF would participate in humanitarian operations under UN auspices to assist Rwandan refugees in Kenya and Zaire.[10] In January 1994, however, Japan had declined a request from Yasushi Akashi, head of UN peacekeeping in former Yugoslavia and previously head of UNTAC, for four or five Japanese military personnel to join a group of unarmed observers in Macedonia.[11] By September, Japan had passed legislation providing for Japanese military personnel to participate in both peacekeeping and enforcement operations under UN auspices, but the issue remained very sensitive.

The question of Japanese involvement in UN operations had come to a head at the time of the Gulf conflict in 1990–1991. Japan gave political support to the U.S.-led coalition that acted under UN authority in an attempt to reverse Iraq's occupation of Kuwait. However, Japan's concrete contribution to the allied effort was mainly financial. Initially, the government under Toshiki Kaifu offered U.S. $1 billion to support the coalition. After the offer was widely criticized, the amount was increased to U.S. $4 billion on 14 September 1990. When war erupted in January 1991, the Japanese increased their contribution by a further U.S. $9 billion.[12] Nevertheless, Japan was criticized, by the United States in particular, for its reluctance to make a military contribution. As U.S. secretary of state James Baker said in a speech in Tokyo in November 1991, "Your checkbook diplomacy, like our dollar diplomacy of an earlier era, is clearly too narrow."[13]

In August 1990 the Kaifu government had introduced a Peace Cooperation Bill in the Diet with a view to authorizing the involvement of the SDF in UN peacekeeping operations and in measures of "collective security" (as opposed to the "collective defense" barred by Article 9). However, widespread opposition led to the bill's abandonment in November 1990.[14] In January 1991 the U.S. proposal that Japan provide aircraft for transporting refugees was accepted, despite considerable public opposition, but not implemented; it was only in April 1991 that the Japanese government committed itself to sending six minesweepers to the Persian Gulf.[15]

In June 1992 the upper house of the Diet approved legislation submitted by the Kiichi Miyazawa government to enable the SDF to take part in UN peacekeeping operations. Although the role of the SDF in these operations would be heavily circumscribed, the passage of the legislation represented a stronger Japanese commitment to an active role in support of UN peacekeeping. The legislation was generally justified as part of Japan's "international contribution."[16] It was argued that if Japan was to play a more significant international role, then it had to be more active in contributing to world order.

A more active international role was presaged in the proposal that Japan become a permanent member of the UN Security Council. In the context of discussions about this proposal, Prime Minister Morihiro Hosokawa said in September 1993 that Japan "is prepared to do all it can to discharge its responsibilities."[17] One concern for Japan was that permanent membership in the UN Security Council would mean pressure for Japan to assume a more significant international role, including making a military contribution to UN peace enforcement activities. This concern led the Socialist-LDP (Liberal Democratic Party) government under Prime Minister Tomiichi Murayama to adopt a more cautious attitude. When Foreign Minister Yohei Kono addressed the UN General Assembly on 27 September 1994, he said that Japan was willing to become a permanent member of the Security Council but that it would not contribute to military activities.[18]

Post-Cold War Asia Pacific

The Japanese approach to post–Cold War Asia Pacific must be seen in the context of the development of Japan's international role more generally. Although Japan has a global interest in maintaining a liberal economic system, it also has a more specific interest in ensuring continued access to the economies of the Asia Pacific region.

The economic significance of the region to Japan is evident in a number of areas, including trade, investment, and foreign aid. In the period 1985–1990, 28.9 percent of Japan's total trade was with Asia (overwhelmingly East Asia), as compared with 29.5 percent with the United States and 14.7 percent with Europe.[19] In the period April 1986–March 1991, 17.2 percent of Japan's direct foreign investment went to Asia Pacific—the Association of Southeast Asian Nations (ASEAN), Oceania, and the newly industrializing countries (NICs)—as compared with 10.9 percent to Latin America, 21.2 percent to Europe, and 48.1 percent to North America.[20] In 1989 East Asia received 46.4 percent of Japan's bilateral foreign aid; the five most important recipients of Japanese bilateral aid between 1985 and 1989 were Indonesia, China, the Philippines, Thailand, and Bangladesh.[21]

Although these figures indicate the economic importance of Asia Pacific to Japan, Japan's crucial economic role in the region should also be made clear. In 1991 Japan was a more important exporter to the five major ASEAN countries, South Korea, and Taiwan than the United States was. However, the United States was a more important destination for exports from these countries, except for Malaysia (where the difference was marginal) and (more significantly) Indonesia, which was a supplier of oil and natural gas to Japan.[22] Japan's share of ASEAN exports (excluding Singapore) fell from 34.5 percent to 25 percent of the total between 1980 and 1989, when the NICs and Europe grew in importance as destinations; the proportion of Japan's exports to ASEAN also fell from 7 percent to 6.1 percent during the same period.[23] In the period 1980–1988, the proportion of NIC exports going to Japan rose from 10.1 percent to 12.5 percent; in the same period, the proportion of Japan's exports going to the NICs increased from 14.9 percent to 19.4 percent.[24]

Japan is also the most important foreign investor in East Asia; its investments there are worth nearly twice those of the United States. Initially Japanese investment had been directed toward ensuring the supply of raw materials (Indonesia was particularly important in this regard), but since the 1970s, there has been a focus on the development of the NICs. Since the revaluation of the yen following the Plaza Accord of 1985, there has been a shift of emphasis to investment that utilizes the availability of cheap labor in Southeast Asia.[25] In 1988–1989 the five most important recipients of Japanese investment in East Asia (in order) were Hong Kong, Thailand, Singapore, Indonesia, and South Korea; the order over the entire 1951–1990 period was Indonesia, Hong Kong, Singapore, Thailand, and South Korea.[26] Some 60 percent of official aid in Asia (including South Asia) comes from Japan.[27]

Japan's economic importance in the region can also be seen in the high level of intraregional trade within East Asia: In 1990 42 percent of East Asian imports originated in East Asia, and 39 percent of East Asian exports went to East Asian destinations.[28] The increasing level of economic integration in East Asia has led to speculation about the development of a "yen bloc."[29] In general, this would simply be a way of referring to the greater emphasis on economic interactions within the region. Since Japan is overwhelmingly the most important economy in the region, the expansion of intraregional economic interactions could be expected to strengthen its position even further. More specifically, the development of a yen bloc would mean that an increasing proportion of regional trade and finance was being conducted in yen.[30] Although economic regionalism in East Asia has not developed with the aim of excluding others, the potential is there if protectionism should start to gain hold in other parts of the world. Japan would clearly be the leader of such an economic bloc.[31] Whether this could be characterized as a revival of the "Greater East Asia Co-Prosperity Sphere" is debatable.[32]

Japan's approach to its role in Asia Pacific is greatly influenced by the need to protect its economic interests in the region. Essentially, this means that Japan must maintain regional stability and continued access to markets and investment opportunities. The way in which Japan has pursued this goal in particular countries and regions will be considered in more detail in subsequent chapters. However, a number of general features of Japan's approach can be identified.

One such feature is Japan's belief that the United States has a continuing relevance to Asia Pacific security in the post–Cold War era. As Foreign Minister Michio Watanabe observed in November 1992: "In the long term it won't be possible for the US to continue playing the role of world policeman because the American budget won't stand it. But in the short term an American military presence is a must for Asian stability and security."[33] Japan has been unable to make an overtly military contribution to regional security because of Article 9, domestic politics, and regional opposition and therefore views the U.S. military presence in the region as essential. In the same interview, Watanabe argued, "There's clearly a long way to go before Japanese troops would be trusted in Southeast Asia in the same way as American troops. . . . I myself think we need to establish a track record. Some more history has to be put in place before we can be accepted as a truly peace loving nation. So we don't have any desire to send troops abroad in a security-maintenance capacity."[34]

Watanabe's statement suggests a second feature of Japan's approach: the continuing relevance of comprehensive security. Japan sees itself as contributing to regional security through various nonmilitary means, such as taking a more active political role and becoming involved in UN peace-keeping in the region. Prime Ministers Kaifu and Miyazawa attempted to expand Japan's regional involvement. On a tour of ASEAN countries in May 1991, Kaifu made an important speech regarding Japan's role in the region. "Amidst these changing times . . . ," Kaifu noted, "Japan is expect-ed to make even greater contributions in the Asia Pacific region—not only in the economic sphere but in the political sphere as well." The "appropri-ate role" in the political sphere was as "a nation of peace." The continued security relationship between Japan and the United States was vital, but Japan also envisaged the development of a "partnership" with ASEAN. In developing a regional role, Kaifu said, "we need to go beyond the econom-ic realm and work in political, social, and foreign policy realms as well to become a major force for stability grounded in freedom and democracy."

Prime Minister Miyazawa expressed similar sentiments in a major speech delivered in Bangkok in January 1993. Asia Pacific countries, Miyazawa said, needed to "develop a long-term vision regarding the future order of peace and security for their region." He continued: "Various ideas should be thrashed out through political and security dialogue among the countries of the region. . . . Japan will actively take part in such discus-sions."[35]

These statements by Kaifu and Miyazawa indicated the general role they envisaged for Japan. Although controversial in Japan itself, an expand-ed Japanese peacekeeping role has been relevant to the Asian region.[36]

Impact of Domestic Politics

In examining the development of Japan's role in post–Cold War Asia Pacific, some attention should be given to the impact of domestic politics. After World War II, policy formulation in Japan was traditionally based on the interaction of business interests, the bureaucracy, and the factions of the ruling Liberal Democratic Party.[37] The ruling group tried to achieve con-sensus in its decisionmaking, an effort that explained the cautious and fre-quently indecisive nature of Japanese foreign policy.

In the early 1990s, important changes occurred in Japanese politics, and these changes in turn had implications for Japanese foreign policy. The most important change was the apparent end of the LDP's dominance of politics and the emergence of coalition-based government. The impetus for this change came from the fragmentation of the LDP. Following elections in July 1993, a seven-party coalition government was formed with Morihiro Hosokawa as prime minister. Three of the parties (the Japan Renewal Party, the Japan New Party, and Sakigake) were conservative reform groups; the others were the Komei Party (Buddhist), the Social Democratic Party of Japan (SDPJ, formerly the Socialist Party), the Democratic Socialist Party, and the United Social Democratic Party.[38] Hosokawa himself was from the Japan New Party. Difficulties in maintaining this broad coalition caused it to collapse in April 1994. Foreign policy was one source of conflict between the right and the left of the coalition. In particular, Ichiro Ozawa, former power broker in the LDP and leader of the Japan Renewal Party (also known as the New Frontier Party), believed that Japan should become a "normal country" in matters of defense and foreign policy,[39] a view that was unacceptable to the left of the coalition. Hosokawa's successor, Tsutomu Hata of the Japan Renewal Party, lasted for less than two months after the SDPJ defected from the coalition.[40]

At the end of June 1994 Tomiichi Murayama of the SDPJ became prime minister on the basis of an SDPJ-LDP coalition. Although this combination appeared unlikely in light of the two parties' histories, the SDPJ had become far less pacifist and more realist, and LDP leader Yohei Kono, the deputy prime minister and foreign minister, was regarded as a "dove."[41] With the SDPJ policies largely emasculated as a result of its coalition with the LDP, Murayama resigned as prime minister and was replaced by the LDP's Ryutaro Hashimoto in January 1996. When elections were held in October 1996, the SDPJ was effectively eliminated, the LDP failed to win an absolute majority, and the opposition New Frontier Party lost some seats.[42] Hashimoto, who was regarded as a nationalist in foreign policy matters, formed a minority government. Coalition politics had made it difficult for Japan to play a more active foreign policy role,[43] but the situation might prove different under an LDP minority government.

Japan's Military Power

What military power would Japan have available if it felt required to use that power as part of its international role? Between 1985 and 1992, Japanese defense spending increased from U.S. $13.151 billion to U.S. $16.901 billion (1985 prices) but remained constant at 1 percent of GNP.[44] China's defense spending over the same period increased from U.S. $19.85 billion to U.S. $22.364 billion (1985 prices); this represented 5.1 percent of

GDP (gross domestic product)/GNP in 1985 and 5 percent in 1992.[45] By 1996, Japan's defense budget was U.S. $45.1 billion at current prices.[46] As *The Military Balance 1995–1996* commented, the appreciation of the yen against the dollar means that "with the possible exception of Russia, Japan now spends appreciably more on defence than any other country apart from the US."[47] The goal of the armed forces remained the defense of the home islands and the sea lanes up to 1,000 miles from Japan. In 1996, total armed forces numbered 235,500, with 148,000 in the Ground Self-Defense Force, 43,000 in the Maritime Self-Defense Force, and 44,500 in the Air Self-Defense Force. There has been a steady increase in the size of Japan's equipment holdings since the early 1980s, including a spectacular increase in the number of attack helicopters, of which there had been only two in 1984.[48] In 1996, major items of equipment included some 1,130 main battle tanks, 680 surface-to-air missiles, 80 attack helicopters, 17 submarines, 9 destroyers, 51 frigates, and 379 combat aircraft.

Modernization is planned of various elements of the SDF, including new submarines, destroyers, and frigates, and the new *Kongo*-class destroyer has been equipped with a helicopter deck.[49] Japan is not a nuclear weapons state, but it could easily acquire a nuclear capability; the Japanese have been somewhat ambiguous on this issue.[50] Japan's defense concerns have been heightened by developments in North Korea; the 1994 white paper of the Defense Agency gave particular attention to this matter.[51]

The changes in Japan's defense capability have been evolutionary rather than radical. Nevertheless, with the declining U.S. military presence in Asia Pacific, Japan's own defense forces could expect to become more significant.[52]

Notes

1. Shinohara, "Japan as a World Economic Power," p. 18.
2. Ibid.
3. Akaha, "Japan's Comprehensive Security Policy," pp. 324–325. See also Tetsuya, "Comprehensive Security and the Evolution of the Japanese Security Posture."
4. Drifte, *Japan's Foreign Policy,* p. 34.
5. Ibid., p. 35.
6. Scalapino, "Perspectives on Modern Japanese Foreign Policy," pp. 399–400.
7. See Akaha and Langdon, *Japan in the Posthegemonic World.*
8. Akaha, "Japan's Comprehensive Security Policy," p. 329.
9. See *The Military Balance 1993–1994,* p. 159; *The Military Balance 1994–1995,* p. 178.
10. "SDF Chiefs Ordered to Prepare for Rwanda Mission," *Japan Times* (Weekly International Edition), 12–18 September 1994, p. 3.
11. Charles Smith, "Request Denied," *Far Eastern Economic Review,* 3 February 1994, p. 13.

12. Malik, *The Gulf War*, pp. 81, 84.

13. Quoted in George, "Japan's Participation in U.N. Peacekeeping Operations," p. 564.

14. Malik, *The Gulf War*, pp. 82–83.

15. Ibid., pp. 84, 86; Akaha, "Japan's Comprehensive Security Policy," p. 332.

16. Gordon, "Japan: Searching Once Again," p. 60. For a critique, see Yoshitaka, "Japan's Undue International Contribution."

17. Quoted in Ako Washio, "Tokyo Wants to Join the Club." *Japan Times* (Weekly International Edition), 26 September–2 October 1994, p. 7.

18. "Kono Explains Japan's Bid for UNSC Seat Before Assembly," *Japan Times* (Weekly International Edition), 3–9 October 1994, p. 1.

19. Rowley and do Rosario, "Japan's View of Asia," p. 9.

20. Ibid.

21. "Appendix," in Holloway, *Japan in Asia*, pp. 207–208.

22. Gordon, "Japan: Searching Once Again," pp. 62–64.

23. Rowley and do Rosario, *Japan in Asia*, p. 13.

24. Ibid.

25. Ibid., pp. 9–10.

26. Stefan Wagstyl, "Japan Sets Its Stamp on East Asia," *Financial Times*, 30 January 1990, p. 22; Rowley and do Rosario, *Japan in Asia*, p. 11.

27. Rowley and do Rosario, *Japan in Asia*, p. 15.

28. Arase, "Japan in East Asia," pp. 128–129.

29. E.g., Emmott, *The Sun Also Sets*, chap. 9; Holloway and Rowley, "Towards a Yen Bloc."

30. See Holloway and Rowley, "Towards a Yen Bloc," p. 186.

31. See Patrick L. Smith, "Japan in East Asia: A Boom Pays Off," *International Herald Tribune*, 30 May 1990, p. 1.

32. See Ayako Doi and Kim Willenson, "Japan: Greater East Asia Co-Prosperity Sphere?" *International Herald Tribune*, 12 August 1991, p. 6.

33. Charles Smith and Robert Delfs, "Activism in Asia: Foreign Minister Reasserts Tokyo's Regional Role," *Far Eastern Economic Review*, 10 December 1992, p. 10.

34. Ibid.

35. Paul Handley, "Japan's Clarion Call," *Far Eastern Economic Review*, 28 January 1993, p. 10. See also Brown, "The Debate over Japan's Strategic Future," pp. 551–552; "Japan Seeking to Strengthen Ties in Asia," *Nikkei Weekly*, 8 February 1993, p. 26.

36. See Michael Richardson, "Japan Moving Toward Regional Security Role," *Asia-Pacific Defence Reporter*, May 1991, pp. 18–19; Brown, "The Debate over Japan's Strategic Future," pp. 550–551.

37. Rothacher, "The Formulation of Japanese Foreign Policy," p.1. See also Tanaka, "The Transformation of Domestic Politics and Its Implications for Foreign Policy in Contemporary Japan."

38. Louise do Rosario, "Moment of Truth," *Far Eastern Economic Review*, 12 August 1993, p. 10.

39. Charles Smith, "The Battle to Come," *Far Eastern Economic Review*, 21 April 1994, p. 15.

40. Charles Smith, "Shackled Premier," *Far Eastern Economic Review*, 5 May 1994, pp. 14–15; Charles Smith, "Prisoners of Politics," *Far Eastern Economic Review*, 7 July 1994, pp. 14–15.

41. Charles Smith, "Strange Bedfellows," *Far Eastern Economic Review*, 14 July 1994, pp. 22–23; Charles Smith, "Right Turn," *Far Eastern Economic Review*, 15 September 1994, p. 20.

42. Sebastian Moffett, "Back to the Future," *Far Eastern Economic Review,* 31 October 1996, pp. 14–15.

43. See Michael Richardson, "Asians Worry About Weak Tokyo Rule," *International Herald Tribune,* 19 July 1993, p. 7.

44. *The Military Balance 1993–1994,* p. 226.

45. Ibid.

46. This figure and subsequent data are from *The Military Balance 1996/97,* p. 184f.

47. Ibid., p. 172.

48. "Asia: The Rise in Defence Capability, 1984–1993," map accompanying *The Military Balance 1993–1994.*

49. *The Military Balance 1993–1994,* p. 148.

50. See ibid., p. 147; Charles Smith, "Unclear Signals," *Far Eastern Economic Review,* 30 September 1993, p. 24; Charles Smith, "Touchy Subject," *Far Eastern Economic Review,* 29 September 1994, pp. 16, 18.

51. Charles Smith, "Western Front: Defence Strategists Plan for a Post–Cold War World," *Far Eastern Economic Review,* 28 July 1994, p. 16.

52. See Michael Richardson, "Asia Fears New Tokyo Sea Thrust," *International Herald Tribune,* 20 February 1990, pp. 1, 4.

5

THE SOVIET UNION AND RUSSIA

The post–Cold War period saw the disintegration of the USSR at the end of 1991. In the Asia Pacific region, Russia was the successor state to the USSR. This chapter will examine the international role of both the USSR and Russia in Asia Pacific during the post–Cold War period. Was the USSR still a power to be reckoned with in Asia Pacific during the Gorbachev era? Has post-Soviet Russia remained a significant Asia Pacific power or is it essentially a power in decline? In looking at these questions, we will need to be aware of the more general circumstances affecting the USSR and Russia, including the domestic and international dimensions, and focus particularly on the role of the Soviet/Russian Far East.

The Soviet Role Under Gorbachev

In czarist times, Russian involvement in the Asia Pacific region dated to the seventeenth century; political control followed in the aftermath of traders and fur trappers.[1] From the late eighteenth century to 1867, the Russian Empire crossed the Bering Straits to include Alaska (Russian America). To the south, Russia expanded its empire into Siberia and the Far East at the expense of the Chinese Empire. In the late nineteenth and early twentieth centuries, Russia also clashed with Japan in areas such as Manchuria and Korea. The Russo-Japanese War of 1904–1905 resolved the conflict in Japan's favor, but the underlying tension between the two powers in this region continues to the present. In the aftermath of the Russian Revolution, central control over the Russian Far East was weakened for a time. An Allied force (predominantly U.S. and Japanese) intervened in the region between 1918 and 1920, ostensibly as part of wartime strategy. An "independent" Far Eastern Republic existed between 1920 and 1922, largely in response to the threat posed by continuing Japanese involvement in the region after the withdrawal of other Allied forces.

Although the USSR's relationship with Japan was a key factor in Soviet involvement in the Asia Pacific region, the situation became more complex after Japan's defeat in World War II in 1945. In some respects,

47

Joseph Stalin saw Soviet territorial gains at this time (the Kurils and south-ern Sakhalin) as avenging Russia's defeat in 1905. The USSR also had to contend with the emergence in 1949 of China as a major power and the for-ward presence of the United States in the northern Pacific, particularly in Japan. Throughout the Cold War, the geopolitical role of the Soviet Far East was particularly important to the USSR. Vladivostok became a major Soviet naval base for the projection of Soviet power in the Pacific and Indian Oceans. In 1990, for example, the Pacific Fleet, which was based at Vladivostok, had 110 (including 24 nuclear-armed) submarines and 69 principal surface combatants. The Pacific Fleet Air Force had 233 combat aircraft and 89 combat helicopters.[2]

Economically, the region was important for its natural resources such as fish, timber, energy sources (particularly coal, oil, and natural gas), and minerals (including gold, silver, diamonds, tin, mercury, tungsten, lead, and zinc).[3] There were also important reserves of iron ore, but their exploitation was economically difficult. The population in 1986 of the two administra-tive regions of East Siberia and the Far East was only 16.4 million; three-quarters of the inhabitants were of Russian ancestry.[4] The region was treat-ed mainly as a frontier, an outpost of a Europe-centered Soviet state, but it was particularly important to the Soviet Union's geopolitical position.

Mikhail Gorbachev attempted to reorient the role of the USSR in Asia Pacific. Underlying the themes of glasnost (openness) and perestroika (restructuring), Gorbachev's aim was to renovate the USSR so that it would be better able to function in the modern world. Gorbachev's plan involved, among other things, the development of an economy that could compete with the Western capitalist economies. It also involved a move toward a political system based on popular consent so that some measure of demo-cratic legitimacy could be achieved. Less emphasis was to be placed on the USSR's role as a military power and on its links with ideological allies. Gorbachev hoped that the USSR would benefit from the economic dynamism of the Asia Pacific region. He wanted to encourage links with "Asian tigers" such as South Korea and downplay relations with ideologi-cal allies such as North Korea and Vietnam.

Gorbachev addressed his new approach in two important speeches. In the first speech, at Vladivostok in July 1986, he paid lip service to tradi-tional ideological allies in the region, focusing much more on Soviet rela-tions with China, Japan, the United States, and ASEAN (the Association of Southeast Asian Nations) and the possibility of economic cooperation with these countries.[5] Gorbachev also addressed security issues and proposed the idea of a Pacific conference (comparable to the Helsinki Conference of 1973) as part of "the general process of creating an all-embracing system of international security." Gorbachev also proposed to settle the Cambodian conflict by encouraging the normalization of Sino-Vietnamese relations, to support dialogue on the Korean issue, and to begin the withdrawal of

Soviet forces from Afghanistan. Gorbachev also suggested regional arms control measures for nuclear weapons, naval forces, and conventional armed forces and weapons, as well as confidence-building measures.

In the second important speech, at Krasnoyarsk in September 1988, Gorbachev discussed the progress being made in a number of conflicts and renewed his call for new arms control measures in the region. He believed that economic reform and restructuring in Siberia and the Far East could facilitate economic links with neighboring countries. Gorbachev also proposed a conference of foreign ministers "to discuss initial approaches to building new relations in the Asian-Pacific Basin."[6]

Gorbachev succeeded in improving the general climate of international relations in Northeast Asia. The Sino-Soviet summit in Beijing in May 1989 symbolized the end of the conflict between the two Communist powers and also facilitated a settlement in Cambodia. Improvements in relations with Japan proceeded more slowly, largely because of the problem of the Northern Territories, the southernmost islands of the Kurils occupied by the USSR but claimed by Japan. In Southeast Asia, the Soviet relationship with Vietnam remained of some importance but received less emphasis than it had previously. The ending of the Cold War between the United States and the USSR at a global level was reflected more specifically in improved relations between the two powers in Asia Pacific. This was reinforced when Soviet foreign minister Eduard Shevardnadze met U.S. secretary of state James Baker in Irkutsk in late July 1990. There they declared that the United States and the USSR were no longer adversaries in Europe or Asia.[7]

The main economic relationship that the USSR developed under Gorbachev was with South Korea. After diplomatic relations between the two countries were established in 1990, trade grew. In 1991 the USSR received exports from South Korea worth U.S. $625 million; imports from the USSR to South Korea amounted to U.S. $577 million.[8] The USSR saw South Korea as one of the most likely prospects for undertaking investment in Siberia and the Soviet Far East.

Gorbachev's hopes for reconstituting the USSR were destroyed by the domestic turmoil that his reforms unleashed. Rather than giving a new legitimacy to the USSR, democratization gave vent to the forces of ethnic nationalism. After an attempted conservative coup failed in August 1991, these forces led fifteen union republics of the USSR to become independent post-Soviet states by the end of that year.

Even before the Soviet collapse, the USSR had become much less significant as a military power in Asia Pacific. In line with Gorbachev's speeches at Vladivostok and Krasnoyarsk, Soviet troop strength in Siberia and the Far East had been reduced to 200,000 by 1990; Soviet forces were also being withdrawn from Mongolia and the Soviet presence at Cam Ranh Bay was reduced.[9] Given the turmoil in the USSR, however, the reduction in Soviet military power was even greater than these changes indicate. Reduced morale, lack of leadership, and poor or nonexistent maintenance all contributed to the USSR becoming less significant as a military power in Asia Pacific.

The Russian Role Under Yeltsin

Under Boris Yeltsin, the question was whether Russia would continue as a declining power in Asia Pacific or whether it would regain a role as a major power in the region. Developments to date suggest the former situation is more likely. Nevertheless, Yeltsin and his government have given some attention to the role they would like Russia to play in Asia Pacific.

This role needs to be placed in the context of Russian foreign policy in general. Alexei Arbatov has identified four main forces shaping foreign policy: a pro-Western group, moderate liberals, centrist and moderate conservatives, and neo-Communists and nationalists.[10] The pro-Western group, identified particularly with Andrei Kozyrev (Russia's foreign minister until December 1995), sees "political and economic integration of Russia into the West" as the main goal of foreign policy. The moderate liberals stress "the necessity for distinctly Russian foreign policy and security priorities, based on the specifics of Russia's geopolitical position and its transitional domestic situation." Accordingly, this group focuses on Russia's relations with the other Soviet successor states. The centrist and moderate conservatives favor better relations with the West but not at the expense of Russia's independent role, particularly within the sphere of the former USSR. The neo-Communists and nationalists are anti-Western and favor a restoration of Russia's imperial and world role.

These varying perspectives are also found in the more specific issue of Russia's role in Asia Pacific. Underlying these views are certain assumptions about geographical priorities in Russia's foreign policy. Although the groups differ as to whether Russia should see itself as Western, Eurasian, or distinctively Russian, they all seem to agree that Russia's role in Asia Pacific is not a priority. Russia's relations with the Soviet successor states and the Western powers are generally regarded as more important.

Although Yeltsin has made no statement on Russia's role in Asia Pacific comparable to Gorbachev's 1986 Vladivostok speech, any comments that he has made have generally been consistent with Gorbachev's vision. In an address to South Korea's National Assembly in November 1992, Yeltsin said:

In order to link the economy of our Far East with the economic complex of East Asia we consider it important to begin the formation of a mechanism for multilateral talks in the Asian-Pacific region, to work out a system of crisis settlement in order to prevent an increase in military tension in this region, and to create, together with other interested states, a center for the prevention of conflict situations.[11]

In a press conference on 25 January 1993, before a visit to India, Yeltsin spoke of Russia as a "Eurasian state" and referred to the need "to balance the policy between the East and Europe and Asia." Yeltsin concluded that Russia needed to give attention to "such major countries as China and India, such economically strong states as South Korea."[12] In June 1994 both Yeltsin and Defense Minister Pavel Grachev spoke of the need to develop effective security systems in Asia Pacific.[13]

In January 1994 Andrei Kozyrev enunciated some features of Russian foreign policy in a speech to the Chinese People's Diplomacy Association in Beijing.[14] These included Asia Pacific's economic importance to Russia and Russia's reduced military role in the region. With multipolarity as the basis of interstate relations, Kozyrev said, Russia aimed for "stable, balanced relations with all Asia-Pacific states."

On 4 July 1995 Kozyrev made another important statement at a meeting of Russian ambassadors to Asia Pacific countries.[15] He said he saw the region changing from "a complex theater of military-political and quite often . . . ideological confrontation" to a "sphere of economy [and] scientific-technical, cultural cooperation." Kozyrev foresaw "strategic partnerships" developing with a number of key states, including the United States and Canada (Asia Pacific's "Eastern neighbors"), China, India, and South Korea. Kozyrev diplomatically described relations with Japan as having "far from exhausted their potential of positive development" and emphasized relations with the members of the Commonwealth of Independent States (CIS). He also called for more active support for Russian "peacemaking" in Tajikistan, the protection of the Tajik-Afghan border, and greater international involvement in Afghanistan and hoped to "actively develop cooperation with Australia, New Zealand and the South Pacific."

Whereas Yeltsin and Grachev had earlier supported the development of a security system in Asia Pacific, Kozyrev suggested that "processes there will develop in their own original way" rather than necessarily following the European model. Russia was also keen to become involved in "economic integration processes" such as APEC (Asia-Pacific Economic Cooperation). Summing up, Kozyrev declared that Russian policy in Asia Pacific was based on

development of normal goodneighborly mutually beneficial relations of partnership with all the countries in the region without exception, ensuring, by political means [the] conditions for reliable security on the Eastern direction. We do not consider a single state as a potential enemy. The creation, in the Eastern direction, of favorable conditions for economic transformations in Russia, the speeding up of the country's economic development, in particular its Far Eastern and Siberian regions.

In practice, Russia's geographical proximity to Northeast Asia has tied the two regions, but Russia has also established links with Southeast Asia, particularly Indonesia. Between 28 July and 1 August 1995, Kozyrev attended a consultative meeting at the ASEAN foreign ministers conference during which closer ties between ASEAN and the CIS as regional organizations were promoted.[16] On a broader level, Russia has participated in the ASEAN Regional Forum, which addresses Asia Pacific security issues, since its formation in 1994 and also sought to be included in the Asia-Europe summit meetings, the first of which was held in 1996.[17]

Yevgeny Primakov replaced Kozyrev in December 1995. Many viewed the replacement as an attempt by Yeltsin to modify the pro-Western orientation espoused by Kozyrev and to be more assertive about Russian interests. In a press conference on 12 December 1995,[18] Primakov stated: "Russia was and remains a great power. Her foreign policy should correspond to that status. The point also is to create an external environment that would favor to the greatest possible extent economic growth and the development of democratic processes in Russian society." Primakov's priorities were strengthening Russia's territorial integrity; promoting the processes of economic reintegration of the former USSR; achieving international stabilization at a regional level, particularly in the former Yugoslavia and the CIS; and precluding "the emergence of new centers of tensions and primarily the proliferation of weapons of mass destruction." Although Asia Pacific per se was not listed as a priority, Primakov noted the need for Russia to diversify its relations with China, India, and Japan.

From the perspective of Russian domestic politics, Kozyrev's replacement by Primakov could be viewed as an attempt by Yeltsin to shore up his own position in response to the gains made by the neo-Communists and nationalists in the December 1995 parliamentary elections. This political imperative became even more urgent with the threat posed by Gennady Zyuganov as the Communist challenger to Yeltsin during the June–July 1996 presidential elections. Although Yeltsin was ultimately successful in retaining the presidency, this was by no means a foregone conclusion. The assertive nationalism and anti-Western orientation of Zyuganov's supporters was evident in a press conference held by the parliamentary coalition "Russian Union" on 17 September 1992.[19] The coalition argued that because "the prospects of facing economic, political and military might of Japan and the United States in the area contradicts the interests of quickly growing China . . . China would be interested in strong economic, political relations with Russia." Furthermore, "the development of relations between China and Russia is vital for Russia as an important factor of economic renovation and protection of its territorial integrity, stability in the East." Russian Union also saw opportunities for promoting cooperation between Russia and India, as well as between Russia and traditional allies such as North Korea, Vietnam, Mongolia, and Laos. The coalition feared that

Western economic domination would separate certain regions from Russia, including the Far East, to "create a kind of sanitary cordon around Russia increasing the distance between us and the more developed and economically promising partners."[20]

Although this fear may be exaggerated, the Far East is an important aspect of Russia's role in Asia Pacific. Not only is the region economically important but there is considerable potential for the further development of its natural resources. Exploration of this potential has been complicated by the terrain and climate and by the political situation in Russia. Another obstacle is the tension between Moscow and political leaders in the Far East. Former Communist leaders in the region have tended to be critical of Yeltsin at crucial times, such as the presidential-parliamentary clash in 1993. Other leaders, such as Governor Valentin Fyodorov of Sakhalin (1991–1993), believe that Moscow has inhibited their own developmentalist plans.

Although these tensions have contributed to regionalist sentiment in the Far East, the central government has generally had the upper hand. Governors who become too outspoken are likely to be dismissed. (Nevertheless, governors such as Evgeny Nazdratenko of the Maritime Province [1993–] have been able to achieve a large measure of autonomy for themselves.) Apart from the political constraints deriving from the structure of the Russian Federation, Far Eastern autonomy is inhibited by its continuing economic dependence on the central government and by its exposed security situation. An autonomous or even independent Far East would be more open to domination by neighboring countries such as China, Japan, and South Korea. However, if the Russian Federation as a whole should disintegrate, there would of course be a greater possibility of the Far East becoming an independent state.[21]

Let us consider the extent of Russian power in Asia Pacific in more recent times. Asia Pacific has become increasingly important for Russian trade (it represented 33 percent of Russia's total trade in 1992[22]), but Russia is less important for the trade of Asia Pacific countries. In 1995 China took 4.3 percent of Russia's exports and provided 1.86 percent of its imports; Japan took 4.09 percent of Russia's exports and provided 1.64 percent of its imports. In 1995 Russia took 1.12 percent of China's exports and provided 2.87 percent of its imports; in the same year, Russia took 0.26 percent of Japan's exports and provided 1.41 percent of its imports.[23]

Russia's military power in Asia Pacific has also declined.[24] Vladivostok remains important as the headquarters for Russia's Pacific Fleet, with 43 submarines (14 carrying strategic missiles) and 45 principal surface combatants in 1996. However, it appeared that the combat readiness of these forces was low and that they had significantly deteriorated.[25] The Far Eastern Military District (with its headquarters at Khabarovsk) included 10 of Russia's 28 motor rifle divisions. By 1996 the Russian army had been reduced to 460,000 troops for the entire country. This total shows the significance of reductions in the early 1990s of 120,000, or about one-third of troop strength, along the Sino-Russian border.[26] In 1996 Russia retained some 700 military personnel in Vietnam and about 500 in Mongolia.

The decline in Russian military strength must be seen in the context of the international situation. Although Russian naval forces in the Far East may no longer be relevant to a global nuclear strategy, they would be important if Russian relations with Japan were to deteriorate, over the Kurils, for example. They might also be significant if Russian-U.S. relations were to deteriorate, for example, if there were a nationalist resurgence in Russia. Russian land forces are mainly relevant to its relations with China. They could play some role in the calculus of power should there be a deterioration in that relationship.

Whatever Russia's aspirations in Asia Pacific, its political and economic circumstances have combined to limit its influence in the region. Russia appears to be a power in decline. Gerald Segal has compared its influence in the region to that of Australia,[27] and Robert Legvold similarly argues that Russia "is not likely to be a factor affecting the basic equilibrium in East Asia."[28] A nationalist Russia aligning with an anti-Western China could exacerbate tensions in the region, as would a deterioration in relations between Russia and Japan or between Russia and the United States. Russia may have influence in some regions, particularly in Northeast Asia, but it is unlikely to have a major impact. This situation is unlikely to change in the near future.

Notes

1. For historical background on the Russian Far East, see Stephan, *The Russian Far East.*
2. *The Military Balance 1990–1991,* pp. 42–43.
3. See *Pacific Russia,* pp. 103–111.
4. Segal, *The Soviet Union and the Pacific,* p. 7.
5. See "Text of Speech by Mikhail Gorbachev in Vladivostok, 28 July 1986," pp. 201–227.
6. See "Gorbachev Offers New Bids on Asian Policy," *Current Digest of the Soviet Press,* vol. 40 no. 38 (19 October 1988), pp. 1–7.
7. Chufrin, "The USSR and Asia-Pacific in 1990," p. 18.
8. *Direction of Trade Statistics Yearbook 1996,* p. 276.
9. Ibid., p. 17.
10. Arbatov, "Russia's Foreign Policy Alternatives," pp. 8–14.
11. "Yeltsin in South Korea, Pushes Rapprochement," *Current Digest of the Post-Soviet Press,* vol. 44 no. 46 (16 December 1992), p. 15.
12. "Press Conference by Boris Yeltsin," Official Kremlin International News Broadcast, 25 January 1993.
13. "Boris Yeltsin's Address to Russian Military," Official Kremlin Inter-

national News Broadcast, 28 June 1994; Pavel Grachev, "Military Doctrine and Russia's Security: The Nuclear Weapon Is Deterrent of Any Aggression Against Russia," Official Kremlin International News Broadcast, 9 June 1994.

14. Cited, Akaha, "Russia in Asia in 1994," p. 100.

15. Official Kremlin International News Broadcast, 4 July 1995.

16. "Foreign Ministry Press Briefing," Official Kremlin International News Broadcast, 8 August 1995.

17. "Press Briefing by Foreign Ministry Vice Spokesman Mikhail Demurin," Official Kremlin International News Broadcast, 1 August 1995.

18. "Press Conference with Foreign Minister Yevgeny Primakov," Official Kremlin International News Broadcast, 12 December 1995.

19. "Press Conference by the Parliamentary Group Russian Union," Official Kremlin International News Broadcast, 17 September 1992.

20. "Will There Be a Change of Course? Foreign Policy Problems and Election Programs of Various Parties," *Nezavisimaya Gazeta,* 10 December 1995 and 13 December 1995.

21. See Valencia, *The Russian Far East in Transition,* p. 3.

22. Austin and Callan, "Russia," p. 86.

23. Figures calculated from *Direction of Trade Statistics Yearbook 1996.*

24. Figures cited here are from *The Military Balance 1996/97.*

25. Austin and Callan, "Russia," p. 87.

26. Segal, "Russia as an Asian-Pacific Power," p. 76.

27. Ibid., pp. 69, 82.

28. Legvold, "Russia and the Strategic Quadrangle," p. 19. See also Ziegler, "Russia in the Asia-Pacific."

PART III

MAJOR POWER RELATIONSHIPS

6

THE JAPANESE-
U.S. RELATIONSHIP

Since 1945, the relationship with Japan has been of major importance to the United States. The relationship with the United States has been of even greater importance to Japan. This chapter provides an overview of the development of Japanese-U.S. relations in the postwar period and focuses on the issues that have been particularly significant since the end of the Cold War.

The Postwar Context

As a consequence of U.S. occupation immediately after World War II, Japan came to assume an important role in the strategy of containment, serving as the linchpin for U.S. efforts to counter the Communist powers (the USSR and, after 1949, China as well) in Northeast Asia. When the occupation ended in 1951, this role was formalized with the concurrent signing of a Mutual Security Treaty between Japan and the United States. The security and political relationship was further consolidated with the signing of a new Treaty for Mutual Cooperation and Security in 1960.

Essentially, Japan's role was to play host to U.S. forces deployed as part of the U.S. defense strategy in the Asia Pacific region. In this respect, Japan played a significant role in both the Korean and Vietnam Wars. Japan's own military role was circumscribed by Article 9[1] in the U.S.-designed constitution for 1947. Ostensibly, this article proscribed the development of armed forces by Japan, but it was subsequently interpreted to allow for the development of Self-Defense Forces. Under the Yoshida Doctrine, Japan was content to rely on the U.S. security guarantee while concentrating on its own economic development.

By the 1970s and 1980s, however, Japan's situation had changed considerably; the country had become a major economic power in its own right. During the 1980s, the United States emerged as the world's major debtor country, Japan being responsible for the financing of much of this

59

debt. The increasing deficit of the U.S. government became a major political issue. U.S.-Japanese trade relations were characterized by the large surplus in Japan's favor. Many in the United States argued that the inferior U.S. position in the trade relationship was exacerbated by restrictions on access to Japan's domestic market.

In these circumstances, the U.S.-Japan security relationship was increasingly scrutinized. The cry arose in the United States that Japan was having a free ride and had exploited the situation to its own benefit and to the detriment of the United States. Paul Kennedy popularized the concept of "imperial overstretch," whereby great powers were undermined by the economic costs of their need to maintain large military forces. Many people voiced their support of increased Japanese defense spending and defense "burden sharing." In the early 1980s, under Prime Minister Zenko Suzuki, Japan did modify its approach to defense: One percent of GNP was no longer the absolute limit for defense spending; Japan would defend its sea lanes to a distance of 1,000 nautical miles. Japan's defense spending in absolute terms was exceeded only by that of the United States and the USSR.[2]

During the 1980s, technology transfer issues caused some tensions in Japanese-U.S. relations; the Toshiba episode of 1987 is a good example. The Toshiba Corporation illegally sold U.S.-imported equipment to the USSR, which in turn made it easier for Soviet submarines to escape detection by the United States. The United States therefore had to improve its own technology if its submarine detection capability were to remain effective. This meant that the overall cost of deterrence increased. U.S. outrage over the incident was symbolized by the members of Congress who smashed a Toshiba radio–cassette player with a sledgehammer outside the Capitol.

A more crucial issue for the security relationship was the FSX episode of the late 1980s. The issue arose originally in 1986, when Japan's Defense Agency put forward a proposal for Japan to construct its own fighter aircraft to be known as the FSX. Japan hoped that building the FSX would help the country develop an internationally competitive aircraft industry, even though fighter aircraft could be purchased more cheaply from the United States. The United States subsequently pressured Japan to make the project a joint one, on the grounds that it would lead to the development of a more effective fighter. An agreement providing for joint development was concluded in November 1988.

In the meantime, the issue became mired in U.S. domestic politics. The U.S. State and Defense Departments had actively pushed for joint development. The Commerce Department, however, was concerned that the project would give Japan access to U.S. technology, which in turn would bring economic benefits to Japan. If Japan were serious about reducing its trade surplus with the United States, the Commerce Department reasoned, it should simply buy the U.S. F-16 aircraft. The issue was taken up in Congress and the Bush administration was forced to negotiate a revised agreement whereby the United States would perform about 40 percent of the work involved in the production of the FSX. The agreement was narrowly approved by the Senate in May 1989.[3]

The relationship of defense to technology was examined in a 1987 Pentagon report on the semiconductor industry. The report pointed out that Japan dominated the semiconductor industry and that because the nature of much modern weaponry was high-tech, this had implications for U.S. defense. The report recommended that the United States reduce its dependence on Japan in the semiconductor industry and, by implication, in all other defense-related areas of advanced technology where Japan played the leading role.[4]

The question of defense burden sharing, especially the cost of maintaining U.S. forces in Japan, has been of continuing importance in the U.S.-Japan security relationship. Congressional critics have charged that Japan, with its healthy economy and trade surplus with the United States, should be responsible for the cost of U.S. forces stationed there. In 1989, at a time when Japan was paying 40 percent of the costs of U.S. forces in Japan, Congress passed legislation requiring the administration to negotiate for full payment. The outcome was that Japan agreed to pay all yen-based expenses by 1995, or about one-half of the full cost.[5]

The Debate About Japan's Role in the World

In the Japanese context, much of the debate about Japan's role in the world concerns the future of its relationship with the United States. The idea that Japan should become a "normal" country is largely propounded by the political right. Within this part of the political spectrum, there have been two major perspectives on Japan's security role as it relates to the United States. According to Masaru Tamamoto, these two views are espoused by the "political realists" and the "military realists."[6] The political realists argue that Japan should primarily make an economic contribution to the alliance but not become involved in significant political and military commitments. The military realists claim that an economic contribution is insufficient and that Japan should be prepared to make more significant political and military commitments.[7] An important leader among the political realists was Kiichi Miyazawa (prime minister, 1991–1993). Yasuhiro Nakasone (prime minister, 1982–1987) played a major role in advancing the position of the military realists, who come predominantly from the nationalist right.

Another advocate of the military realist position is Shintaro Ishihara, a leading figure in the Liberal Democratic Party and the author of *The Japan*

That Can Say No.[8] The main message of the book is that Japan should be more assertive in its negotiations with the United States over economic issues, but Ishihara applies the same argument to the security relationship. It is not that Japan wishes to undermine its relationship with the United States, but that it should be more vigorous in defending its own interests. As Tamamoto suggests, "the picture that emerges from a closer look at the nationalist right is a more or less centrist vision that amounts to preserving Japan as number two in Pax Americana."[9] In a similar vein, Ishihara says, "Japan and the United States should constitute a Group of Two that works to solve global issues. An equal partnership would help confirm Japan's status in the world, and I think Washington would see the advantages."[10]

Because Nakasone was prime minister for much of the 1980s, the position of the military realists was strengthened. Japan increased its defense expenditure, partly in response to U.S. criticism and also as a means of gaining more influence with the United States. When Nakasone visited President Ronald Reagan in January 1983, he discussed Japan's strategic significance, describing it as an "unsinkable aircraft carrier" off the coast of East Asia.[11]

The "Ron-Yasu relationship" signified the close ties between the United States and Japan at this time. Critics such as Ishihara, however, believed that Japan was still too passive in its relationship with the United States. Ishihara thought that the way forward in U.S.-Japan relations was "not the Nakasone way—the famed Ron-Yasu relationship, with Nakasone insinuating himself next to the U.S. president at the summit meetings of the seven industrial democracies."[12] Critics interpreted Japan's concession to U.S. pressure over the FSX issue as typifying Japan's failure to defend its own interests.

Post-Cold War Strategic Issues

With the end of the Cold War, economic differences have become prominent in Japanese-U.S. relations. Nevertheless, the broader strategic context of the relationship has also required reassessment. In the aftermath of the Cold War, would Japan continue to play an important role in the U.S. approach to Asia Pacific security?

This question was taken up by U.S. defense secretary Richard Cheney during a visit to Tokyo in February 1990. Cheney announced that although there would be a 10 percent reduction in U.S. military personnel in the Pacific, a "major portion" of the U.S. presence would remain. Without such presence, according to Cheney, "a vacuum would quickly develop. . . . There almost surely would be a series of destabilizing regional arms races [and] an increase in regional tension." With potential instability in Burma, Cambodia, China, North Korea, and Vietnam, noted Cheney, "it's an open question as to how those changes will affect regional stability." China and India would "continue to emerge as regional powers. We don't know what the regional effects will be. . . . Given these potential dangers to regional security, it should be clear that the United States could not ever think of a withdrawal from Asia."[13] Selig Harrison and Clyde Prestowitz reported that privately U.S. officials also argued that the U.S. presence was important in constraining eventual Japanese military domination of the region.[14] U.S. Marine commander in Japan, Major General Henry Stackpole III, echoed this sentiment in March 1990 when he said that U.S. forces in Japan provided "a cap in the bottle" to prevent a revival of Japanese military power.[15]

A broader political basis for the Japanese-U.S. security relationship was proposed by Richard Solomon, U.S. assistant secretary of state for East Asian and Pacific Affairs, in a speech in Tokyo on 10 April 1990. This was an elaboration of President George Bush's previous offer to Prime Minister Toshiki Kaifu to develop a "global partnership" with Japan.[16] Solomon said that "the US-Japan partnership . . . [i]s of paramount importance to the future of international economic, security, and political relations in Asia— and, indeed, in the world at large. . . . A restructured and reinvigorated US-Japan relationship—along with a united, integrated Europe—will be one of the pillars of the international architecture of the 21st century."[17]

Solomon identified four components in the new "global partnership": a reaffirmed defense relationship; foreign policy coordination; economic cooperation (which would involve solving bilateral trade problems and cooperating on multilateral matters such as the General Agreement on Tariffs and Trade); and Japan's global role (including the enhancement of "Japan's institutional position in multilateral economic and political institutions").[18] On the first point, Solomon's statement echoed what Cheney had said earlier in the year:

> In the many-centered world that we see emerging, the US-Japan security tie can only become more important to maintaining the strategic balance. Regardless of the Soviet threat . . . our role as a regional balancer, honest broker, and ultimate security guarantor cannot be replaced by any other power. Such a role for the United States will become more important in East Asia in the decades to come. And our security cooperation with Japan will become ever more important to our ability to sustain that role.[19]

The Gulf Conflict, 1990–1991

Despite the views advanced by spokespeople for the Bush administration, the achievement of a U.S.-Japan global partnership was not necessarily straightforward. Sentiment associated with Article 9 of the Japanese constitution acted as a powerful restraint in the security sphere. This was well illustrated when Japan, despite U.S. urging, found it difficult to assume a more active role during the Gulf conflict of 1990–1991. In 1987 political opposition had prevented the Nakasone government from sending minesweepers to the Persian Gulf to assist Western efforts to keep sea lanes open during the Iran-Iraq War. In the end, Japan provided financial aid only, setting a precedent for its actions during the Gulf conflict.

The United States wanted Japan to become directly involved in the crisis through the provision of personnel and equipment, as well as financial assistance to both the multinational forces and the countries affected by the crisis.[20] In October 1990, the Kaifu government was defeated in the Diet when it proposed sending Japanese military personnel in a noncombat role to assist the operations of the U.S.-led coalition in the Gulf. Again, Japanese involvement took a financial form; U.S. $13 billion was provided to underwrite the costs of the operation (roughly one-quarter of the total cost). Two Japanese relief planes were sent carrying food and medical supplies to multinational forces.[21] In the aftermath of the war, Japan sent six ships, including four minesweepers, to join minesweeping operations in the Persian Gulf.[22] In spite of these efforts, Japan was criticized in the United States for the tardiness of its contribution and its unwillingness to assume the military burden expected of a major power.

Beyond the Gulf Conflict

The frictions experienced over the Gulf conflict could also occur within the Asia Pacific region. Without the perception of a Soviet threat as a unifying factor in Asia Pacific, there is more scope for differences to arise. Thus, Japan tends to be more pragmatic than the United States on issues involving China, North Korea, and Vietnam. However, aid to Russia is more difficult for Japan than for the United States because the issue of the Northern Territories has not been settled. A regional partnership, let alone a global partnership, has been difficult to achieve.

Both U.S. and Japanese leaders have continued to use the language of cooperation in their rhetoric. In the Tokyo Declaration, issued by George Bush and Kiichi Miyazawa in January 1992, the two leaders spoke of the "US-Japan Alliance" as "the political foundation on which the two countries cooperate in assuming their respective roles and responsibilities for securing world peace and stability in their Global Partnership."[23] Similarly, in an address to the Diet on 22 January 1993, Miyazawa proposed that Japan and the United States should work together in "coordinated leadership under a shared vision."[24] He argued that "the U.S. military presence in the Asia-Pacific region will be more important than ever for stability . . . and close Tokyo-Washington ties will be essential as Japan pursues a greater role in the region."[25]

Although the Clinton administration has placed an even stronger emphasis on economic issues in Japanese-U.S. relations, security issues continue to play a role. In February 1993, Secretary of State Warren Christopher said that trade issues should "not overshadow the many areas where we work together on global, bilateral and regional issues."[26] Whether the security relationship can be insulated from the continuing frictions over trade issues is more problematical.

On the Japanese side, the instability resulting from domestic political realignment—during the coalition governments of Morihiro Hosokawa (August 1993–April 1994) and Tsutomu Hata (April–June 1994); in a coalition of the Liberal Democratic Party and the Social Democratic Party of Japan under Tomiichi Murayama (June 1994–January 1996); and in the Ryutaro Hashimoto government (January–October 1996)—has affected the process of redefining the security relationship.

One problem for the Hosokawa government in approaching the security relationship with the United States was that its members covered such a broad spectrum. In his search for a new basis for Japanese-U.S. relations, Hosokawa was conscious of "the domestic political scars caused by the Cold War. . . . The international polarity epitomized by the United States and the Soviet Union generated a bipolarity in Japanese politics as well."[27] His implication was that in the future attitudes toward the United States would be less significant as a polarizing factor in Japanese politics.

Nevertheless, differences over the security relationship with the United States did cause tensions within the Hosokawa government from time to time. For example, Kosuke Uehara, head of the National Land Agency and a member of the SDPJ, told the Diet on 26 August 1993 that the U.S.-Japan security relationship should be revised in light of the international changes that followed the end of the Cold War. Keisuke Nakanishi, head of the Defense Agency and a member of the conservative Shinseito, believed that the U.S.-Japan security treaty "should be a permanent treaty."[28]

Concerns about North Korea, among other factors, led to discussions between Japan and the United States about the development of a Theater Missile Defense (TMD) system.[29] A problem with the proposal was that both sides feared it might become "the son of FSX"; it also might violate Japanese policy about avoiding involvement in collective defense.[30] In a visit to Tokyo on 2 November 1993, U.S. defense secretary Les Aspin stressed that technological collaboration would not be required in the development of a TMD directed against North Korea.[31] When Hosokawa visited Washington, D.C., in February 1994, Japanese officials discussed the need to balance the emphasis on trade issues, suggesting that attention be given to security issues in Asia and to "global cooperation" programs in areas such as AIDS and space research. Japanese officials viewed the coordination of policy on North Korea as particularly significant at this time.[32]

Without the SDPJ, the short-lived Hata government (April–June 1994) was in a position to move more to the right on foreign policy issues. Leading figures within coalition parties, such as Ichiro Ozawa of the Japan

Renewal Party (New Frontier Party) and Yuichi Ichikawa of the Komei Party, favored changes in Japan's Self-Defense Law to enable active logistical support for the United States in the event of a conflict with North Korea.[33] Foreign Minister Koji Kakizawa favored a more cautious approach: "Issues facing us are U.S.-Japan economic problems and North Korea's suspected nuclear development. Japan will fulfil its responsibility and cooperate with the United Nations and other nations so that suspicions over North Korea will be cleared."[34]

Tomiichi Murayama, of the SDPJ, became prime minister in late June 1994, leading a coalition of the SDPJ, the LDP, and the reformist Sakigake. He committed himself to uphold the U.S.-Japan Mutual Security Treaty, which had previously been strongly opposed by his party.[35] When Murayama met Bill Clinton at the Group of Seven (G7) summit in Naples in July 1994, he said he would both "continue to follow the diplomatic policies of previous governments and . . . maintain the U.S.-Japanese security system."[36]

During 1995, largely on the initiative of U.S. assistant secretary of defense Joseph Nye, a Japanese-U.S. declaration was prepared reaffirming the security ties between the two countries. The declaration was to have been signed at the time of Clinton's visit to Osaka in November, for the meeting of the Asia-Pacific Economic Cooperation (APEC). When Clinton had to cancel his visit because of the budgetary impasse with Congress, the signing of the declaration was postponed. The issue was further clouded by the alleged rape of a girl on Okinawa by three U.S. servicemen.[37] The incident highlighted the ambivalent feelings many Japanese have toward the U.S. defense presence in their country.

When Clinton did visit Japan in April 1996, the joint security declaration was finally issued. The commitment by both countries to "bilateral policy coordination, including studies on bilateral cooperation in dealing with situations that may emerge in the areas surrounding Japan" was widely taken to mean that Japan could become more involved in regional security issues such as those in Korea, Taiwan, and the South China Sea, particularly by providing increased logistical support to the United States.[38] Okinawa is likely to become less significant as a center for U.S. military deployment in Japan; in September 1996, Okinawa passed a referendum opposing the U.S. military presence.[39] Indeed, some claimed that after the alleged rape in Okinawa in 1995, the continuation of the U.S.-Japan alliance had only minority support in Japan.[40]

Post–Cold War Economic Issues

With the end of the Cold War, the economic differences between Japan and the United States have become more important in their relationship.

Without a sense of a common threat, economic tensions have become more prominent. These differences are not directly related to security issues, but insofar as they weaken the relationship, they do have security implications. Japan has had to respond to the widespread U.S. perception that the United States has been disadvantaged by unfair Japanese trading practices. Prominent Japanese figures have made extreme and even racist statements attributing U.S. economic problems to an underlying malaise in U.S. society. Professor Aida Yuji of Kyoto University, for example, has suggested that "Iberian and African cultural traits seem to impede industrialization"; the United States, "with its vast human and technological resources . . . could become [simply] a premier agrarian power—a giant version of Denmark, for example—and the breadbasket of the world."[41] In January 1992 Yoshio Sakurauchi, speaker of the House of Representatives in the Diet, spoke of the United States as "Japan's subcontractor" and described many U.S. workers as "lazy and illiterate."[42] Prime Minister Miyazawa also caused a stir with his comment that the United States had lost its "work ethic."[43]

During most of the Bush presidency, Japan was led by Toshiki Kaifu (August 1989–October 1991) and Kiichi Miyazawa (November 1991–July 1993). Kaifu has been described as belonging to "the postwar Japanese tradition of nonideological, pragmatic leadership."[44] His response to the economic differences between Japan and the United States was essentially pragmatic. When George Bush began his presidential term in 1989, the United States had an annual trade deficit of nearly $52 billion with Japan. In July 1989, Japan and the United States agreed to participate in a Structural Impediments Initiative (SII).[45] The agreement was a concession to the U.S. view that access to the Japanese market was often impeded by the organization of the Japanese economy. In June 1990, Japan committed itself to action in six SII-related areas: the reform of savings and investment patterns, land policy, the distribution system, restrictive business practices, *keiretsu* relationships (groupings of companies), and pricing. The United States committed itself to reducing the federal deficit.[46] The two countries conducted negotiations on specific sectors and products; meetings between Bush and Kaifu in September 1989 and March 1990 had helped facilitate progress in these negotiations.[47] Japan, however, was placed on the defensive by comments such as Bush's statement in March 1990 that trade problems were a threat to the proposed global partnership between the United States and Japan.[48]

In Miyazawa, the United States found itself dealing with a leader who was assertive in defending Japanese interests but diplomatic in pursuing an accommodation. When he was elected prime minister, Miyazawa said that Japan's trade surplus was a "fundamentally insoluble problem" deriving from demand for Japan's superior products,[49] a comment that suggested an unyielding position on Miyazawa's part. Nevertheless, despite George

Bush's unfortunate collapse at a Japanese state dinner in January 1992, the two leaders agreed in the Tokyo Declaration "to enhance openness and oppose protectionism in their commercial, financial and investment markets. To this end, Japan and the United States will strengthen policy initiatives to reduce structural impediments."[50]

When Bill Clinton was elected as president in November 1992, Japan was concerned that the United States would move toward "managed trade." Clinton's platform had given primacy to economic concerns, and he was expected to be more assertive in dealing with Japan. Initially, Japanese officials favored a macroeconomic approach to the trade imbalance; this approach focused on Japan's demand for imports and a reduction in the U.S. fiscal deficit.[51] When Finance Minister Yoshiro Hayashi visited Washington, D.C., in February 1993 (along with Foreign Minister Michio Watanabe), he rejected suggestions that the yen should be appreciated against the dollar as a means of reducing Japan's trade surplus.[52] Clinton did not clearly specify a solution to the trade surplus issue; instead, he told Watanabe that Japan had "to demonstrate to the American people that they have the opportunity to compete abroad."[53] The possibility of reinstating the Super 301 provision against "unfair traders" was on the U.S. agenda.

U.S. pressure on Japan continued when President Clinton met Prime Minister Miyazawa on 16 April 1993. Announcing that "the Cold War partnership between our two countries is outdated," Clinton presented demands for sectoral quotas for U.S. exports to Japan and supported a revaluation of the yen.[54] Underlying Clinton's approach was the idea that the United States had sacrificed too much economically in maintaining the Western alliance against the USSR.[55] Japan in particular had benefited from this arrangement, but with the end of the Cold War, it was time to rectify the balance. Miyazawa's concern was that the United States would seek targets for specific types of imports into Japan. In his view, the relationship should be based on "the principle of free trade. . . . [It] cannot be realized with managed trade nor under the threat of unilateralism."[56] Both leaders agreed to replace the SII and sector-specific talks with a new framework for trade talks.[57] Japan subsequently attempted to win support from other Asia Pacific countries in its campaign against "managed trade."[58]

When Clinton and Miyazawa met in Tokyo at the G7 summit in July 1993, they were able to reach a broad agreement on trade issues. The United States agreed to abandon its aim of numerical targets and accept instead "objective criteria" as the basis for evaluating market access. Japan promised to reduce its trade surplus, and the United States its budget deficit. The two sides agreed to negotiations on motor vehicles and insurance, government procurement of high-technology products such as computers and satellites, and the reform of regulations affecting imports and direct investment. Whether this compromise would satisfy the long-term goals of the two countries remained to be seen.[59]

With the inauguration of coalition governments in Japan under Morihiro Hosokawa (August 1993–April 1994), economic issues continued to loom large in Japanese-U.S. relations. Although Hosokawa was regarded as a reformist (he reiterated the view that "free trade and free market economic principles are the basis on which we would like to correct the imbalance"[60]), his ability to move in the direction favored by the United States was limited. On his first visit to the United States as prime minister, in September 1993, Hosokawa stated his opposition to reducing Japan's trade surplus on the basis of a numerical target.[61] In some areas, however, Hosokawa did make concessions. In October 1993, his government announced that for public works projects it would "adopt an open competitive bidding system so that foreign companies can participate in bidding."[62] There were also suggestions that Tokyo would modify its position on rice imports in the conclusion of the Uruguay Round.[63]

Clinton and Hosokawa were scheduled to meet again on 11 February 1994, and the resolution of various issues from the Clinton-Miyazawa agreement of July 1993 remained difficult. The major problems concerned government procurement, autos and auto parts, and insurance; access to the Japanese construction market and cellular telephones were other issues requiring resolution.[64] When Clinton and Hosokawa did meet, it proved impossible to reach an agreement. In implementing "objective criteria," Japan was reluctant to consider "quantitative indicators," which it believed could become "numerical targets." Although Clinton denied that the United States sought numerical targets, Hosokawa was cautious: "We don't want numerical targets to gain a life of their own . . . because at the end of the day we believe that will lead to managed trade."[65]

U.S. dissatisfaction with Japan was made clear when U.S. trade representative Mickey Kantor announced that the United States would impose restrictions on selected Japanese imports in retaliation for Japan's restricting access of a U.S. company (Motorola) to the Japanese market for cellular telephones.[66] To avoid U.S. sanctions, the Hosokawa government agreed on 25 February 1994 to prepare a plan that would reduce the trade surplus to 2.8 percent of gross domestic product in 1994 from a surplus of 3.1 percent in 1993.[67] Ichiro Ozawa of the Japan Renewal Party and rival to Hosokawa reportedly favored targets if they were introduced by Japan and were not subject to U.S. sanctions.[68] The plan that was produced involved some deregulation and the promotion of domestic demand. Japanese carmakers were also to boost their purchases of U.S. car parts (cars and car parts accounted for over half of Japan's U.S. $60 billion trade surplus with the United States in 1993).[69]

The United States regarded these measures as insufficient. Prime Minister Tsutomu Hata assumed office in April 1994, and on 9 May he told President Clinton that he wished to see trade talks resumed. In April–May 1994, the Clinton administration adopted a more flexible approach to trade negotiations with Japan as part of a reevaluation of Asia Pacific policy and in late May announced that the trade talks would be resumed. U.S. trade representative Mickey Kantor said the United States had "confirmed that we are not seeking numerical targets or managed trade. . . . The purpose of each agreement is to achieve concrete and substantial results in the market, increased access and sales."[70] Nevertheless, the United States wanted the negotiations to be "results-oriented," which led to Foreign Minister Koji Kakizawa expressing concern "that something like a request for numerical targets could emerge."[71]

Agreement on these issues was not reached during the Hata government. However, in October 1994 (by which time Tomiichi Murayama had become prime minister), agreements had been concluded on government procurement, insurance, window glass, and the criteria for determining the extent to which Japan was opening its markets. Although numerical targets were avoided, the United States could claim that market access for procurement, insurance, and window glass would be judged by objective criteria.[72]

For procurement it was agreed that the objective criteria to be used were not numerical targets but "annual evaluation of progress in the value and share of procurement of foreign products and services" (the agreement for insurance was similar).[73] Agreement on cars and car parts proved more elusive, prompting the United States to begin investigating Japan's imports of car parts under Section 301 of its 1988 trade law. Chief Cabinet Secretary Kozo Igarashi saw this decision as "totally inconsistent with the objective of maintaining . . . free trade."[74] When Clinton met Murayama in January 1995, they reached agreement on the opening of Japan's market for financial services.[75] The Clinton administration's more flexible approach had produced results, though it remained to be seen just how much the Japanese market would open up in light of the agreed-upon "objective criteria."

Cars and car parts were one area in which the United States wished to pursue negotiations with Japan. This became a major issue during 1995 because the United States was dissatisfied with what it saw as restrictions limiting the Japanese market for U.S.-made products. An agreement was finally reached at the end of June 1995, but not before the United States had threatened to impose tariffs of 100 percent on luxury cars imported from Japan. The United States had sought numerical targets as a means for measuring whether the Japanese market was becoming more accessible. The five major Japanese carmakers announced that the production of their vehicles in the United States would increase to 2.65 million units by 1998 from 2.1 million units in 1995. Consequently, U.S. officials estimated that the purchase of parts in the United States would increase by U.S. $6.75 billion over the same period.[76] U.S. $6 billion would be spent on foreign car parts in Japan by 1998.[77] Ryutaro Hashimoto, Japan's minister of international trade and industry, considered this a matter for the companies concerned rather than for the Japanese government: "The government of Japan has had no involvement in this calculation because it is beyond the scope and responsibility of government."[78]

It appeared that the strong yen was having some effect in reducing Japan's trade imbalance with the United States; however, it also appeared that the Japanese market was opening up because of changes in consumer preferences in Japan and concessions made by Japan in the Uruguay Round and APEC. Under these circumstances, it seemed that the United States would lessen bilateral pressure on Japan. Japan was more inclined to deal with such pressure by taking issues to multilateral institutions such as the World Trade Organization.

Conclusion

The impact of revisionism underlies these developments in Japanese-U.S. relations in the post–Cold War period. The conventional U.S. view of Japan upholds the importance of maintaining and strengthening the security relationship. Economic concerns are important but should not be allowed to disrupt the security relationship. Against this view, the revisionists have argued that Japan has for too long had a free ride at the United States' expense.[79] The United States should begin to treat Japan as a normal country; Japan should look after its own security needs. If the United States does contribute to Japanese security, this contribution should be used as leverage to exact economic concessions from Japan. In particular, the United States should not hesitate to pressure Japan to improve U.S. access to the Japanese market as a means of managing the trade imbalance between the two countries.

This type of thinking has been an influence, though not necessarily a dominant influence, on the Clinton administration's policy toward Japan. Although the administration has stated that it intends to maintain the security relationship with Japan, it has also not been averse to playing hardball with Japan on economic issues. It is an exaggeration to say that there has been a move in the direction of managed trade, but there has been some ambiguity on the matter.

U.S. policy in turn reinforces the position of those people in Japan who argue that Japan should regard itself as a normal country and not give any special deference to the United States. Although it is too early to tell what the long-term impact will be, it appears that the economic tensions between the two countries will lead to a recasting of their security relationship. This likelihood is reinforced by the fact that the post–Cold War international situation reduces the pressure on the two countries to act in concert on security issues. Without a perception of a common threat, there is more scope for Japan and the United States to pursue security policies independently of each other.

Notes

1. "Aspiring sincerely to an international peace based on justice and order, the Japanese people forever renounce war as a sovereign right of the nation and the threat or use of force as a means of settling international disputes.

"In order to accomplish the aim of the preceding paragraph, land, sea and air forces, as well as other war potential, will never be maintained. The right of the belligerency of the state will not be recognized."

2. Mochizuki, "To Change or to Contain," p. 348.

3. Holland, *Japan Challenges America,* p. 117.

4. Destler and Nacht, "U.S. Policy Toward Japan," p. 295.

5. Mochizuki, "To Change or to Contain," p. 350; Brock, "The Theory and Practice of Japan-Bashing," p. 39.

6. Tamamoto, "Japan's Search for a World Role." An updated version of this essay is reprinted in Bienen, *Power, Economics, and Security,* chap. 10.

7. Tamamoto, "Japan's Search for a World Role," p. 496.

8. Ishihara, *The Japan That Can Say No.*

9. Tamamoto, "Japan's Search for a World Role," pp. 496–497.

10. Ishihara, *The Japan That Can Say No,* p. 62.

11. Nish, "The United States in East Asia: Japan's Perspective," p. 37.

12. Ishihara, *The Japan That Can Say No,* p. 62.

13. Based on Harrison and Prestowitz, "Pacific Agenda: Defense or Economics?" p. 68.

14. Ibid.

15. Ibid., p. 62.

16. Polomka, "Towards a 'Pacific House,'" p. 177.

17. Richard Solomon, "US and Japan: An Evolving Partnership," *Current Policy* (U.S. Department of State), no. 1268, p. 2.

18. Ibid., p. 5.

19. Ibid.

20. Purrington and A. K., "Tokyo's Policy Responses During the Gulf Crisis," pp. 308–309.

21. Ibid., p. 309.

22. Purrington, "Tokyo's Policy Responses During the Gulf War and the Impact of the 'Iraqi Shock' on Japan," p. 171.

23. "Tokyo Declaration Issued by Bush, Miyazawa," *Japan Times,* 10 January 1992, p. 33.

24. "Miyazawa Vows Reform, 'Shared Vision' with U.S.," *Japan Times* (Weekly International Edition), 1–7 February 1993, p. 6.

25. Ibid.

26. "Still on Honeymoon: Japanese Visit to Washington Smoother than Feared," *Far Eastern Economic Review,* 25 February 1993, p. 13.

27. James Sterngold, "To U.S., Hosokawa Says 'Yes' but 'No,'" *International Herald Tribune,* 11 August 1993, p. 4.

28. "Security Ties with U.S. Questioned: Coalition Moves to Close Ranks," *Japan Times* (Weekly International Edition), 6–12 September 1993, pp. 1, 5.

29. Susumu Awanohara, "My Shield or Yours?" *Far Eastern Economic Review,* 14 October 1993, p. 22.

30. Ibid.; Ako Washio, "Diplomatic Efforts to Continue to End Pyongyang Standoff," *Japan Times* (Weekly International Edition), 15–21 November 1993, p. 3.

31. *Keesing's Record of World Events,* vol. 39 (1993), p. 39738.

32. David E. Sanger, "Clinton-Hosokawa: Hopes Dashed," *International Herald Tribune,* 10 February 1994, pp. 9, 13.

33. Charles Smith, "Flawed Alliance," *Far Eastern Economic Review,* 28 April 1994, p. 16.

34. "Key Ministers State Policy Goals," *Japan Times* (Weekly International Edition), 9–15 May 1994, p. 6.

35. *Keesing's Record of World Events,* vol. 40 (1994), p. 40100.

36. "Security Ties to Remain, Murayama Tells Clinton," *Japan Times* (Weekly International Edition), 18–24 July 1994, p. 6.

37. Nigel Holloway and Sebastian Moffett, "Patchwork Diplomacy," *Far Eastern Economic Review,* 23 November 1995, pp. 16–17; Nigel Holloway, "Missed Opportunity," *Far Eastern Economic Review,* 30 November 1995, p. 16.

38. *The Military Balance 1996/97,* p. 170.

39. Sebastian Moffett, "Back to the Barracks," *Far Eastern Economic Review,* 19 September 1996, pp. 16–17.

40. *Strategic Survey 1995–1996,* p. 187.

41. Quoted, Johnson, "History Restarted," p. 52.

42. T. R. Reid, "Tokyo Official Calls U.S. 'Subcontractor' to Japan Economy," *International Herald Tribune,* 21 January 1992, p. 1.

43. Johnson, "History Restarted," p. 59.

44. Tamamoto, "Japan's Search for a World Role," p. 516.

45. Marshall, "The U.S. and Japan," p. 334.

46. Ibid. See also Margaret Shapiro, "Wide Agreement Reached on Trade by U.S. and Japan," *International Herald Tribune,* 29 June 1990, pp. 1, 16.

47. See Fred Hiatt and Margaret Shapiro, "Kaifu to Fight Protectionism," *International Herald Tribune,* 29 June 1990, pp. 1, 2; Don Oberdorfer, "Bush Meets Japanese Leader and Cites 'Broad Agreement,'" *International Herald Tribune,* 2–3 September 1989, p. 2; Peter Riddell, "Economic Reforms a Priority Says Kaifu," *Financial Times,* 5 March 1990, p. 1.

48. Patrick L. Smith, "Japan-U.S. Crisis Over Trade," *International Herald Tribune,* 14 March 1990, p. 1.

49. *Keesing's Record of World Events,* vol. 37 (1991), p. 38558.

50. "Tokyo Declaration Issued by Bush, Miyazawa," *Japan Times,* 10 January 1992, p. 33.

51. Michiyo Nakamoto and Charles Leadbeater, "Japan Ready to Come Out Fighting," *Financial Times,* 8 February 1993, p. 3.

52. Steven Brull, "Japan Is Cool to Rise in Yen as Way to Cut Trade Gap," *International Herald Tribune,* 15 February 1993, pp. 1, 9.

53. See "Still on Honeymoon: Japanese Visit to Washington Smoother than Feared," *Far Eastern Economic Review,* 25 February 1993, p. 13.

54. Robert Delfs, "A New Ball Game," *Far Eastern Economic Review,* 3 June 1993, p. 49; Maya Maruko, "Clinton Remark Causes Yen to Rise," *Japan Times* (Weekly International Edition), 26 April–2 May 1993, p. 5.

55. Susumu Awanohara, "US Aims: Starting Over," *Far Eastern Economic Review,* 3 June 1993, p. 52.

56. "Clinton Targets Japan's Trade Surplus: New U.S. Policy Worries Tokyo," *Far Eastern Economic Review,* p. 5.

57. Susumu Awanohara, "A Promise Kept," *Far Eastern Economic Review*, 29 April 1993, p. 15.

58. David E. Sanger, "Japan Rallies Asia Against U.S. Push for Trade Quotas," *International Herald Tribune*, 7 June 1993, pp. 1, 3.

59. Steven Brull, "Price of Victory: Trouble Seen in U.S.-Japan Trade," *International Herald Tribune*, 12 July 1993, pp. 1, 16.

60. James Sterngold, "To U.S., Hosokawa Says 'Yes' but 'No,'" *International Herald Tribune*, 11 August 1993, p. 4.

61. "Japan Asks U.S. to Be Patient: Hosokawa Arrives for Talks with Clinton," *International Herald Tribune*, 27 September 1993, p. 5.

62. Paul Blustein, "Japan Bows to U.S. on Construction: Tokyo Unveils Plan to Open Market, and U.S. Postpones Sanction Threat," *International Herald Tribune*, 27 October 1993, p. 1.

63. Charles Smith and Jonathan Friedland, "Staple of Dispute: Tokyo Hints at Concessions on Rice Trade," *Far Eastern Economic Review*, 28 October 1993, p. 22.

64. Susumu Awanohara, "Washington's Ire," *Far Eastern Economic Review*, 20 January 1994, p. 56.

65. Susumu Awanohara and Charles Smith, "Trade Tantrums," *Far Eastern Economic Review*, 24 February 1994, p. 17.

66. "Shake Your Partners," *Economist*, 19 February 1994, p. 33.

67. *Keesing's Record of World Events*, vol. 40 (1994), p. 39864.

68. Charles Smith, "Second Thoughts," *Far Eastern Economic Review*, 10 March 1994, p. 56.

69. Jonathan Friedland, "Not Good Enough," *Far Eastern Economic Review*, 7 April 1994, p. 74.

70. Susumu Awanohara and Jonathan Friedland, "Agree to Agree," *Far Eastern Economic Review*, 2 June 1994, p. 61. On the change of emphasis in U.S. policy toward Japan at this time, see Susumu Awanohara, "Golden Opportunity," *Far Eastern Economic Review*, 21 July 1994, pp. 24–25.

71. "Japan-U.S. Talks Progressing," *Japan Times* (Weekly International Edition), 13–19 June 1994, pp. 1, 6.

72. Nigel Holloway and Charles Smith, "To Fight Another Day," *Far Eastern Economic Review*, 13 October 1994, p. 18.

73. Ako Washio and Maya Maruko, "Despite Breakthrough, Trade 'Deal' Remains Ambiguous," *Japan Times* (Weekly International Edition), 10–16 October 1994, p. 3.

74. Nigel Holloway and Charles Smith, "To Fight Another Day," *Far Eastern Economic Review*, 13 October 1994, p. 18.

75. "Open Sesame," *Economist*, 14 January 1995, p. 72.

76. Nigel Holloway, "Collision Averted," *Far Eastern Economic Review*, 13 July 1995, p. 76.

77. Ibid.

78. Ibid.

79. The leading revisionist is Chalmers Johnson. See, for example, his "Japan in Search of a 'Normal' Role." Other examples include Thurow, *Head to Head,* and Prestowitz, *Trading Places.*

7

THE SINO-U.S. RELATIONSHIP

Sino-U.S. relations have passed through a number of phases since 1945. This chapter summarizes those phases and then examines the post–Cold War era in more detail.

The Postwar Context

Sino-U.S. relations were antagonistic for more than two decades following the establishment of the People's Republic of China (PRC) in 1949. Initially, the United States saw China as part of a single Communist bloc led by the USSR. The U.S. policy of containment therefore applied just as much to China as to other parts of the bloc. U.S. hostility to China was reinforced by the Korean War, when Chinese "volunteers" entered the conflict on the side of North Korea. At the same time, the United States' relationship with the Nationalist government on Taiwan (the Republic of China, or ROC) was strengthened, leading to the signing of a mutual security treaty in 1954.

The U.S. view of China as the major threat to security in the Asia Pacific region was reciprocated by China's view of the United States as the major threat to its own security. The development of the Sino-Soviet conflict complicated this situation, but certainly in the 1950s, the United States was preeminent in China's perception of external threats. Reinforcing the perception were such developments as the strengthening security relationship between the United States and the Nationalist government on Taiwan (including U.S. support for that government's claim to be the legitimate government for the whole of China), the Taiwan Straits crises of 1955 and 1958, and the establishment of the Southeast Asia Treaty Organization (SEATO) in 1954. The Chinese viewed SEATO—which was complemented by U.S. defense treaties with Australia and New Zealand (ANZUS), Japan, and the ROC—as a manifestation of the U.S. "encirclement" of China. Apart from its extensive naval forces in the region, U.S. forces were stationed in countries such as Japan, South Korea, and the Philippines.

By the 1960s, the United States had become aware of the intensity of the Sino-Soviet conflict. U.S. hostility to China remained strong, however, and it was one of the factors leading to U.S. intervention in Vietnam, where Communist success was seen as assisting Chinese expansionist designs. For its part, China was hostile to any shift by the United States toward a "two Chinas" policy (which was contemplated, for example, by the Kennedy administration). In addition, the onset of the Vietnam War meant that again there was a major military conflict on China's borders. The escalation of that war coincided with an intensification of the Sino-Soviet conflict. China thus felt threatened by both superpowers, a feeling that was heightened by the xenophobia of the Cultural Revolution.

By the late 1960s, the situation was beginning to change again. The Nixon administration sought improved relations with China as part of its strategy for stabilizing international politics and, more particularly, as a means for facilitating a settlement in Vietnam. China was influenced by a desire to avoid simultaneous conflicts with both the United States and the USSR. Although the more radical elements preferred to maintain China's opposition to "imperialism" and "social imperialism," the dominant view was that it was better to come to terms with one of China's foes.

The rapprochement between China and the United States was formalized with the signing of the Shanghai communiqué in February 1972.[1] This development coincided with a period of détente in Soviet-U.S. relations. Thus, China and the USSR remained in conflict with each other but were simultaneously trying to improve relations with the United States. This meant that the United States could use its relationship with one of the Communist powers as a means of putting pressure on the other. When Soviet-U.S. relations deteriorated in the late 1970s, there was talk in the Carter administration of "playing the China card." A de facto Sino-U.S. alliance could provide a means of containing the USSR.

In 1978 the Carter administration and the PRC agreed to full diplomatic normalization, an agreement that required the severing of official U.S. diplomatic relations with the ROC on Taiwan. However, the Taiwan Relations Act of 1979 allowed the United States to continue an "unofficial" relationship with Taiwan and signaled the United States' interest in a peaceful resolution of the Taiwan issue. U.S. arms sales to Taiwan continued to be a problem for Sino-U.S. relations. A resolution of the issue was attempted in the Sino-U.S. joint communiqué of 17 August 1982, in which the United States stated its intention "to reduce gradually its sales of arms to Taiwan."[2]

An indication of the changing Sino-U.S. relationship was the large-scale arms sales during the 1980s to China by the United States. In 1979 China and the United States had reached an agreement to establish a joint missile monitoring station in Xinjiang. The United States also assisted China in the peaceful development of nuclear energy under the 1985 nuclear cooperation agreement.[3] The Sino-U.S. military relationship was formalized in September 1983 by U.S. defense secretary Caspar Weinberger as a "three pillars" approach involving senior visits, exchanges, and technological cooperation.[4] By 1986, U.S. military sales to China under FMS (foreign military sales) agreements exceeded U.S. $37 million; commercial sales were nearly U.S. $20 million.[5]

Despite these developments, by this stage there was less talk of Sino-U.S. "strategic cooperation." In March 1983 U.S. secretary of state George Shultz had stated that Japan was the most important U.S. ally in Asia and that China, though important, was a regional power.[6] This attitude was reinforced by the improved Soviet-U.S. relationship that developed during the Gorbachev period. A cooperative security relationship with China was important to the United States, but not in terms of a global strategy. An irritant in the Sino-U.S. relationship was the sale of Silkworm antiship missiles by China to Iran. After July 1987, when the United States began escorting reflagged Kuwaiti tankers in the Persian Gulf, it had to contend with the possibility of Iranian attacks using these missiles. China's subsequent agreement to supply CSS-2 ballistic missiles to Saudi Arabia also exacerbated Middle East tensions.

Even before the end of the Cold War, then, changes in Soviet-U.S. relations had made China less strategically significant to the United States. The relationship remained important in terms of security because of China's regional role and the influence it could exert in areas such as the Middle East. At the same time, improvements in PRC-Taiwan relations augmented the U.S. perception that China was mostly playing a constructive role in international affairs. The improved relations between Taiwan and the PRC were prompted by Beijing's switch to "peaceful reunification" in 1979 and its subsequent adoption of the goal of "one country, two systems" in 1983 (which was also the basis for the 1984 agreement to transfer Hong Kong from British to Chinese sovereignty in 1997).[7]

The Impact of Tiananmen Square

All aspects of the Sino-U.S. relationship were jeopardized by the massacre at Tiananmen Square on 4 June 1989. Let us look first at the U.S. response to the massacre before turning to the Chinese response.

The U.S. Response

Tiananmen Square led to a much stronger emphasis on human rights considerations in the United States' relations with China. These considerations were articulated most clearly through Congress. President Bush attempted to maintain the substance of the U.S. relationship with China but was forced to make modifications. President Clinton has had to wrestle with the same issues.

In the immediate aftermath of Tiananmen Square, Bush announced that U.S. military sales and visits by military personnel to China would be suspended. At the same time, he said, "I don't want to see a total break in this relationship and I will not encourage a total break in the relationship."[8] Subsequently, it was announced that high-level exchanges would be suspended and that the United States and its allies would oppose loans to China by international financial institutions.[9] Bush suggested that the United States could exert some influence to ameliorate the human rights situation in China by maintaining the existing relationship. The U.S. relationship with China was also important in terms of regional security if conflicts in countries such as Afghanistan and Cambodia were to be resolved. The relationship with China also provided the United States with a means of pressuring North Korea.

Bush had been the U.S. representative in China in 1974–1975, and this appointment influenced the formulation of policy toward China during his administration. Because maintaining the relationship with China was important to Bush, even in the aftermath of the massacre, National Security Adviser Brent Scowcroft and Deputy Secretary of State Lawrence Eagleburger were sent on a secret mission to Beijing on 1–2 July 1989 and on another mission in December 1989.[10] Although it is questionable whether any significant changes resulted from these missions, their purpose was to secure some modification in China's domestic policies and to maintain the momentum of Sino-U.S. relations.

Bush's weak response to the Beijing massacre provoked widespread criticism in Congress. On 22 June 1989 Senate Majority Leader George Mitchell, referring to the execution of dissidents in China, said: "I am saddened by the president's refusal to give outlet to the feelings of the American people about these executions which now have reached the point which can only be described as organized murder."[11] Similarly, after the second Scowcroft-Eagleburger mission, Mitchell said that Bush had "kowtowed to the Chinese government." Arguing that the administration had adopted a "business as usual" approach, Mitchell continued: "There are times when what America stands for and believes in is more important than economic or geopolitical considerations. This is one of those times."[12] Stephen Solarz, the Democratic chairman of the House Foreign Affairs Subcommittee on Asian and Pacific Affairs, took the view that Bush "has demonstrated that he is far more concerned about the sensibilities of the Chinese leadership than the aspirations of those in China who hope to bring a greater measure of democracy to their homeland."[13]

The Chinese Response

In his study of Chinese elite perceptions of the United States, David Shambaugh distinguishes between Marxist and non-Marxist perspectives on U.S. foreign policy. The Marxists, following Lenin, see the "motive force" of U.S. foreign policy as "monopoly capitalists who seek ever-higher profits and ever-expanding areas of control abroad."[14] The non-Marxists, by contrast, see "a more variegated, ad hoc U.S. foreign policy" deriving from "a multiplicity of interests that are defined in the context of this or that specific region, country, or domestic interest group."[15] These different perspectives paralleled political divisions within the Chinese leadership that were exacerbated by the crisis of mid-1989. Conservative leaders saw Sino-U.S. relations from a Marxist ideological perspective; moderate leaders saw the relationship in more pragmatic terms.[16] Whereas the former group advocated responding in kind to Western sanctions after Tiananmen, the latter group counseled patience and a conciliatory stance. Deng Xiaoping's position was ambiguous: At times he blamed the United States for the troubles China experienced; in the long term, however, he worked toward achieving accommodation.[17]

Even before the crisis of mid-1989, Chinese leaders had warned the United States against interfering in China's domestic affairs. When Bush visited Beijing in February 1989, he was told by Zhao Ziyang, the reformist general secretary of the Chinese Communist Party, that "the fact that there are some people in American society who support people dissatisfied with the Chinese government will not contribute to the stability of China's political system and the process of reform, nor will it be conducive to relations with the USA."[18] U.S. support for dissidents such as astrophysicist Fang Lizhi was likely to undermine the position of reformists within the Chinese leadership.[19]

In the aftermath of the Beijing massacre, the official Chinese response was to declare: "What is happening in China is China's internal affair. . . . [The] Chinese government is completely capable of quelling the current rebellion in Beijing."[20] The imposition of sanctions by the United States was angrily rejected. This sentiment was clearly expressed in a statement by the Foreign Affairs Committee of the National People's Congress on 19 July 1989:

> We hereby express our utmost indignation at such acts by the US Congress of grossly interfering in China's internal affairs. . . . [The Beijing disturbances] were a planned, organized and premeditated political turmoil started by a tiny number of people in collusion with some hostile forces abroad through taking advantages [*sic*] of student demonstrations. The turmoil later escalated into a counter-revolutionary rebellion in Beijing.[21]

The Marxist ideological perspective was evident in an article entitled "Anti-China Clamour Cannot Intimidate Chinese People" by the *People's Daily* commentator.[22] The actions of the U.S. Congress derived from "anti-communist class instincts." The quelling of the "counter-revolutionary rebellion" was "a justifiable and legitimate measure that any sovereign country in the world would take when faced with a similar situation." The advocates of sanctions in the U.S. Congress were responsible for "persistent, flagrant interference in China's internal affairs, such as on the question of Taiwan, the 'Tibetan question' and the so-called 'human rights question.' . . . [Only] a China practising bourgeois liberalization and taking a capitalist road will please them."

It is interesting to observe that the commentary distinguishes between the advocates of sanctions in Congress and the Bush administration:

> We have noted the Bush administration's opinion that the United States should make a discreet response to events in China and that it is in accord with US national interests to keep good relations with China. . . . We hope that the US government and the majority of American Congressmen will not do things which damage bilateral relations out of consideration for maintaining the fundamental interests of the Chinese and American people and the overall situation in Sino-US relations.

Speaking in New York on 2 October 1989, Foreign Minister Qian Qichen of China rejected U.S. interference in "China's internal affairs" but advocated reconciliation on the basis of the Five Principles of Peaceful Coexistence.[23] The first two principles were perhaps most important to the improvement of Sino-U.S. relations: "It is essential to recognize and respect differences, and seek and enlarge common ground" and "The domestic politics of a country should not be taken as a precondition for the restoration and development of bilateral relations."

Deng Xiaoping made his views clear when he spoke to Richard Nixon in Beijing on 31 October 1989.[24] On the one hand, he said, "Frankly speaking, the US was involved too deeply in the turmoil and counter-revolutionary rebellion which occurred in Beijing not long ago. China was the real victim and it is unjust to reprove China for it." On the other hand, the influence of the non-Marxist perspective can be seen in Deng's argument that "national interest" should be taken as the "highest criterion" in the conduct of a country's affairs. In Deng's view, "We can never forget state sovereignty and national honour, nor can we do away with national self-respect." Stability was crucial to China: "Without a political situation marked by stability and unity, and without a stable social order we can accomplish nothing in a country with such a huge population and poor foundation."

China protested against amendments on sanctions adopted by Congress in mid-November 1989; China also objected to U.S. measures making it easier for Chinese students to stay in the United States.[25] The December

1989 visit to Beijing by National Security Adviser Scowcroft and Deputy Secretary of State Eagleburger benefited those elements favoring a return to normality in Sino-U.S. relations and undermined the more conservative elements. As Deng said on this occasion, "Despite certain disputes and differences, ultimately Sino-US relations must be improved. It is necessary for world peace."[26]

1990–1992

Although the sharp deterioration in Sino-U.S. relations after the Beijing massacre did not lead to a permanent rupture, the issues that came to the fore at the time continued to be important. On the one hand, the United States had to balance the strategic and economic importance it assigned to China against China's violation of human rights. On the other hand, China rejected interference in what it saw as domestic matters and at the same time attempted to demonstrate that it could not be ignored on major international issues.

Bush and His Critics

A clear statement of the Bush administration's objectives in China was given by Acting Secretary of State Lawrence Eagleburger before the Senate Foreign Relations Committee on 7 February 1990. Apart from the desire to influence Chinese domestic policies and to promote economic relations, the Bush administration wished to advance security objectives, both global and regional. China retained its strategic importance in the post–Cold War world:

> China remains relevant in resolving the conflicts left over from an earlier time of Soviet expansionism. But of even greater importance is the fact that, as the world's most populous nation, a country with great economic potential, and the possessor of a significant military capability, China's participation is essential to coping successfully with a number of transnational issues. These include, among others, the proliferation of missiles and nuclear weapons, chemical weapons proliferation, and environmental pollution. Thus China's strategic significance needs to be seen not simply through the narrow prism of the Soviet factor but on the far broader scale of its place in an increasingly polycentric world.[27]

According to Eagleburger, China's regional role was even more self-evident; Korea and Cambodia were specifically mentioned. The Bush administration did not want to see China return to a "spoiler" role; hence it must be engaged in dialogue on regional issues. China's role during the Gulf conflict of 1990–1991 bore out Eagleburger's argument. Although not actively involved with the coalition forces against Iraq, China chose not to obstruct these forces (through its membership on the UN Security Council, for example).[28] China's actions during the conflict were related to a desire to decrease its diplomatic isolation after Tiananmen Square.

The problem for the Bush administration was how to pursue its objectives in China in light of the different priorities emanating from Congress. Essentially, the administration continued to pursue its goals while attempting to compromise with Congress when necessary. One issue of conflict between the president and Congress was the question of MFN (most-favored-nation) status for China.

This status had originally been granted by Carter in 1980, and despite what the term might suggest, it simply meant that normal economic relations existed between the United States and China. Any tariffs imposed on imports from a country with MFN status would be no greater than whatever the lowest prevailing tariffs happened to be. There were moves within Congress to attach conditions to the granting of MFN status to China as a means of influencing human rights issues in that country. Bush resisted these moves on the grounds that they would jeopardize any influence the United States had in China (on human rights and other issues). Bush also believed these moves would adversely affect the burgeoning free market sector in China and the interests of Americans who benefited from Chinese imports or sold products to China.[29]

Despite these arguments, lobbying on the issue came primarily from U.S. interests that would suffer from a revocation of China's MFN status—wheat exporters and retail interests (importers of Chinese toys and textiles) in particular.[30] Although China maintained its MFN status, Bush nevertheless needed to show that he would take an active role in pressuring China on various issues. Indicative of this role was Bush's letter to Democratic senator Max Baucus in July 1991, in which he outlined steps to ensure better access to China for U.S. exports.[31] Similarly, the Dalai Lama's visit to Washington, D.C., in April 1991 demonstrated that Bush was active in pursuing human rights issues in China.[32] Nevertheless, in 1992 Bush was forced to veto two bills linking the renewal of China's MFN status to improvements in China's human rights policies and better access to its markets.[33]

China's Response

In response to the conflict between Bush and Congress, China attacked its critics in Congress and elsewhere and simultaneously encouraged Bush's viewpoint. In pursuit of this latter goal, China increasingly attempted to show its importance to the United States in a variety of international situations.

Chinese protests against "interventionist" U.S. policies continued throughout 1990. When Congress passed legislation to codify existing U.S.

sanctions in January 1990, Vice Foreign Minister Liu Huaqiu protested to U.S. ambassador James Lilley against the "hegemonist act of the US Congress, which, basing its legislation on rumours, has wilfully trampled on the basic norms governing international relations and wantonly interfered in China's internal affairs."[34] The State Department's annual human rights report was attacked soon after in a *People's Daily* commentary as a "New Demonstration of Hegemonism."[35] Claiming that "some anti-China elements of the United States were deeply involved in the turmoil . . . [of] the counter-revolutionary rebellion last June in Beijing," the commentator went on to reject criticisms of "the situation in Tibet" and "China's domestic policies and some administrative measures that have nothing to do with human rights." The "peaceful evolution" strategy of the United States would not force China "to give up its Four Cardinal Principles—adherence to the socialist road, the leadership of the Communist Party, the people's democratic dictatorship and Marxism-Leninism and Mao Zedong Thought."

Although this commentary was written from a Marxist ideological perspective, in practice a number of steps of a more pragmatic nature were taken. In June 1990, following Bush's renewal of China's MFN status in May, the leading dissident Fang Lizhi was allowed to leave China (where he had taken shelter in the U.S. embassy).[36] China also made itself useful to the United States in the Gulf conflict, which developed after August 1990. At the same time, China attempted to improve its relations with the USSR and Japan, as well as with other countries in the Asia Pacific region, such as Vietnam.[37] This last relationship was particularly relevant to achieving a settlement of the conflict in Cambodia.

Chinese success in showing its continued importance to the United States was highlighted when Foreign Minister Qian Qichen visited Washington, D.C., in November 1990 for talks with President Bush and Secretary of State James Baker.[38] China also agreed to visits by Assistant Secretary of State for Human Rights and Humanitarian Affairs Richard Schifter and Under Secretary for International Security Affairs Reginald Bartholomew (regarding weapons proliferation issues). When Schifter visited China in December, a spokesperson for the Chinese foreign ministry said, "To exchange views on human rights is one thing; to interfere in internal affairs under the pretext of human rights is another."[39] Whether this amounted to an acceptance of discussions on human rights issues as part of the bilateral relationship was difficult to say. Written from a Marxist ideological perspective, the *People's Daily* commentary of 23 December 1990 was negative on this point: "Everyone can see that human rights clamoured for by these 'guardians' have been used to oppress the masses, interfere in others and protect the hegemony of rule by the bourgeoisie and dollar imperialists."[40]

China's relationship with the United States continued along similar lines during 1991. Issues concerning its territorial integrity were of some concern to China. The government issued a protest when Bush received the Dalai Lama in April; China believed the United States was supporting a person who "advocates 'Tibetan independence' and seeks to split China and undermine the unity of her nationalities."[41] Similarly, China was critical of remarks by James Lilley, the former U.S. ambassador to China, who criticized the Chinese principle of "one country, two systems" as the basis for reunification with Taiwan.[42] In November 1991, China took issue with proposed U.S. legislation to express support for the 1984 Sino-British Joint Declaration on Hong Kong.[43]

The MFN issue also remained important in 1991. China was hostile to U.S. attempts to link renewal of MFN status to progress on human rights issues. At the same time, tensions in the Sino-U.S. relationship were exacerbated by a growing trade deficit in China's favor and U.S. allegations of unfair trade practices.[44] The United States was concerned by Chinese missile sales to Pakistan, Syria, and Iran. China attempted to alleviate this concern by "seriously considering" signing the Nuclear Nonproliferation Treaty (NPT).[45] Many of these issues were discussed when Secretary of State Baker visited China from 15 to 17 November 1991. China indicated to Baker that it would adhere to the NPT within three months and that it would observe the guidelines for the Missile Technology Control Regime. It also expressed support for turning the Korean peninsula into a "nuclear-free zone." Some progress was made on trade issues, but China maintained its stance that human rights issues were an internal matter.[46]

While the MFN and human rights issue continued to strain Sino-U.S. relations during 1992, a new issue arose that had implications for China's security: Bush's decision in September to allow the sale of up to 150 F-16 fighter aircraft to Taiwan.[47] In the words of the *People's Daily* commentary: "This decision flagrantly violates the Sino-US joint communique of August 17, 1982, grossly interferes in China's internal affairs, seriously jeopardizes Sino-US relations, and obstructs and undermines the cause of China's peaceful reunification. The Chinese people have expressed their great outrage with and strong protest against such hegemonistic behavior."[48] Vice Foreign Minister Liu Huaqiu put the matter more moderately when he said to U.S. ambassador J. Stapleton Roy that the decision "would lead to a major retrogression in Sino-US relations and would inevitably cause a negative impact on Sino-US co-operation in the United Nations and other international organizations."[49]

Issues in Sino-U.S. Relations Since 1993

Since 1993, the issues that were important in the early 1990s have continued to dominate Sino-U.S. relations. We will focus on the initial approaches of both the Clinton administration and China before turning to the issues of trade and human rights, concerns about nuclear and chemical weapons and missile technology, Taiwan, and the broader security relationship.

Initial Approaches

Although it was expected that Bill Clinton would align himself with the Democrats in Congress who were critical of China, he has largely continued Bush's policies. An early indication of the new administration's policy toward China was given in the confirmation hearings of Warren Christopher (as secretary of state) and Winston Lord (as assistant secretary of state for East Asian and Pacific Affairs). Christopher spoke in favor of renewing China's MFN status, "but conditioned on their making very substantial progress" in areas such as human rights and "abusive trade practices."[50] Lord, who had been U.S. ambassador to China between 1985 and 1989 (during Ronald Reagan's second term in office), gave geopolitical reasons for maintaining links with China, in particular the hope that China could restrain North Korea in the development of nuclear weapons.[51]

Although he had a reputation as a Clinton supporter and advocate of human rights, Lord had earlier indicated his preference for a "balanced" approach to China in an article published soon after Tiananmen Square: "While I consider the encouragement of human rights an important dimension of our foreign policy, I also weigh heavily the geopolitical and economic factors. . . . My strong natural impulse is to refrain from commenting on China's internal difficulties."[52] Essentially, Lord argued in favor of the policy adopted by Bush after Tiananmen Square. At the same time, he believed that strategic factors were important in Sino-U.S. relations, in particular Indochina, Korea, and South Asia, as were China's involvement in the Middle East and its missile sales to Third World countries.[53]

One measure of the Clinton administration's desire to maintain a working relationship with China was the emphasis it placed on restoring meetings between high-level officials. A meeting between Secretary of State Warren Christopher and Foreign Minister Qian Qichen at the UN in September 1993 was followed by visits to Beijing by Agriculture Secretary Mike Espy, Defense Undersecretary Charles Freeman, and Treasury Secretary Lloyd Bentsen and culminated in November 1993 at the meeting between Clinton and China's president, Jiang Zemin, at the conference of the Asia-Pacific Economic Cooperation in Seattle.[54] This last meeting was the highest-level Sino-U.S. exchange since Tiananmen Square. Despite concern in the United States about China's human rights policies in general and issues such as Tibet and democratic reform in Hong Kong in particular, the welcome given to the Dalai Lama in Washington, D.C., in April 1993 was more cautious than that extended by Bush two years earlier.[55] Although the two administrations were different, their perceptions of the importance of China to the United States were remarkably similar.

Despite Clinton's campaign rhetoric that was critical of Bush's China policy, China initially expressed a willingness to work with the new president "on the basis of principles enshrined in the three Sino-US joint communiques."[56] On 30 November 1992, General Secretary Jiang Zemin emphasized to visiting U.S. congressmen the broader international context of Sino-U.S. relations when he said they had "a major impact on peace and stability in the Asia-Pacific region and the world as a whole."[57] However, because China feared a more difficult relationship with Clinton, it was reportedly taking steps to accelerate sales of weapons (including missile technology) to countries such as Iran, Syria, and Pakistan (and possibly Libya).[58]

Trade and Human Rights

The MFN issue remained important to Sino-U.S. relations, particularly during the early part of the Clinton administration. Congress strongly supported the view that MFN should be used as a lever in China's human rights performance. Clinton supported MFN renewal, but subject to conditions. Although the administration favored consensus with Congress on the issue, it argued that determining conditions on the basis of presidential policy rather than through legislation would be more flexible. It was expected that these conditions would relate to progress on human rights, trade issues, and the proliferation of missiles, but the 1993 renewal confined itself solely to human rights.[59]

By 1994, the Clinton administration had concluded that linking MFN to human rights was an ineffective way to achieve change and jeopardized the ability of the United States to work with China on other areas of common interest. On 24 May Clinton announced that China's MFN status would be extended; trade would not be used to pressure China on human rights issues. In Clinton's words, his decision "offers us the best opportunity to lay the basis for long-term sustainable progress in human rights and for the advancement of our other interests with China."[60]

China's position all along had been that it would not allow the MFN issue to be a pretext for interference in its internal affairs. As Jiang Zemin commented in 1993, MFN "should be the basis for normal economic relations and trade between the two countries and should not have become an issue."[61] China continued to advance its own position vigorously in 1994.[62] This might have partly been an attempt to disarm criticism from more conservative elements at home. It might have also been related to a perception that Clinton's own domestic position on this issue was weak.

In any event, China sought to demonstrate to critics the adverse economic implications both for Hong Kong as a transshipment center and for Taiwan as a source of investment in mainland industries oriented to the U.S. market. Secretary of State Warren Christopher was given short shrift when he visited Beijing in March 1994 to press for Chinese action on human rights issues. In April 1994, a Chinese delegation visited the United States to lead a trade promotion, to elicit bids for investment projects, and to spend hundreds of millions of dollars on the purchase of U.S. goods for government agencies in China. China believed that such action would strengthen support for its position in the U.S. business community, which in turn would lead to further lobbying of the Clinton administration.

Human rights issues remained influential in Sino-U.S. relations, but henceforth the Clinton administration attempted to deal with these issues in the context of the relationship as a whole rather than focus on one in particular. (Any attempt by Congress to use MFN differently would most likely have been subject to a presidential veto.) Whether the new approach would be more effective was doubtful given China's position on the matter. China's treatment of human rights activists and the Dalai Lama's role in publicizing the plight of Tibet highlighted China's stance on human rights in general.

Trade between the United States and China continued to expand. China estimated that by 1995 the United States took 16.6 percent of its total exports (the United States put the figure at 30 percent, allowing for the shipment of goods through Hong Kong). The trade deficit (which the United States estimated at U.S. $33.8 billion in 1995, though U.S. $23 billion, allowing for the Hong Kong factor, seems more accurate) was growing.[63] The deficit increased U.S. demands that China should take action against copyright piracy. The United States also insisted that China implement the liberal trading rules of the World Trade Organization before it would support Chinese membership in that organization.

Weapons and Missile Proliferation

A source of tension in Sino-U.S. relations is the United States' view that China has undermined its attempts to restrict the spread of nuclear and chemical weapons and missile technology. Secretary of State James Baker had secured promises from China in November 1991 to adhere to the Missile Technology Control Regime (MTCR) and to the Nuclear Nonproliferation Treaty; (the latter was signed in March 1992).[64] In 1993, when it became clear that China was selling M-11 missiles (capable of delivering nuclear weapons) to Pakistan, the United States invoked various electronics export bans on China.[65] The resumption of Chinese nuclear testing in October 1993 also damaged Sino-U.S. relations.[66] Tensions developed in the area of chemical weapons proliferation when the United States claimed that the Chinese ship *Yinhe* was carrying chemical weapons ingredients for use by Iran.[67] Subsequent Sino-U.S. inspection showed this claim to be without foundation, but the perception remained that China's involvement in Middle East weapons sales was detrimental to U.S. interests. Possibly influenced by this perception, the Senate Foreign Relations

Committee voted in July 1993 to reject the gradual reduction guidelines in the 1982 Sino-U.S. communiqué concerning arms sales to Taiwan.[68]

China argued that the U.S. response to these incidents was unwarranted. When the U.S. government barred the sale of some advanced technology to China in reaction to Chinese sales of missile technology to Pakistan, these sanctions were rejected by the Chinese foreign ministry as "entirely unjustifiable."[69] The *Yinhe* incident was described by the foreign ministry as "a show of hegemony and power politics, pure and simple."[70]

Talks in Washington, D.C., between Secretary of State Warren Christopher and Foreign Minister Qian Qichen indicated an improved Sino-U.S. understanding on proliferation issues. On 4 October 1994, the two sides agreed that they would work for "the earliest possible achievement" of an international convention "banning the production of fissile materials for nuclear weapons." In addition, China agreed to accept the internationally agreed definition of a violation of the MTCR.[71]

U.S. concerns again came to the fore in May 1995, when China tested a solid-fuel ballistic missile (the East Wind 31),[72] and in early 1996, when allegations surfaced that China had transferred nuclear weapons-related technology to Pakistan.[73] In mid-1996, there were further allegations that Pakistan had deployed M-11 ballistic missiles provided by China.[74] Since Pakistan was engaged in developing a nuclear capacity, the substantiation of these allegations would have pressured the U.S. government to invoke sanctions against China.

Taiwan

Taiwan is a major source of conflict in Sino-U.S. relations not only because the United States has continued to sell arms to Taiwan but also because China has opposed Taiwan's attempts to improve its international status. In September 1993, China protested reports that the United States would sell to Taiwan forty-one Harpoon antiship missiles and four Hawkeye E-2T airborne early warning command and control aircraft.[75] China also took exception to U.S. legislation in May 1994 that, among other things, removed the limit on U.S. arms sales to Taiwan (arguing that Section 3 of the Taiwan Relations Act took precedence over the communiqué of 17 August 1982).[76]

During 1995, Clinton found himself under increasing pressure from the Republican-dominated Congress to adopt a more critical stance toward China and to make concessions to Taiwan. Leading Republican figures such as Senator Jesse Helms, chairman of the Senate Foreign Relations Committee, and Newt Gingrich, Speaker of the House of Representatives, openly espoused a pro-Taiwan position. On 9 July 1995, Gingrich called for U.S. diplomatic recognition of Taiwan.[77]

The Taiwan issue came to a head when the Clinton administration granted a visa on 22 May 1995 for President Lee Teng-hui of Taiwan to attend an alumni reunion at Cornell University in June. Although ostensibly a private occasion, the visit was seen by China as undermining the "one China" policy that the United States officially supported. The Chinese foreign ministry accused the United States of "brazenly creating 'two Chinas,' or 'one China, one Taiwan.'"[78] China subsequently increased pressure on Taiwan (and indirectly on the United States) by holding missile tests close to northern Taiwan in July and August 1995.[79]

The Taiwan issue also came to the fore in March 1996, in the first democratically conducted presidential elections in Taiwan. China was particularly concerned that the pro-independence Democratic Progressive Party would make gains. China communicated its opposition to an independent Taiwan by conducting missile tests close to the island. The United States responded by moving naval forces into a protective position in the Taiwan Straits. Although Lee Teng-hui was successful in the elections, the episode did show that the development of a more independent status for Taiwan could lead to tensions in Sino-U.S. relations.

China saw Taiwan as an issue relating to its territorial integrity, and it viewed Tibet and Hong Kong in a similar light. The United States often saw Tibet as a human rights issue or a situation in which the right of self-determination should be exercised. And although the United States had accepted the 1984 Sino-British agreement on reversion in Hong Kong, there is the potential for damage to Sino-U.S. relations should there be problems after Chinese rule is restored on 1 July 1997.

The Security Relationship

Since 1993, there has been the question of whether the broader security relationship between the United States and China should be seen as cooperative or conflictual. This is not simply a matter of how the two countries have dealt with issues such as Taiwan but also a matter of how they have related to the pattern of security in the region as a whole. From the U.S. perspective, the question is sometimes posed in terms of whether or not China should be seen as a security threat. Although the United States has often been negative about some of China's actions regarding nuclear proliferation and the transfer of missile technology to countries such as Pakistan and Iran, China has been in a position where it could cooperate or not with the United States on issues such as North Korea. Chinese policy and actions in relation to the South China Sea could also undermine the United States' goal of achieving stability in the region.

There is also the broader question of how China positions itself in the multipolar pattern of the region; this position directly affects Sino-U.S. relations. If China tries to develop relationships with the United States and Japan, this is likely to lead to a large measure of cooperation between

China and the United States. However, if the relationship is primarily antagonistic, then China is more likely to develop relations with countries that also have problematic relationships with the United States. If China were to develop a relationship with Russia, for example, the two conservative leaderships could well have a common anti-U.S. agenda. Such a situation would be a serious problem for the United States.

The Clinton administration concluded by 1996 that it should pursue a strategy of engagement rather than containment in China. It argued that the likelihood of China's becoming a threat could be minimized by engaging in dialogue with China and developing common interests between the two countries. China tended to be suspicious of engagement; in the words of one Chinese analyst, it was "an attempt to pervade China with U.S. economic, political, cultural and ideological influences."[80] The United States found that although achieving its objectives through engagement was not necessarily straightforward, a strategy based on containment would more likely exacerbate tensions between the two countries. Although the crisis of March 1996 demonstrated that the United States was prepared to provide military support to Taiwan, in opposition to China, the Clinton administration concluded that, on the whole, more could be gained by developing links with China in the hope that they would integrate China more effectively with the region and the world.

Notes

1. The development of Sino-U.S. relations since 1972, including the period since 1989, is covered in detail in Harding, *A Fragile Relationship*.
2. "U.S.-China Joint Communique, August 17, 1982," *Department of State Bulletin*, vol. 82 no. 2067 (October 1982), p. 20.
3. See Tan, "U.S.-China Nuclear Cooperation Agreement."
4. Woon, "Chinese Arms Sales and U.S.-China Military Relations," p. 602.
5. McLaurin and Moon, *The United States and the Defense of the Pacific*, p. 165.
6. Ross, "National Security, Human Rights, and Domestic Politics," p. 282.
7. On PRC-Taiwan relations and their implications for the United States, see, for example, Lasater, *Policy in Evolution;* Copper, *China Diplomacy;* Zhan, *Ending the Chinese Civil War.*
8. *Congressional Quarterly Weekly Report,* 10 June 1989, pp. 1411, 1426.
9. Richard L. Williams, "U.S. Response to Changes in China," *Current Policy,* no. 1195, p. 2.
10. Lawrence S. Eagleburger, "U.S. Actions Toward China," *Current Policy,* no. 1247, pp. 3–4.
11. "A Policy Confrontation on China?" *Congressional Quarterly Weekly Report,* 24 June 1989, p. 1564.
12. "Bush Bid to Fix Beijing Ties Strains Those with Hill," *Congressional Quarterly Weekly Report,* 24 June 1989, pp. 3434–3435.
13. Ibid., p. 3435.

14. Shambaugh, *Beautiful Imperialist*, pp. 226–227.

15. Ibid., p. 235. See also Wang and Lin, "Chinese Perceptions in the Post–Cold War Era," which suggests that elite views of the United States can be seen in terms of "ideological," "geopolitical," and "global interdependence" perspectives.

16. Harding, "China's American Dilemma," pp. 14–15.

17. See Yahuda, "Sino-American Relations," pp. 188–189.

18. *Keesing's Record of World Events*, vol. 35 (1989), p. 36455.

19. Robert Delfs, "Regrets Only," *Far Eastern Economic Review*, 9 March 1989, p. 11.

20. "US Interference Protested," *Beijing Review*, 12–25 June 1989, p. 7.

21. "US Congress' Bill Refuted," *Beijing Review*, 31 July–6 August 1989, p. 6.

22. "Anti-China Clamour Cannot Intimidate Chinese People," *Beijing Review*, 17–23 July 1989, pp. 14–15.

23. Qian Qichen, "Current International Situation and Sino-US Relations," *Beijing Review*, 9–15 October 1989, pp. 7–9.

24. "US Must Take Steps to Patch Up Sino-US Rift," *Beijing Review*, 13–19 November 1989, pp. 5–6.

25. "China Protests US Congress Bill," *Beijing Review*, 27 November–3 December 1989, p. 7; "US Bill on Student Visas Censured," *Beijing Review*, 4–10 December 1989, p. 7.

26. Robert Delfs and Susumu Awanohara, "Angling for Influence," *Far Eastern Economic Review*, 21 December 1989, p. 10.

27. Eagleburger, "U.S. Actions Toward China," p. 2.

28. See Malik, *The Gulf War*, pp. 57–79.

29. The arguments of the Bush administration are well presented in the statement by Richard Solomon, assistant secretary of state for East Asian and Pacific Affairs, to the Subcommittee on East Asian and Pacific Affairs of the Senate Foreign Relations Committee, 6 June 1990. See Richard H. Solomon, "China and MFN: Engagement, not Isolation, Is Catalyst for Change," *Current Policy*, no. 1282.

30. Ross, "National Security, Human Rights, and Domestic Politics," pp. 305–306.

31. Ross, "U.S. Policy Toward China," p. 354.

32. "Bush Meets with Dalai Lama; Visit Highlights China Policy," *Congressional Quarterly Weekly Report*, 20 April 1991, p. 1002.

33. "Issue: MFN Status for China," *Congressional Quarterly Weekly Report*, 31 October 1992, p. 3459.

34. Susumu Awanohara, "China Card Shuffled," *Far Eastern Economic Review*, 15 February 1990, p. 12. This reference gives Liu Huaqing as vice foreign minister rather than Liu Huaqiu. Liu Huaqing was vice chair, Central Military Commission.

35. "New Demonstration of Hegemonism," *Beijing Review*, 12–18 March 1990, pp. 9–10.

36. *Keesing's Record of World Events*, vol. 36 (1990), p. 37531. See also the comment in Lepage, "Sino-American Relations Post-Tiananmen," pp. 65–66.

37. Harding, "China's American Dilemma," pp. 21–22. See also Xinghao, "Managing Sino-American Relations in a Changing World," p. 1166. The implications of Chinese policies in Southeast Asia for the United States are discussed in Bert, "Chinese Policies and U.S. Interests in Southeast Asia."

38. Susumu Awanohara, "Mutual Abstainers," *Far Eastern Economic Review*, 13 December 1990, pp. 10–11.

39. Quoted, "Quarterly Chronicle and Documentation (October–December 1990)," *China Quarterly*, no. 125 (March 1991), p. 215.

40. Quoted, Susumu Awanohara and Tai Ming Cheung, "Abusive Treatment," *Far Eastern Economic Review,* 3 January 1991, p. 9.

41. Quoted, "Quarterly Chronicle and Documentation (April–June 1991)," *China Quarterly,* no. 127 (September 1991), p. 681.

42. "Quarterly Chronicle and Documentation (July–September 1991)," *China Quarterly,* no. 128 (December 1991), p. 886.

43. Laurence Zuckerman, "Hong Kong Looms as U.S.-China Issue," *International Herald Tribune,* 7 November 1991, p. 6.

44. Susumu Awanohara, "Falling from Favour," *Far Eastern Economic Review,* 2 May 1991, pp. 10–11.

45. *Keesing's Record of World Events,* vol. 37 (1991), p. 38340.

46. Ibid., pp. 38574–38575; "Baker's China Mission Called a Success," *Beijing Review,* 25 November–1 December 1991, pp. 4–5.

47. *Keesing's Record of World Events,* vol. 38 (1992), p. 39095.

48. "A Grave Move to Sabotage Sino-US Relations," *Beijing Review,* 14–20 September 1992, p. 5.

49. "Proposed F-16 Sale Draws Strong Protest," *Beijing Review,* 14–20 September 1992, p. 4.

50. "Christopher Weighs In on China, Empty Embassy in Moscow," *Congressional Quarterly Weekly Report,* 13 March 1993, p. 622.

51. "Lord Seeks China Consensus," *Congressional Quarterly Weekly Report,* 3 April 1993, p. 855.

52. Lord, "China and America," p. 2.

53. Ibid., pp. 15–16.

54. *Asia 1994 Yearbook,* p. 117; Susumu Awonohara, "No Ground Given: US-China Talks Cordial but Inconclusive," *Far Eastern Economic Review,* 2 December 1993, pp. 13–14.

55. Susumu Awanohara, "Lukewarm Welcome: Dalai Lama Gets Cautious Reception in Washington," *Far Eastern Economic Review,* 6 May 1993, p. 13.

56. "China Ready to Work with Clinton," *Beijing Review,* 16–22 November 1992, p. 5.

57. "Jiang: Improve Sino-US Relations," *Beijing Review,* 7–13 December 1992, p. 5.

58. "Fearing Clinton Line, China Steps Up Arms Deals," *International Herald Tribune,* 8 December 1992, p. 2.

59. Shirley A. Kan, "Clinton's China Syndrome," *Far Eastern Economic Review,* 1 July 1993, p. 23.

60. Susumu Awanohara, "Full Circle," *Far Eastern Economic Review,* 9 June 1994, p. 15.

61. "Jiang on Sino-US Relations," *Beijing Review,* 31 May–6 June 1993, p. 4.

62. See Tony Walker, "China Goes on Offensive over MFN," *Financial Times,* 17 March 1994, p. 7; Patrick E. Tyler, "Ready to Revert to Cold War, China Says," *International Herald Tribune,* 21 March 1994, pp. 1, 4; "A Mixed Approach by Beijing to U.S.," *International Herald Tribune,* 7 April 1994, p. 6.

63. Nigel Holloway and Shada Islam, "Artillery Exercises," *Far Eastern Economic Review,* 30 May 1996, pp. 49–50; Nigel Holloway, "Damned Lies and Statistics," *Far Eastern Economic Review,* 30 May 1996, p. 50.

64. Shirley A. Kan, "Clinton's China Syndrome," *Far Eastern Economic Review,* 1 July 1993, p. 23.

65. *Asia 1994 Yearbook,* p. 116.

66. Ibid., p. 117.

67. Ibid., pp. 116–117.

68. Melana Zyla, "Socking It to China: US Senate Acts on Arms Sales to Taiwan," *Far Eastern Economic Review*, 5 August 1993, p. 15.

69. *Keesing's Record of World Events*, vol. 39 (1993), p. 39598.

70. "Foreign Ministry on 'Yinhe' Incident," *Beijing Review*, 13–19 September 1993, p. 4.

71. Nigel Holloway, "Goodwill Proliferates," *Far Eastern Economic Review*, 20 October 1994, p. 20.

72. Nigel Holloway, "A Chill Wind," *Far Eastern Economic Review*, 15 June 1995, pp. 15–16.

73. Nigel Holloway and Ahmed Rashid, "Sparks for Tinder," *Far Eastern Economic Review*, 22 February 1996, pp. 14–16.

74. Nigel Holloway et al., "Going Ballistic," *Far Eastern Economic Review*, 27 June 1996, pp. 14–15.

75. *Keesing's Record of World Events*, vol. 39 (1993), p. 39638.

76. "US Act Called 'Oar on Others' Boat,'" *Beijing Review*, 16–22 May 1994, pp. 5–6; "U.S. Envoy Gets Protest by Beijing Over Taipei," *International Herald Tribune*, 6 May 1994, p. 6.

77. Simon Reeve, "Thanks, but No Thanks," *Far Eastern Economic Review*, 27 July 1995, p. 19.

78. Nigel Holloway, Julian Baum and Lincoln Kaye, "Shanghaied by Taiwan," *Far Eastern Economic Review*, 1 June 1995, p. 15.

79. Julian Baum, "Pressure Cooker," *Far Eastern Economic Review*, 1 June 1995, pp. 16–17.

80. Matt Forney and Nigel Holloway, "Out of Synch," *Far Eastern Economic Review*, 5 December 1996, p. 16.

8

THE SINO-
JAPANESE RELATIONSHIP

In addition to the Japanese-U.S. and the Sino-U.S. relationships, the Sino-Japanese relationship has been essential to the dynamics of international politics in post–Cold War Asia Pacific. Whereas the United States theoretically has the option of reducing its presence or even withdrawing from the region, China and Japan are inextricably part of its future. To understand the development of the Sino-Japanese relationship in the post–Cold War era, it is helpful to consider how it developed in the past, particularly in the postwar period.

The Postwar Context

From China's perspective, Japan's international role in the postwar period was closely related to the U.S.-Japan Mutual Security Treaty of 1951. This meant that insofar as there was an antagonistic relationship between China and the United States, there was also hostility between China and Japan. Conversely, when the Sino-U.S. relationship improved, so did the relationship between China and Japan. When antagonism prevailed, it tended to be reinforced by the historical memories China had of Japan. In recent years, these memories concerned imperialist depredations, beginning with the loss of Taiwan in 1895. Japan's occupation of Manchuria in 1931 and its launching of war against China in 1937 were very fresh in Chinese minds. During the 1950s and 1960s, antagonism prevailed in Sino-U.S. relations, and this was likewise the case in Sino-Japanese relations.

Japan's view of China was greatly influenced by the cultural similarities of the two peoples and the nature of their long-term historical relationship. Hidenori Ijiri sums up the situation: "The Japanese have an inferiority complex due to their cultural debt to China and the sense of original sin stemming from their past aggression against China, while having a superiority complex based upon their assistance to China's modernization and contempt for China's backwardness."[1]

In the postwar period, Japan's relationship with the United States had a major bearing on its relationship with China. In the 1951 peace treaty, Japan concluded peace with the Republic of China on Taiwan rather than with the People's Republic of China. It followed the United States' lead in not extending diplomatic recognition to the PRC and it supported the U.S. policy of containing China. At the same time, Japan developed trade relations with China under the guise of "the separation of politics from economics." By 1965 Japan had succeeded the USSR as China's most important trading partner,[2] but Japan still maintained strong links with Taiwan.

Sino-Japanese diplomatic normalization came in the aftermath of the Sino-U.S. rapprochement proclaimed in the Shanghai communiqué of February 1972. The Sino-Japanese communiqué of September 1972, which prepared the way for full diplomatic relations, stated: "Neither power should seek hegemony in the Asia Pacific region and each is opposed to the efforts by any other country or group of countries to seek such hegemony."[3] The Chinese believed that the first part of this statement placed limits on Japan's role in the region and that the second part was directed against the USSR.

The Sino-Japanese relationship was further consolidated by the signing in 1978 of the Long-Term Trade Agreement and the Treaty of Peace and Friendship. By this stage, Soviet-U.S. relations had deteriorated again after a period of détente earlier in the decade. Since the Sino-Soviet conflict continued as before, this meant that there was a convergence in Chinese and U.S. perceptions of the USSR, which had implications for Sino-Japanese relations. China now looked favorably on Japanese rearmament; a stronger Japan could make a positive contribution to a China-U.S.-Japan alignment arrayed against Soviet hegemonism.

Following the Long-Term Trade Agreement, there was considerable growth in Sino-Japanese trade. The total trade between the two countries rose from U.S. $5 billion in 1978 to U.S. $19.3 billion in 1988.[4] It has been argued that Japan was motivated not so much by economic factors as by a "long-term political interest in a stable China."[5] Japan's problems in dealing with China were clearly shown in 1982, when China unilaterally canceled Japanese contracts worth 300 billion yen for the construction of the Baoshan steelworks near Shanghai.[6] Despite China's claims that the location of the works was faulty, it appeared that the real reason for China's action was the effect on revenue of its inability to produce and export crude oil to the level provided for under the Long-Term Trade Agreement.[7] This episode understandably contributed to Japanese caution about investing in China.

During the 1980s, there were further changes in the strategic situation, particularly with the development of Soviet-U.S. détente during the Gorbachev era. One effect of the détente was that China became less strategically significant to the United States, a factor that encouraged Sino-

Soviet rapprochement. Economic tensions between Japan and the United States led to questions about the future of the U.S.-Japan security relationship. Increasingly, Japan was seen as a more independent element in Asia Pacific. Given that Japan was a potential future rival, China was less encouraging about Japanese rearmament and preferred to see Japan have a more limited defense role.

A number of episodes during the 1980s illustrated the importance of cultural and political sensitivities in the Sino-Japanese relationship.[8] In 1982 and 1986, there were Chinese protests against watered-down accounts in Japanese textbooks of Japanese actions in China during the Sino-Japanese war of 1937–1945. In August 1985, China took strong exception to an official visit paid by Prime Minister Yasuhiro Nakasone of Japan to the Yasukuni Shrine in Tokyo. This shrine honored Japan's war dead, including those who had been convicted as war criminals. China was also sensitive to Japan's development of closer relations with Taiwan, albeit on an unofficial level. This sensitivity was illustrated in China's reaction in February 1987 to a decision by the Osaka High Court, which said that ownership of a student hostel (Kokaryo) in Kyoto could be retained by Taiwan rather than switching to the PRC as a consequence of diplomatic normalization.

By 1989, then, Japan and China were clearly more involved with each other at both political and economic levels, but the relationship remained sensitive. Economically, Japan was much more significant to China than China was to Japan. In 1990 China accounted for 3.1 percent of Japan's exports and 5.3 percent of its imports. Japan's share of China's total trade in 1990 was 15.1 percent.[9] In that year, there was a trade surplus in China's favor of nearly U.S. $6 billion; textiles, energy (coal and oil), and food were China's main exports, and machinery, manufactured goods, and chemical products its main imports.[10] Although Japan's direct foreign investment in China was limited, it was an important source of foreign aid. In 1988 Japan provided 36.3 percent of China's foreign aid, excluding multilateral sources.[11] Japan's interest in the long-term political stability of China was still a major consideration. Japan's private investors were wary about the investment climate in China, but the Japanese government wanted to support developments that would encourage greater stability.

The economic ties between China and Japan have been appropriately described as "the ties that bind."[12] That is, whatever the political tensions and cultural sensitivities in the relationship, both China and Japan have had a strong incentive to promote their mutual economic interests. By the early 1990s, Japan was China's most important trading partner, accounting for about one-fifth of its foreign trade; by comparison, China accounted for 4–5 percent of Japan's foreign trade.[13] For the most part, trade balances have been in Japan's favor, although the balance has changed more recently. China supplies foodstuffs, textiles, and energy sources to Japan and takes consumer goods, finished steel products, and fertilizers in return. Japan has been generous in providing official development assistance and loans to facilitate China's modernization, but private long-term investment (including technology transfer) has lagged.[14] On the basis of interviews, Allen Whiting reports a Chinese perception that Japan is "determined to hold China back,"[15] but Japanese investment behavior is linked more closely to an assessment of risks.

Post-1989 developments in the Sino-Japanese security relationship must be analyzed in the context of the economic relationship. China and Japan may see each other as potential political rivals, but economic realities encourage some modification in behavior that might otherwise lead to conflict. Although there have been some tensions in the relationship, in general China and Japan have not been involved in any major conflict in the post–Cold War period. Even Tiananmen Square resulted in only a minor setback to Sino-Japanese cooperation. China and Japan are concerned about how they relate to each other in the evolving strategic situation in post–Cold War Asia Pacific, but some issues have impinged on the broader relationship. These include not just the Beijing massacre, but also the Gulf crisis, the questions of Hong Kong and Taiwan, the Senkakus issue (known as the Diaoyus to the Chinese), and the "war guilt" issue. These issues will be considered in turn, as will the impact of political visits and the significance of the various Japanese coalition governments between 1993 and 1996.

Tiananmen Square

During the first part of 1989, the issues in Sino-Japanese relations were reflected in the official visits made by the two countries' leaders. China was represented at Emperor Hirohito's funeral in February 1989 by Foreign Minister Qian Qichen. China failed to send a more senior representative because of its anger at a statement by Prime Minister Noboru Takeshita that Hirohito held no responsibility for Japanese atrocities in China during World War II.[16] Premier Li Peng visited Japan in April 1989. According to Li, the bases of Sino-Japanese relations were the Joint Statement of 1972, the Treaty of Peace and Friendship of 1978, and the four principles of "peace and friendship, equality and mutual benefit, mutual trust, and long-term stability."[17] Some hurdles in the relationship included the question of interpreting the past and Japanese-Taiwan relations. On the first point, Li said, "In order to further Japan-China relations, it is important to correctly assess the past history and draw lessons from that."[18] On the second point, Prime Minister Takeshita said Japan would uphold the "one-China" principle and not develop official relations with Taiwan.[19]

Like China's relations with other countries, its relations with Japan were interrupted by the massacre at Tiananmen Square in June 1989. Japan was cautious in responding to this event. On the one hand, Japan did not want to be out of line with its Western allies, who were generally more forthright in condemning China's actions. On the other hand, there were special factors affecting Japan's relationship with China, including the legacy of Japan's past aggression against China, particularly in the 1930s and 1940s, that led Japan to be less critical of the event.

Prime Minister Sosuke Uno commented: "I say clearly that Japan invaded China 40 years ago. Japan cannot do anything against a people who experienced such a war. Sino-Japanese relations differ from Sino-United States relations."[20] Japan's foreign ministry cautiously stated on 4 June that it was "very much concerned about the Chinese government's suppression with force of anti-government demonstrations"; on 5 June, Uno expressed his "regret."[21] Deputy Foreign Minister Ryohei Muratata took a stronger stance on 7 June, informing Yan Zhenya, the Chinese ambassador in Tokyo, that "Japan has been adhering to a stance of maximum restraint on internal matters of China, but the Chinese government's actions are intolerable from a humanitarian standpoint."[22]

Although initially reluctant to follow the Western countries in applying sanctions to China, Japan did announce on 20 June 1989 that it would suspend a five-year aid program amounting to U.S. $5.5 billion in "soft" loans that had been due to commence the following April.[23] At the same time, Japan remained reluctant to isolate China. While Foreign Minister Hiroshi Mitsuzuka criticized China for actions "not compatible with the basic values of our country," he also said that it was "China's internal affair."[24] A Japanese foreign ministry official made the point that "sanctions by definition mean punishment. . . . But even if you want to punish the Chinese, you don't get the results you wish. We don't think sanctions are an appropriate response for the Western democracies to make."[25] Finance Minister Tatsuo Murayama told the Diet, "We should bear in mind that China is unquestionably an important neighbor" and "both economic and political considerations" should affect any decision about resuming aid.[26] When the Group of Seven leaders met in Paris in mid-July 1989, Uno and Mitsuzuka lobbied in favor of a conciliatory approach and against the imposition of joint sanctions.[27] Nevertheless, Japan supported the G7 declaration, which said: "We look to the Chinese authorities to create conditions which will avoid their isolation and provide for a return to cooperation based upon the resumption of movement towards political and economic reform and openness."[28]

When Japan attempted to explain its position to China, the acting Chinese ambassador in Tokyo said that the declaration was a "reckless interference" in China's internal affairs.[29] In a meeting with Japanese foreign minister Hiroshi Mitsuzuka in Paris on 1 August 1989, Chinese foreign minister Qian Qichen similarly objected to the declaration.[30] President Jiang Zemin of China told a visiting delegation from the Japanese Diet that talks on the loans program should be resumed.[31] The issue was also pressed when a Japanese business delegation visited China in November 1989, but again without effect.[32] In January 1990, China recommenced high-level visits to Japan, with Zou Jiahua (minister in charge of the State Planning Commission) making a trip to Tokyo. The resumption of official Japanese loans was high on his agenda.[33]

Japan was reluctant to ease its sanctions against China without modification in U.S. policy. Prime Minister Toshiki Kaifu emphasized the need for a joint approach when he visited Washington, D.C., in September 1989.[34] At the same time, Japan maintained contact with China through various business and unofficial political delegations.[35] For example, a business delegation organized by the Japan-China Association on Economy and Trade and the Federation of Economic Organizations (Keidanren) visited China from 9 to 13 November 1989 to "seek methods for resuming bilateral economic cooperation."[36] Japan viewed the visit by U.S. national security adviser Brent Scowcroft to Beijing in December 1989 as an indication that the United States was modifying its approach to China.[37] Nevertheless, while the United States continued its sanctions policy, it remained difficult for Japan to resume its aid program to China. In July 1990, at the G7 summit in Houston, Kaifu finally gained Bush's tacit approval for resuming Japan's proposed soft loans to China for 1990–1995. According to Kaifu, the loans would "encourage the process of reform and open-door policy" in China.[38]

In an article published later in 1990, Kaifu wrote:

> Maintaining and developing a good, stable relationship between Japan and China is important not only for our own country but for the peace and stability of the entire Asia-Pacific region. While we strongly criticized the suppression of human rights during the Tiananmen incident and continue to do so, we consider it important to keep China from falling into isolation and to encourage it to continue its reform process and open-door policy. Our aim is for China to become an integral part of the regional framework of peace and prosperity.[39]

With this objective in mind, in August 1991 Kaifu became the first leader from a major Western country to visit China following Tiananmen Square. The visit was indicative of the changing emphases in Sino-Japanese relations. Whereas in the past economic issues had been a priority in the relationship, the focus of this visit was on broader international issues in which Japan and China were both involved.[40] Kaifu said that China's agreement to sign the Nuclear Nonproliferation Treaty, announced at the time of his visit, would "strengthen the regime of nuclear non-proliferation"; in his view, the fact that China made the announcement during his visit "demonstrates the importance China attaches to its ties with Japan." Kaifu also urged China to support the establishment of an arms transfer register under UN auspices. This was part of a broader strategy to enhance cooperation between Japan and China through the UN, not just on arms control but on issues such as Cambodia and Korea. By acting as a bridge between China and the West, particularly in the regional context, Japan was attempting to develop a more significant international role for itself.

The Gulf Conflict

Even before Kaifu's visit to China, the Gulf crisis of 1990–1991 had had some effect on Sino-Japanese relations. There was some concern in China that the Japanese debate about sending its troops to assist in peacekeeping operations might presage a more ambitious Japanese military role. Commentary in the Chinese press suggested that the proposed UN Peace Cooperation Bill allowing the dispatch of Japanese forces on such missions would cause "severe and emotional repulsion" from the Chinese people, who "worry that there will be a repetition of history."[41] Official reactions were more restrained.[42] Although the bill was not passed at the time of the Gulf crisis, a similar peacekeeping operations bill was passed in June 1992. Chinese concerns about the bill were similar to those expressed in 1990.[43]

The Hong Kong, Taiwan, and Senkakus/Diaoyus Issues

Hong Kong

The Hong Kong and Taiwan issues have also had a bearing on the development of Sino-Japanese relations. Japan's interest in these two "newly industrializing economies" has been primarily economic. Hong Kong ranks second only to Indonesia as a destination for Japanese investment in Asia and ranks fifth in the world as a market for Japanese exports.[44] Hong Kong is important to Japan not only for the economic access it provides to China but also as a regional and global economic center in its own right.[45]

For these reasons, the Japanese government was active in lobbying the Chinese and British governments and the Hong Kong authorities about issues relating to Hong Kong. Japan's main concern was to preserve Hong Kong as an economic center; questions relating to the political system were regarded as secondary. Foreign Minister Taro Nakayama visited Hong Kong in November 1989, and Liberal Democratic Party faction leader Michio Watanabe visited Beijing in 1990.[46] The Hong Kong situation was also discussed by Premier Li Peng and Foreign Minister Sosuke Uno in Tokyo in April 1989.[47] When Chinese foreign minister Qian Qichen visited Japan in June 1991, Prime Minister Kaifu told him, "It is important for Hong Kong to maintain its economic freedom and vitality for the development of China's reform and Open Door policy, as well as for Sino-Japanese and Sino-British relations."[48]

Taiwan

Japan's links to Taiwan date to the period between 1895 and 1945, when the island was a Japanese colony. Taiwan is actually of greater economic significance to Japan than is China. By 1990 Taiwan ranked fourth among the destinations for Japan's exports, and sixth as a supplier of Japan's imports. Total bilateral trade in 1990 was U.S. $23.9 billion, exceeding Japan's trade with China by U.S. $5.7 billion.[49] Taiwan's trade deficit with Japan in 1990 was U.S. $6.9 billion.[50]

Despite these economic links with Taiwan, since 1972 Japan has assiduously avoided having official relations with Taiwan. Despite Taiwanese resentment, Japan did not want to anger China, which was far more important to Japan politically and strategically.[51] For its part, China wanted Japan to continue to adhere to the "one China" policy as agreed to in 1972. China believed that Japan's economic and political links with Taiwan tended to undermine its commitment to the policy.[52]

Prime Minister Morihiro Hosokawa's statement in March 1994 that Japan would abide by the principles of the Joint Statement of 1972 and would not establish official relations with Taiwan was pleasing to China.[53] It followed a more ambiguous statement in January 1994 by Foreign Minister Tsutomu Hata, who had said, "For the development of China and the development of Asia, we cannot deny the development of Taiwan."[54] At the time of the Taiwan crisis, in March 1996, Japan adopted a cautious line, expressing understanding for the U.S. position but also noting, "China is a very important neighbour for us."[55]

The Senkaku/Diaoyu Islands

The Sino-Japanese dispute over the sovereignty of the Senkaku or Diaoyu islands in the East China Sea flared in late 1990. In October, the Kaifu government, in response to strong protests from both China and Taiwan, announced that it was withdrawing recognition of a lighthouse built on the islands by a Japanese rightist group. The Chinese press saw this "brazen invasion" of Chinese territory as evidence of Japan's "expansionist mentality" and the "resurgence of the ghost of Japanese militarism."[56] As was the case in the Gulf crisis, however, the official Chinese reaction was more cautious. On 27 October Vice Foreign Minister Qi Huaiyuan declared China's "indisputable sovereignty" over the islands to the Japanese ambassador and also pointed out that in 1972 the two countries had agreed to "shelve the dispute." He proposed that China and Japan should discuss "shelving the sovereignty, jointly developing the resources in the waters around the Diaoyu Islands, and opening the local fishing resources to the outside world."[57]

The dispute over the Senkakus/Diaoyus flared again in 1996, when Japanese rightists once more erected a lighthouse and other structures on the islands. Activists from Hong Kong and Taiwan vehemently protested Japanese actions. Japan was less than forthright in dealing with its own rightists, possibly because of Prime Minister Ryutaro Hashimoto's identification with a more nationalistic position. China, which maintained its claim on the islands, had a pragmatic interest in obtaining oil from this region and approached the dispute with caution.[58]

The War Guilt Issue

Following Toshiki Kaifu's visit to China in August 1991, Jiang Zemin, general secretary of the Chinese Communist Party, visited Japan in April 1992 and held discussions with Prime Minister Kiichi Miyazawa.[59] Miyazawa was cautious about an invitation for Emperor Akihito to visit China because of the scope for embarrassment over unresolved issues such as the Senkakus and war reparations claims. Miyazawa was also concerned about China's human rights issues and its arms exports. Despite these concerns, Emperor Akihito visited China in October 1992; his trip was the most significant official visit of the year.

Following the enthronement of Emperor Akihito in November 1990, China had been keen to host an official visit by the new emperor as part of the process of restoring China's place in the international community. The problem for Japan, and right-wing nationalists in particular, was that such a visit might pressure the emperor to apologize for Japan's wartime behavior in China. In August 1992, however, Prime Minister Miyazawa said that the visit would take place to commemorate the twentieth anniversary of Sino-Japanese diplomatic normalization. In Beijing, on 23 October, Akihito spoke of his "deep sadness" about "an unfortunate period in which my country inflicted great sufferings on the people of China," but he did not give a formal apology.[60]

The issue of war guilt also featured in Japan's relations with China during the period of coalition governments, which was inaugurated under Morihiro Hosokawa in August 1993. Hosokawa stated on 10 August that Japan had fought "a war of aggression" and that he "would like to sincerely express [his] feelings for all war victims and their surviving families in the neighbouring nations of Asia as well as all the world."[61] During a visit to China in March 1994, he spoke in similar terms: "We deeply deplore [the suffering caused by Japan in the past] and we will, on the basis of the study of history, make continuing efforts to establish friendly ties with China."[62]

On 7 May 1994, Shigeto Nagano was forced to resign as justice minister in the Hata government after he claimed that the 1937 Nanjing massacre was a "hoax" and had "never really happened." He denied that Japan was the aggressor in World War II, saying, "We really believed in the Greater East Asian Co-prosperity Sphere."[63] Tsutomu Hata reiterated his "deep remorse and convictions over the Japanese military's aggressive behavior and colonial rule [in Asia]. . . . Looking ahead to the 50th anniversary of the end of the war next year, we must express to future generations [our remorse]."[64]

The war guilt issue was prominent in 1995 but was not resolved in Sino-Japanese relations. Prime Minister Tomiichi Murayama visited the Marco Polo Bridge in Nanjing (where hostilities in the Sino-Japanese war had commenced in 1937) during his visit to China in May 1995,[65] but efforts to pass a war apology resolution in the Diet proved less than satisfactory. The resolution as approved by the lower house on 9 June qualified "a sense of deep remorse" by referring to "many instances of colonial rule and aggression . . . in the modern history of the world."[66] Within the coalition government, the Socialists and the smaller Sakigake supported an apology, which much of the Liberal Democratic Party opposed. Murayama used the word "apology" when he spoke on 15 August, the anniversary of Japan's surrender in World War II.[67] Ryutaro Hashimoto, Murayama's successor, was unlikely to use such language given his links to the right. His visit to the Yasukini war shrine on 29 July 1996 caused some controversy.[68] Because the issue has been left unresolved, China has been able to use it as a bargaining tool in a range of matters with Japan.

Interpretation

Underlying the development of Japan's relations with China in the post–Cold War period is the question of whether these relations have been primarily cooperative or conflictual.[69] Japanese governments have generally sought cooperation, even in the face of the obstacles posed by Tiananmen Square. The economic relationship between China and Japan has for the most part been complementary. Japan has provided economic assistance to China (mainly through soft loans) as a means of encouraging economic modernization and, so it is thought, political stability. Japan sees that political cooperation with China is useful in dealing with regional conflicts such as those in Cambodia and the Korean peninsula. Chinese cooperation would also be important to Japan if it were to enter the UN Security Council.

During the Cold War, Sino-Japanese relations were predominantly a reflection of the state of Japanese-U.S. relations. During the post–Cold War period, the Japanese-U.S. relationship has become looser, with some significant tensions over economic issues. Japan has therefore become relatively more independent as an actor in international politics. China now finds itself in a dilemma. A closer Japanese-U.S. relationship could place some constraints on Japan. At the same time, it would mean the continuation of a strong U.S. influence in the region. A more distant Japanese-U.S. relationship would reduce U.S. influence in the region and make both China and Japan relatively more significant. Given these alternatives, China's preference appears to be the continuation of a close Japanese-U.S. relationship, even though this will restrict its role in the region.[70] In January 1987, China had protested when, for the first time, Japanese defense spending exceeded 1 percent of gross national product.[71] The desire for economic cooperation has restrained China from expressing too vigorously its opposition to an expanded Japanese strategic role. However, issues such as the Senkakus (Diaoyus) and Taiwan could provide a pretext for Sino-Japanese conflict should a leadership with a different set of priorities emerge in Beijing.

The cultural stereotyping that occurs between China and Japan is one factor that exacerbates tensions in the Sino-Japanese relationship. Although Morihiro Hosokawa attempted to lay the war guilt issue to rest, it continues to plague the relationship. China assumes that it should "naturally" be the leading power in Asia Pacific and that Japan owes it a moral debt because of Japan's aggression against China in the 1930s and 1940s. In the context of these attitudes, Japan has been sensitive to what it sees as an undue expansion of China's military forces in recent years.[72] This expansion has included the purchase of advanced aircraft (SU-27) and missiles from Russia, as well as the acquisition of a blue-water capability for the Chinese navy. Tensions over issues such as the Senkakus/Diaoyus and the South China Sea indicate the changing emphasis in China's military power.

Japan has responded to the new situation in a variety of ways. It has attempted to cooperate with China on a number of security issues in the region. Such cooperation is directly relevant to the issues concerned, but it also gives China the sense that it is essential to the conduct of international relations in the region. Japanese diplomacy was instrumental to China's adherence to the Nuclear Nonproliferation Treaty and the Missile Technology Control Regime; Japan also encouraged the PRC to support the proposed UN registry of arms sales.

When Chinese foreign minister Qian Qichen visited Tokyo in June 1993, it was agreed to establish a bilateral security dialogue.[73] China's fears of a revival of Japanese militarism provide a deterrent to an excessive Chinese military buildup. As Professor Yoshihide Soeya of Keio University points out, "They [China] don't want to stimulate a revival of Japanese militarism by moving toward Japan in a military sense. This indirect deterrent is an important asset for Japanese diplomacy."[74]

Notes

1. Ijiri, "Sino-Japanese Controversy Since the 1972 Diplomatic Normalization," p. 639.

2. Johnson, "Japanese-Chinese Relations, 1952–1982," p. 110.

3. Quoted, Iriye, "Chinese-Japanese Relations, 1945–90," p. 628.

4. Arnold, "Political and Economic Influences in Japan's Relations with China Since 1978," p. 419.

5. Arnold, "Japan and China," p. 103.

6. Arnold, "Political and Economic Influences in Japan's Relations with China Since 1978," p. 426.

7. Ibid., p. 428.

8. See Ijiri, "Sino-Japanese Controversy Since the 1972 Diplomatic Normalization"; Whiting, *China Eyes Japan,* chaps. 3, 8.

9. Delfs and do Rosario, "China: Sense or Sensibility," p. 38.

10. Ibid., p. 39.

11. Ibid., p. 40.

12. *Far Eastern Economic Review,* 24 April 1986, as quoted in Delfs and do Rosario, "China: Sense or Sensibility," p. 93.

13. Whiting, "China and Japan," pp. 40–41.

14. Ibid., pp. 42–44. For more detail, see Whiting, *China Eyes Japan,* chap. 6; Newby, *Sino-Japanese Relations,* chap. 2.

15. Whiting, *China Eyes Japan,* p. 127.

16. *Keesing's Record of World Events,* vol. 36 (1990), p. 37341.

17. "Li Peng Scores Tokyo Touchdown," *Beijing Review,* 24–30 April 1989, p. 6.

18. Ibid.

19. Ibid.

20. Quoted, Ijiri, "Sino-Japanese Controversy Since the 1972 Diplomatic Normalization," p. 656.

21. Whiting and Jianfei, "Sino-Japanese Relations," p. 110.

22. David E. Sanger, "Tokyo, in a Shift, Criticizes Beijing for Shooting Civilians," *International Herald Tribune,* 8 June 1989, p. 1.

23. "Japan to Suspend $5.5bn Aid to Peking," *Financial Times,* 21 June 1989, p. 26.

24. Stefan Wagstyl and Robert Thomson, "Japan Caught Between Awe and Contempt for China," *Financial Times,* 22 June 1989, p. 4.

25. Steven R. Weisman, "Japan Cautiously Mutes Its Criticism of Crackdown in China," *International Herald Tribune,* 22 June 1989, p. 2.

26. Ibid.

27. Kesavan, "Japan and the Tiananmen Square Incident," p. 674.

28. Quoted, ibid.

29. Ibid.

30. Ibid.

31. "Quarterly Chronicle and Documentation (July–September 1989)," *China Quarterly,* no. 120 (December 1989), p. 914.

32. *Keesing's Record of World Events,* vol. 36 (1990), p. 37341.

33. Ibid., pp. 37341–37342.

34. Kesavan, "Japan and the Tiananmen Square Incident," p. 675.

35. See Zhao, *Japanese Policymaking,* chap. 8.

36. *Keesing's Record of World Events,* vol. 36 (1990), p. 37341.

37. Robert Thomson, "Japan Looks at Ties with China," *Financial Times*, 12 December 1989, p. 4.

38. "Japan's China Aid Plan Gets Bush's Tacit Support," *Japan Times*, 9 July 1990, p. 14.

39. Kaifu, "Japan's Vision," p. 35.

40. Tai Ming Cheung and Louise do Rosario, "Seal of Approval," *Far Eastern Economic Review*, 22 August 1991, p. 10.

41. Quoted, "Quarterly Chronicle and Documentation (October–December 1990)," *China Quarterly*, no. 125 (March 1991), p. 209.

42. Whiting, "China and Japan," pp. 46–47.

43. *Keesing's Record of World Events*, vol. 38 (1992), pp. 38962–38963.

44. Charles Smith, "Japan's High Profile," *Far Eastern Economic Review*, 9 November 1989, p. 14; Segal, *The Fate of Hong Kong*, p. 166.

45. Segal, *The Fate of Hong Kong*, p. 166; Goldstein and Rowley, "Hongkong: Shogun Wedding," p. 67.

46. Charles Smith, "Japan's High Profile," *Far Eastern Economic Review*, 9 November 1989, pp. 13–14; Anthony Rowley, "Japanese Whispers," *Far Eastern Economic Review*, 28 June 1990, pp. 72–73.

47. Anthony Rowley, "Japanese Whispers," *Far Eastern Economic Review*, 28 June 1990, p. 72.

48. Quoted, Segal, *The Fate of Hong Kong*, p. 167.

49. Baum and do Rosario, "Taiwan: The Sumo Neighbour," p. 54.

50. Ibid., p. 57.

51. See Masahiko Ishizuka, "Wrong End of the Telescope," *Far Eastern Economic Review*, 23 May 1991, p. 26.

52. China has also been concerned about attempts by Taiwan to undermine Japan's position on this matter. An example was the largely unsuccessful unofficial visit to Tokyo by Taiwan's foreign minister, Fredrick Chien, in February 1993. See Robert Delfs and Julian Baum, "Accidental Tourist," *Far Eastern Economic Review*, 4 March 1993, pp. 17–18.

53. "China, Japan Vow Long-Term Friendship," *Beijing Review*, 28 March–3 April 1994, p. 4.

54. Robert Thomson, "Japan Signals China Policy Shift," *Financial Times*, 11 January 1994, p. 4.

55. Nigel Holloway, "Strait Talking," *Far Eastern Economic Review*, 21 March 1996, p. 16.

56. Quoted, "Quarterly Chronicle and Documentation (October–December 1990)," *China Quarterly*, no. 125 (March 1991), p. 209. See also Tai Ming Cheung and Charles Smith, "Rocks of Contention," *Far Eastern Economic Review*, 1 November 1990, pp. 19–20.

57. Quotations from Whiting, "China and Japan," p. 48.

58. See Bruce Gilley et al., "Rocks of Contention," *Far Eastern Economic Review*, 19 September 1996, pp. 14–15; Matt Forney et al., "Ghosts of the Past," *Far Eastern Economic Review*, 10 October 1996, p. 24.

59. "Strains Evident in Far East," *International Herald Tribune*, 7 April 1992, p. 4; Jiang Zemin, "World Situation and Sino-Japanese Relations," *Beijing Review*, 20–26 April 1992, pp. 10–13.

60. *Keesing's Record of World Events*, vol. 38 (1992), p. 39141. See also Lincoln Kaye, "Saving Faces," *Far Eastern Economic Review*, 5 November 1992, pp. 13–14.

61. Jonathan Friedland, "Blood Money," *Far Eastern Economic Review*, 26 August 1993, p. 21.

62. "China, Japan Vow Long-Term Friendship," *Beijing Review,* 28 March–3 April 1994, p. 4.

63. Charles Smith, "Foot in the Mouth," *Far Eastern Economic Review,* 19 May 1994, p. 30.

64. "Justice Chief Resigns After Denying Nanjing Massacre," *Japan Times* (Weekly International Edition), 16–22 May 1994, p. 5.

65. Lincoln Kaye, "Politics of Penitence," *Far Eastern Economic Review,* 6 July 1995, p. 23.

66. Charles Smith, "Sort of Sorry," *Far Eastern Economic Review,* 22 June 1995, p. 21.

67. *Strategic Survey 1995–1996,* p. 186.

68. Matt Forney et al., "Mute Point," *Far Eastern Economic Review,* 15 August 1996, p. 21.

69. For alternative assessments, see Segal, "The Coming Confrontation Between China and Japan?" and Wang, "Toward Political Partnership."

70. See Manning, "Burdens of the Past, Dilemmas of the Future," p. 50.

71. Pollack, "The Sino-Japanese Relationship and East Asian Security," pp. 718–719.

72. See Brad Glosserman, "Japan Is Uneasy Over China's Military Buildup," *Japan Times* (Weekly International Edition), 21 December 1992–3 January 1993, p. 10.

73. Manning, "Burdens of the Past, Dilemmas of the Future," p. 53.

74. Quoted in Brad Glosserman, "Japan Is Uneasy Over China's Military Buildup," *Japan Times* (Weekly International Edition), 21 December 1992–3 January 1993, p. 10.

9

THE SINO-
RUSSIAN RELATIONSHIP

In post–Cold War Asia Pacific, the countries that have had the most significant major power relationships with the USSR and Russia are China and
Japan. U.S. relations with the USSR and Russia have also been significant,
of course, but they have tended to focus more on the global and European
context rather than the Asia Pacific context. For this reason, this chapter
will examine the relationship between China and the USSR and Russia
(post-1991), and Chapter 10 will look at the relationship between Japan and
the USSR and Russia.

Historical Context, 1949–1985

Before discussing the way in which China's relationship with the USSR
and Russia has developed during the post–Cold War period, let us
review briefly the character of the Sino-Soviet relationship from 1949 to
1985.[1] The proclamation of the People's Republic of China in 1949 was
followed in 1950 by the establishment of the Sino-Soviet alliance. In theory, this alliance was intended to provide an important foundation for
Chinese security, although the alliance was directed primarily against Japan
and any state allied with Japan. In practice, tensions soon developed
between China and the USSR over various issues, including security.
Given that both states claimed to be Communist, ideological issues
often featured in Sino-Soviet conflicts and certainly had an exacerbating
effect. This underlying ideological dimension should be kept in mind, even
though the subsequent discussion focuses on the broader international relationship.

During the 1950s Sino-Soviet relations appeared harmonious on the
surface, but tensions were nevertheless developing. One early source of
conflict was the Korean War. From China's perspective, this war posed a
threat to its own security; the USSR was circumspect about supporting
North Korea, even though that state was considered a Soviet ally.

Consequently, China felt forced to intervene in the war and also was resentful about Soviet inaction. Similarly, China viewed the USSR as less than forthcoming over offshore islands crises in 1955 and 1958. China also resented the USSR's unwillingness to provide assistance in the development of nuclear technology; the USSR's reluctance reflected Soviet concerns about China's lack of caution in statements about the consequences of using nuclear weapons.

By the 1960s, the Sino-Soviet conflict was quite public. The USSR was castigated by China for its "revisionist" tendencies, and China was labeled "dogmatist" by the USSR. The conflict manifested itself in a number of issues during this period. The USSR's nonaligned stance during the Sino-Indian war of 1962 offended China. Tensions also flared over the Cuban missile crisis in the same year, with China accusing the USSR of both "adventurism" and "capitulationism." With the onset of the Vietnam War, China and the USSR found themselves competing for influence in North Vietnam. The Sino-Soviet border was also subject to dispute, and major clashes occurred along the Ussuri River in 1969. More broadly, China and the USSR competed for influence in various regions of the world, including Africa and South Asia, and even as far afield as Latin America and Europe.

The death of Mao Tse-tung in 1976 brought no immediate change in the intensity of the Sino-Soviet conflict. Although the more moderate course espoused by Deng Xiaoping did portend the possibility of some improvement in Sino-Soviet relations, in the short term, various issues exacerbated the conflict. Intervention by Vietnam, a Soviet ally, in Cambodia in late 1978 was one of those issues (as was the Chinese military action against Vietnam in early 1979). Another was the Soviet intervention in Afghanistan in late 1979. A third issue was the large Soviet military presence along the Sino-Soviet border. These were the "three obstacles" China saw as impeding Sino-Soviet relations.

Even before the emergence of Gorbachev as Soviet leader in 1985, there were signs of improvement in Sino-Soviet relations. In a speech at Tashkent in March 1982, Leonid Brezhnev made clear his interest in achieving a better relationship. He described China as "socialist," even though its policies were considered contrary to the interests of socialism, and said that the USSR did not constitute a threat to China. Soviet-U.S. relations were deteriorating at this time (Ronald Reagan having described the USSR in March 1983 as an "evil empire"). China had also had problems with the United States because of Reagan's initial desire to improve relations with Taiwan. Nevertheless, from China's perspective, attempts to improve Sino-Soviet relations were hindered by the three obstacles.

The Impact of Gorbachev

After Mikhail Gorbachev became the new Soviet leader in 1985, the prospects for dealing with the three obstacles improved. In a speech on Asia Pacific issues at Vladivostok on 28 July 1986, Gorbachev referred to a number of issues concerning Sino-Soviet relations. The USSR was examining the withdrawal of "a considerable number of Soviet troops from Mongolia."[2] It was also "prepared to discuss with the PRC specific steps aimed at a balanced reduction in the level of land forces."[3] Gorbachev proposed that the Amur River boundary follow the main channel (the Chinese position)[4] and claimed that progress on the Cambodia issue was dependent "on the normalisation of Sino-Vietnamese relations."[5] Some Soviet troops would be withdrawn from Afghanistan, but complete withdrawal depended on a political settlement.[6] From the Chinese perspective, further steps would be necessary to improve Sino-Soviet relations, but it was clear that some progress had been made.

Further progress in clearing these obstacles was made in the succeeding years. In 1987 talks began on the Amur-Ussuri border dispute. These discussions were based on the Soviet acceptance of the *thalweg* principle as enunciated in Gorbachev's Vladivostok speech.[7] In February 1988, Gorbachev announced that all Soviet troops would be withdrawn from Afghanistan by February 1989. Soviet forces stationed along the Sino-Soviet border (including Mongolia) were substantially reduced in 1989–1990.[8]

The most difficult obstacle to overcome was Cambodia. As early as October 1985, Deng Xiaoping had had Romania's Nicolae Ceauşescu pass on a message to Gorbachev, which in effect said: "If the Soviet Union and China are able to reach an understanding and succeed in urging Vietnam to withdraw its troops from Cambodia, I am willing to meet Gorbachev."[9] The Soviets applied pressure to Vietnam and in May 1988 Vietnam proposed to withdraw its forces from Cambodia by the end of 1990.[10] In late August 1988, direct Sino-Soviet talks on the issue took place in Beijing, and in a speech in Krasnoyarsk in September, Gorbachev indicated his commitment to achieving a settlement. Chinese foreign minister Qian Qichen traveled to Moscow for further talks in December, which prepared the way for a Sino-Soviet summit the following year. In January 1989, Vietnam stated that all its forces would be withdrawn from Cambodia by the following September.[11]

A major event in preparation for the summit was Soviet foreign minister Eduard Shevardnadze's visit to Beijing in February 1989. The Cambodian situation was the main issue discussed, with the Chinese urging the Soviets to apply pressure to Vietnam to hasten an internal settlement. An important difference between the two sides was that China supported the establishment of a provisional four-party coalition government in Cambodia, whereas the USSR sought merely a "provisional organ . . . with quadripartite representation" to implement whatever settlement was reached and to conduct free elections.[12]

By the time Gorbachev reached Beijing for the Sino-Soviet summit of 15–18 May 1989, much of the groundwork for normalization had been completed. In this way, the function of the summit was largely symbolic. Although the USSR had hopes for achieving greater Sino-Soviet coopera- tion, China tended to be more cautious. Jonathan Pollack suggests that China's attitude might have been influenced by the limited progress on the Cambodian issue and the Soviet desire to retain control of Black Bear Island near Khabarovsk.[13] The Chinese caution about improving relations with the USSR was underlined when a visit by three U.S. warships to Shanghai was timed to coincide with a visit by Gorbachev to that city; embarrassment was only avoided when the United States delayed the arrival of the ships.[14] China was more embarrassed by the student demon- strations that were occurring in Beijing at the time of Gorbachev's visit.

Gorbachev had talks with a number of Chinese leaders, including Deng Xiaoping, General Secretary Zhao Ziyang, and Premier Li Peng.[15] Many of the issues discussed were covered in the final communiqué. Perhaps the most difficult issue was Cambodia. Essentially, the statement made about the situation was similar to the position adopted at the time of Shevardnadze's visit. Although both sides were committed to a political settlement of the Cambodian issue, there were differences about the nature of the internal process involved. China remained committed to the estab- lishment of "a provisional quadripartite coalition government headed by Prince Sihanouk during the transitional period after the complete Vietnamese troop withdrawal and prior to the end of a general election." The Soviet commitment was merely to "the internal problems of Kampuchea, including preparations for the general election under interna- tional supervision [being] solved by the Kampuchean people them- selves."[16] The Chinese plan would have guaranteed Khmer Rouge partici- pation, whereas the Soviet position favored the Hun Sen government and the two other factions.[17]

The communiqué took a positive view of developments in Soviet mili- tary dispositions along the border (China welcomed plans to withdraw 75 percent of Soviet forces from Mongolia) and in resolving boundary issues. Party-to-party relations were to be developed on the basis of "the principles of independence, complete equality, mutual respect and non-interference in each other's internal affairs."[18] In international relations, the Chinese emphasized the importance of the Five Principles of Peaceful Coexistence, whereas the Soviets wished to foster "new political thinking."[19] Both gov- ernments were committed to economic growth and expressed hope for an expansion in economic relations. Trade had more than doubled in the previous five years, but only 3.1 percent of China's total trade was with the USSR and 2 percent of Soviet trade was with China.[20]

Sino-Soviet normalization, as symbolized by the summit meeting, could be seen as part of the process that ended the Cold War. (Although the term "Cold War" primarily referred to Soviet-U.S. relations, it did encompass the role of other major powers such as China.) However, subsequent events showed that Sino-Soviet normalization was not necessarily a smooth process. The democracy movement in China, which was more than evident when Gorbachev visited Beijing in May 1989, was one element that made the process difficult. The massacre at Tiananmen Square in the following month also disrupted China's relations with the USSR and other states. The collapse of communism in Eastern Europe and the impact of "Gorbachevism" in the USSR had implications for China, as did the Soviet coup of August 1991 and the subsequent disintegration of the USSR. Whatever the portents of the May 1989 summit, China's task ultimately was to develop relations with Russia and the other post-Soviet states.

Tiananmen Square

Tiananmen Square caused some distancing in the Soviet relationship with China. At the same time, both China and the USSR wished to maintain the gains that had been made in achieving normalization. The initial Soviet reaction to the massacre came in a declaration adopted by the Congress of People's Deputies on 7 June. Describing the massacre as simply "clashes," the declaration expressed the hope that the "friendly Chinese people [would] turn this tragic page in their history as quickly as possible and surge ahead along the road of a construction of a strong, peaceful and free socialist China, a great country enjoying the respect and sympathy of its neighbours and of all humanity."[21]

In a visit to West Germany in mid-June, Gorbachev supported a continuation of the reform process in China, also saying that there "could be elements that took advantage of the situation."[22] Gorbachev made a stronger statement at the opening of the new USSR Supreme Soviet at the beginning of August: "We have made clear our attitude to the tragedy in Beijing. We deplore the turn of events. We are in favour of the most acute problems being solved through political dialogue between the authorities and the people. That is our belief. Such is the method we have chosen for ourselves. But a people solves its problem on its own. This is our principled and, I believe, irreversible position."[23]

When China's foreign minister, Qian Qichen, and Eduard Shevardnadze met in Paris on 30 July, they reaffirmed the commitments made at the summit meeting in Beijing.[24] It was reported, however, that the USSR was discouraging an official visit by Premier Li Peng; Anatoly

Lukyanov, deputy chairman of the Supreme Soviet, refused to meet Li during a visit to China in September 1989.[25]

Soviet competition with the United States was another factor affecting Sino-Soviet relations. When Valentin Falin, head of the international department of the Soviet Communist Party, visited Beijing in late December 1989, it was viewed as a response to an earlier visit by Brent Scowcroft, the U.S. national security adviser. Jiang Zemin, general secretary of the Chinese Communist Party, used the occasion to express China's opposition to interference in its internal affairs by other countries.[26]

The Response to Gorbachevism

China, of course, was concerned about the direction of change in the USSR and the collapse of communism in Eastern Europe during 1989. Gorbachev's influence and weak Communist leadership were held responsible by the Chinese leadership for the demise of communism in Eastern Europe.[27] China favored a more conservative Communist direction in the USSR, but it increasingly realized that the real alternative to Gorbachev was the more radical position represented by Boris Yeltsin.[28] In these circumstances, the general thrust of Chinese policy was to support stability in the USSR while also looking to the possibility of strengthening the more conservative Communist forces.

Visits by Chinese leaders to the USSR were an important means of expressing Chinese views; Premier Li Peng's visit in April 1990 and General Secretary Jiang Zemin's visit in May 1991 were particularly significant. Although Li Peng took the view that perestroika was socialist in orientation, he also "earnestly hoped" for stability to prevail in the USSR.[29] Li expressed himself more forcefully during Soviet foreign minister Alexander Bessmertnykh's visit to Beijing one year later, saying that although "the methods of building one's own country and the kind of road to take are matters which should be decided by the people of that country . . . the Chinese side is concerned about the situation in the Soviet Union, hoping that it will enjoy political stability, economic development, and national unity."[30]

The goal of Jiang Zemin's visit, as he said himself, was "to further friendly, good-neighbourly relations."[31] Although much of the visit was important symbolically, Jiang also expressed China's concerns about the future of socialism in the USSR. He reportedly told Gorbachev: "It is our heartfelt hope and conviction that the great Soviet people, who have made a significant contribution to the cause of human progress and who are imbued with a glorious revolutionary tradition, will surmount their existing temporary difficulties and score final victory in their social reform and construction."[32]

Other visits helped give substance to the process of normalization after Tiananmen Square. Igor Rogachev, the Soviet deputy foreign minister, visited Beijing in January 1990 for talks on the Cambodian situation.[33] Talks also took place between Rogachev and Qian Qichen in June 1990, Cambodia again being an important item for discussion.[34] In September 1990, Shevardnadze and Qian met in Harbin and exchanged views on a number of international issues, including the Gulf crisis, Cambodia, Afghanistan, Korea, and German unification.[35] During the first part of 1991, visitors to China included V. A. Ivashko (deputy general secretary of the Soviet Communist Party) in February; Alexander Bessmertnykh from 31 March to 2 April; and Marshal Dmitry T. Yazov (Soviet defense minister) in May.[36] (There was speculation that Soviet arms sales to China were discussed during this last visit.) During Jiang Zemin's visit to Moscow, an agreement on the eastern section of the Sino-Soviet border was signed. In March, China extended a commodity loan worth U.S. $730 million to the USSR.[37]

The Soviet Coup of August 1991 (and Its Aftermath)

China's fears about the stability of the USSR were confirmed by events in the second half of 1991, beginning with the attempted coup by conservative Communist forces in August and culminating in the disintegration of the Soviet state by December. China reacted cautiously to the first event, its foreign ministry stating: "The changes that have occurred in the Soviet Union are its internal affairs."[38] In spite of the official caution, however, it appears that China favored the conservative Communist forces who instigated the coup.[39] China implicitly compared the coup with its own experience, including the events of June 1989.

The Chinese leadership clearly believed that economic reform should come first in the Soviet Union and that the consequence of the Communist Party relinquishing its leading role would be destabilization. In the words of an article in *Wen Wei Po,* "No matter what merits and demerits Gorbachev had, it seems that history has once again shown that if reform goes too fast or if actual conditions are neglected, a tragedy is very likely to occur."[40] Deng's own rejection of Gorbachev's approach was clear: "When Gorbachev was ousted, the Soviet Union declared to the world that Gorbachev alone cannot change the situation of a country ruled by the Communist party for more than seventy years."[41]

However, with the defeat of the coup, China had to modify its stance. It did so by stating again that these developments were an internal affair for the Soviet Union and that "good neighbourly and friendly relations between China and the Soviet Union will continue to develop."[42] The failure of the coup strengthened the position of conservative elements in

China. Vice President Wang Zhen said: "In our opposition to [foreign-insti-gated] peaceful evolution [toward capitalism], a key tenet is to fortify the brains of the entire party—especially top cadres—with Marxism-Leninism and Mao Zedong thought."[43]

Nevertheless, because the disintegration of the Soviet Union was accelerating in the aftermath of the failed coup, China had to come to terms with the new situation. On 7 September 1991, China recognized Estonia, Latvia, and Lithuania as independent states, one day after this status had been recognized by the USSR.[44] On 27 December 1991, one day after the formal dissolution of the USSR, China accorded recognition to the twelve independent states emerging from the former Soviet Union.[45] Xinhua news agency had earlier attacked Gorbachev for policies that had brought about the Soviet collapse and "political chaos, ethnic strife and economic crises."[46]

What were the implications of this new situation for China's own secu-rity? China believed the fate of the USSR demonstrated the wisdom of its own domestic policies, which gave priority to economic reform while maintaining the rule of the Communist Party. On a global level, China was concerned that the collapse of the USSR would augment U.S. hegemony and consequently restrict China's ability to maneuver.[47]

Within the Asia Pacific region, the USSR had already seen its influ-ence decline, and this process would continue under Russia as the major successor state. As Gerald Segal comments: "Even if there should be a suc-cessfully reforming Russia, its status would probably be like an Australia with nuclear weapons."[48] Russia remained a significant influence in the region, but China's relations with the United States and Japan as the other major powers in the region would become more important. Russia was the most important successor state to China, but China would have to deal with other successor states on various issues—in particular, Kazakhstan, Kyrgyzstan, and Tajikistan, with which China now shared a border. Given the ethnic ties between the populations in these republics and the Muslim population in Xinjiang, China wanted to maintain harmonious relations with these newly independent states.[49]

Central Asia

China wished to establish influence in Central Asia in order to forestall any threat to its own stability but also wished to remain sensitive to the extent of Russian influence in that region. J. Richard Walsh argues: "From China's perspective, since both communism and traditional social structures share an authoritarian base, the survival of the post-independent ruling elites is important to regional stability. Russian influence continues to be essential, and there is no interest in championing the cause of the Central Asian republics at the risk of offending Moscow."[50] As early as December 1991, a Chinese delegation visited the five Central Asian republics with a view to developing links with this region.[51] Various Central Asian leaders subsequently visited China as part of the same process, including the prime minister of Kazakhstan in February 1992; the president of Uzbekistan in March 1992; the president of Turkmenistan in November 1992; and the chairman of the Supreme Soviet of Tajikistan in March 1993.[52] In October 1992 a delegation from Kazakhstan, Kyrgyzstan, Russia, and Tajikistan also visited China.[53] Leading Chinese visitors to the region included Foreign Minister Qian Qichen in November 1992 and Premier Li Peng in April 1994. Aside from consolidating Chinese political influence, these visits were designed to develop further economic and transportation links (the latter included the possibility of constructing a natural gas pipeline from Turkmenistan to connect with the Chinese system in Xinjiang's Tarim Basin).[54] Negotiations on China's western border now included Kazakhstan, Kyrgyzstan, and Tajikistan, as well as Russia. Talks in Beijing in May–June 1993 on reducing the border military presence involved all four of these post-Soviet states and China.[55]

Russia

Despite the change in China's relationship with Central Asia after the collapse of the USSR, China's main focus was on Russia as the most significant of the post-Soviet successor states. The ultimate outcome of the USSR's demise was no doubt a disappointment to China, given its barely concealed support for the attempted coup in August 1991 and its distaste for Boris Yeltsin. Some commentators believed that Russia was giving a lower priority to Asia Pacific affairs. Citing various Russian reports, Gerald Segal says: "It is . . . apparent that the Russian Foreign Ministry has its attention firmly fixed on Europe and the Atlantic world—the bear has turned its backside to Asia."[56] Whatever the priorities in Russian foreign policy, there was scope for the two states to make common cause on some issues. Insofar as the importance of the two states in the "main game" of international politics had declined, there might be the basis for an "eastern Rapallo."[57]

In March 1992, during the initial post-Soviet phase, a trade agreement was signed between China and Russia. Russian foreign minister Andrei Kozyrev visited China in the same month, and Chinese foreign minister Qian Qichen visited Russia in November 1992.[58] The most significant official visit, however, was that by Yeltsin to China in December 1992, a visit that formally defined Sino-Russian relations. Although to many in China Russia represented "chaos and economic decline" and therefore a justification for the repressive measures taken in China in 1989, a pragmatic relationship was still possible.[59] The joint declaration resulting from Yeltsin's visit stated: "Differences in social systems and ideology should not affect the normal growth of state-to-state relations."[60] Russia's recognition of Taiwan as "an integral part of Chinese territory" was important to China; the statement that "neither China nor Russia will seek regional hegemony and both oppose hegemonism and power politics in any form" reflected Chinese terminology.[61] Illustrating the pragmatic basis of the relationship, cooperation was promised in areas such as trade, educational and scientific exchanges, border security, the construction of a nuclear power station in northeast China, and military ties (including arms sales).[62] Building on the foundations laid by the Yeltsin visit, pragmatic cooperation was also the theme of visits to China by Foreign Minister Kozyrev in January 1994 and Prime Minister Viktor Chernomyrdin in May 1994.[63] Jiang Zemin reciprocated with a visit to Moscow in September 1994.[64]

An apparent strengthening of the Sino-Soviet relationship in the mid-1990s gave some credence to the possibility of an alignment emerging between China and Russia. This theme was developed during visits by Jiang Zemin to Moscow in June 1995, by Boris Yeltsin to Beijing in April 1996, and by Premier Li Peng to Moscow in December 1996. During Yeltsin's visit the two sides declared "a strategic partnership for the next century."[65] However, given the uncertainties affecting both countries, it would be inaccurate to characterize their relationship as based on a firm alignment. China and Russia enhance their bargaining power in other situations by leaving open the possibility that such an alignment might develop.

Russian arms sales to China (including the acquisition of technology and expertise) were one of the most important concrete aspects of the post-Soviet relationship between the two countries. Russia's need to prop up its ailing military-defense complex coincided with China's desire to provide technological upgrading for its military forces. The willingness of the two sides to engage in these sales indicated that they no longer saw each other as strategic threats. China's enhanced capability could, however, pose problems for Taiwan and for the Southeast Asian countries engaged in disputes with China in the South China Sea. The United States was concerned that the emphasis on the transfer of technology might undermine the Missile Technology Control Regime.[66] By mid-1993, it was reported that Chinese plans for purchases from Russia included: "procurement of a total of 72 Su-27 fighters; the manufacture under licence of 300 MiG-31 interceptors; and orders for SA-10 SAM for which an anti-ballistic missile capability is claimed."[67] In 1992 alone, Russian arms sales to China amounted to U.S. $1.8 billion.[68]

A five-year military cooperation agreement was signed when Russian defense minister Pavel Grachev visited Beijing in November 1993.[69] Subsequently, a leaked copy of the agreement suggested that Sino-Russian military cooperation "could come to include not just weapons sales, but also personnel exchanges, training, intelligence information-sharing and even mutual logistic support."[70] By 1996 China had been licensed by Russia to manufacture up to 150 SU-27 aircraft.[71]

Other Post-Soviet States

China also had security concerns about the other post-Soviet states. These concerns included arms sales and, more broadly, how developments in these states might impinge on Chinese security. The main arms sale issue concerned reports that China was trying to buy an aircraft carrier, the *Varyag,* from Ukraine. Ukrainian president Leonid Kravchuk visited China in late October and early November 1992 but denied that there were negotiations on the matter.[72] When Chinese foreign minister Qian Qichen visited Ukraine in September 1993, he also denied that China had an interest in the carrier.[73] More generally, China had an interest in Ukraine because it was the second most important post-Soviet state and because Russian-Ukrainian relations would affect Russia's own stability and position in the world.

Although there were no major conflicts between Russia and Belarus, China had a similar interest in the latter country; Stanislav Shushkevich, chairman of the Belarus Supreme Soviet, visited China in January 1993.[74] Georgia was of interest to China for similar reasons, which were accentuated by the conflicts in that country. In addition, Georgia occupied a strategically important position in the Caucasus that would be important to Chinese plans for developing a corridor of transportation and economic links between Europe and Asia via Ukraine, the Caucasus, Central Asia, and China (incidentally making Russia less significant). This project was discussed with Eduard Shevardnadze in his capacity as leader of Georgia when he visited China in June 1993.[75]

Economic enticements offered by Taiwan raised the specter of the "two Chinas" policy in some post-Soviet countries. The main example was in Latvia, where China established diplomatic relations in September 1991 but withdrew its diplomats in April 1992 after the opening of a Taiwanese consulate in Riga.[76] In August 1994, it was agreed that the Chinese embassy would reopen, following a Latvian decision to close the Taiwanese consulate.[77]

Notes

1. Useful recent references on Sino-Soviet relations include Nelsen, *Power and Insecurity;* Dittmer, *Sino-Soviet Normalization and Its International Implications, 1945–1990;* Segal, "Sino-Soviet Relations."

2. "Text of Speech by Mikhail Gorbachev in Vladivostok, 28 July 1986," p. 219.

3. Ibid., p. 224.

4. Ibid., p. 220.

5. Ibid., p. 223.

6. Ibid., p. 225.

7. Garver, "The 'New Type' of Sino-Soviet Relations," p. 1138.

8. Ziegler, *Foreign Policy and East Asia*, p. 73.

9. Quoted, Garver, "The 'New Type' of Sino-Soviet Relations," p. 1138.

10. Ibid., p. 1139.

11. Ibid.

12. See the joint statement in Zhou Qingchang, "Sino-Soviet Summit in Sight," *Beijing Review*, 13–26 February 1989, p. 8.

13. Jonathan Pollack, "Gorbachov in Peking," *Far Eastern Economic Review*, 1 June 1989, p. 22.

14. Ibid.

15. See Robert Delfs, "One Stage, Two Plays," *Far Eastern Economic Review*, 25 May 1989, pp. 12–14.

16. "Sino-Soviet Joint Communique," *Beijing Review*, 29 May–4 June 1989, pp. 11–12.

17. Ziegler, *Foreign Policy and East Asia*, p. 77.

18. "Sino-Soviet Joint Communique," *Beijing Review*, 29 May–4 June 1989, p. 12.

19. Ibid.

20. "Trade on Track," *Far Eastern Economic Review*, 25 May 1989, p. 14. See also Goldstein, "Diplomacy Amid Protest," p. 60.

21. Quoted, Lukin, "The Initial Soviet Reaction to the Events in China," pp. 121–122.

22. Daniel Johnson, "China Reform Failure 'A World Threat,'" *Daily Telegraph*, 16 June 1989, p. 13.

23. Quoted, Lukin, "The Initial Soviet Reaction to the Events in China," p. 124.

24. "Quarterly Chronicle and Documentation (July–September 1989)," *China Quarterly*, no. 120 (December 1989), p. 915.

25. Jasper Becker, "Soviet Union Cools Links with China," *Guardian*, 12 October 1989, p. 11.

26. *Keesing's Record of World Events*, vol. 36 (1990), p. 37340.

27. See Daniel Southerland, "Deng Is Said to Warn Against Gorbachev," *International Herald Tribune*, 23 November 1989, p. 2; "In Party Memo, China Leaders Assail Gorbachev," *International Herald Tribune*, 28 December 1989, p. 1.

28. Garver, "The Chinese Communist Party and the Collapse of Soviet Communism," p. 12.

29. *Keesing's Record of World Events*, vol. 36 (1990), p. 37374.

30. Quoted, Garver, "The Chinese Communist Party and the Collapse of Soviet Communism," p. 8.

31. Sophie Quinn-Judge and Tai Ming Cheung, "Market Forces," *Far Eastern Economic Review*, 30 May 1991, p. 18.

32. Quoted, Garver, "The Chinese Communist Party and the Collapse of Soviet Communism," p. 9.

33. "Quarterly Chronicle and Documentation (January–March 1990)," *China Quarterly*, no. 122 (June 1990), p. 370.

34. "Quarterly Chronicle and Documentation (April–June 1990)," *China Quarterly*, no. 123 (September 1990) , p. 593.

35. "Chinese and Soviet Foreign Ministers Conclude Talks," *Beijing Review*, 17–23 September 1990, pp. 8–9.

36. See "Sino-Soviet Relations Promoted," *Beijing Review*, 11–17 March 1991, p. 7; "Li Meets Soviet Foreign Minister," *Beijing Review*, 15–21 April 1991, pp. 7–8; "Soviet Marshal Visits China," *Beijing Review*, 20–26 May 1991, pp. 8–9.

37. *Keesing's Record of World Events*, vol. 37 (1991), p. 38612.

38. "Quarterly Chronicle and Documentation (July–September 1991)," *China Quarterly*, no. 128 (December 1991), p. 885.

39. See Garver, "The Chinese Communist Party and the Collapse of Soviet Communism," pp. 12–19.

40. Quoted, "Quarterly Chronicle and Documentation (July–September 1991)," p. 885.

41. Quoted, Garver, "The Chinese Communist Party and the Collapse of Soviet Communism," p. 15.

42. Catherine Sampson, "Collapse of Junta Shocks Peking," *Times* (London), 23 August 1991, p. 7.

43. Lincoln Kaye, Tai Ming Cheung, and Julian Baum, "Bitter Medicine," *Far Eastern Economic Review*, 5 September 1991, p. 12.

44. Garver, "The Chinese Communist Party and the Collapse of Soviet Communism," p. 18.

45. Ibid.

46. Jeffrey Parker, "China Recognises Twelve Republics," *Times* (London), 28 December 1991, p. 8.

47. Garver, "The Chinese Communist Party and the Collapse of Soviet Communism," pp. 19–20.

48. Segal, "China and the Disintegration of the Soviet Union," p. 860.

49. For discussions of Chinese relations with post-Soviet Central Asia, see Harris, "Xinjiang, Central Asia and the Implications for China's Policy in the Islamic World," and Walsh, "China and the New Geopolitics of Central Asia," pp. 272–284.

50. Walsh, "China and the New Geopolitics of Central Asia," p. 282.

51. Ahmed Rashid, "China Extends a Hand Across the Border," *Independent*, 13 January 1992, p. 10.

52. *Keesing's Record of World Events*, vol. 38 (1992), p. 38814; "Quarterly Chronicle and Documentation (October–December 1992)," *China Quarterly*, no. 133 (March 1993), p. 201; "Quarterly Chronicle and Documentation (January–March 1993)," *China Quarterly*, no. 134 (June 1993), p. 401.

53. "Quarterly Chronicle and Documentation (October–December 1992)," *China Quarterly*, no. 133 (March 1993), p. 201.

54. See "Principles of Relations with the CIS" (interview with Qian Qichen), *Beijing Review*, 14–20 December 1992, pp. 9–10; Steve LeVine, "Li Peng Tip-toes Along the Old Silk Route," *Financial Times*, 29 April 1994, p. 6; Ahmed Rashid, "Chinese Challenge," *Far Eastern Economic Review*, 12 May 1994, p. 30.

55. "Quarterly Chronicle and Documentation (April–June 1993)," *China Quarterly*, no. 135 (September 1993), p. 640.

56. Segal, "China and the Disintegration of the Soviet Union," p. 856.

57. Nguyen, "Russia and China."

58. *Keesing's Record of World Events*, vol. 38 (1992), p. 38814; "Quarterly Chronicle and Documentation (October–December 1992)," *China Quarterly*, no. 133 (March 1993), p. 201.

59. Sheryl WuDunn, "Ready to Deal, Yeltsin in China to Revive Links," *International Herald Tribune*, 18 December 1992, p. 6; Lena H. Sun, "For Moscow, a 'New Stage' with Beijing," *International Herald Tribune*, 19–20 December 1992, p. 5.

60. "Yeltsin's China Visit: A New Era," *Beijing Review,* 28 December 1992–3 January 1993, p. 4.

61. Ibid.

62. Lena H. Sun, "For Moscow, a 'New Stage' with Beijing," *International Herald Tribune,* 19–20 December 1992, p. 5.

63. See "'Trust Us' on Policy, Russia Tells China," *International Herald Tribune,* 29–30 January 1994, p. 4; "China, Russia Ready to Expand Cooperation," *Beijing Review,* 6–12 June 1994, pp. 5–6.

64. "Beneath the Smiles," *Economist,* 3 September 1994, pp. 25–26; "Sino-Russian Ties Set Eye on New Century," *Beijing Review,* 12–18 September 1994, p. 4; "China and Russia Issue Joint Statement," *Beijing Review,* 12–18 September 1994, pp. 18–19.

65. *The Military Balance 1996/97,* p. 171.

66. Tai Ming Cheung, "Arm in Arm," *Far Eastern Economic Review,* 12 November 1992, p. 28.

67. *The Military Balance 1993–1994,* p. 148. See also Tai Ming Cheung, "China's Buying Spree," *Far Eastern Economic Review,* 8 July 1993, pp. 24, 26; Yu, "Sino-Russian Military Relations," pp. 302–316.

68. Tai Ming Cheung, "Sukhois, Sams, Subs," *Far Eastern Economic Review,* 8 April 1993, p. 23.

69. Patrick E. Tyler, "Arms Pact to Bring Russian Expertise to Beijing," *International Herald Tribune,* 10 November 1993, p. 7.

70. Lincoln Kaye, "Courtship Dance," *Far Eastern Economic Review,* 26 May 1994, p. 24.

71. *The Military Balance 1996/97,* p. 171.

72. Tai Ming Cheung, "Arm in Arm," *Far Eastern Economic Review,* 12 November 1992, p. 28; "Quarterly Chronicle and Documentation (October–December 1992)," *China Quarterly,* no. 133 (March 1993), p. 201.

73. "Quarterly Chronicle and Documentation (July–September 1993)," *China Quarterly,* no. 136 (December 1993), p. 1049.

74. "Quarterly Chronicle and Documentation (January–March 1993)," *China Quarterly,* no. 134 (June 1993), p. 401.

75. "Quarterly Chronicle and Documentation (April–June 1993)," *China Quarterly,* no. 135 (September 1993), p. 640.

76. Jeffrey Lilley, "Baltic Two-Step," *Far Eastern Economic Review,* 13 January 1994, p. 27.

77. "Latvian Links," *Far Eastern Economic Review,* 11 August 1994, p. 13.

10

THE JAPANESE-
RUSSIAN RELATIONSHIP

In the aftermath of the Cold War, the relationship between Japan and the Soviet Union and Russia (since 1991) has improved, but tensions remain: mainly, the unresolved issue of the Northern Territories (the term used by Japan but rejected by the Soviet Union and Russia). The issue of the Northern Territories should be examined in the broader context of the way in which the relationship between these countries has developed historically. I will briefly look at the historical development of the relationship before focusing on the post–Cold War period.

Historical Context

Japan and Russia are very close geographically but have had very different historical experiences.[1] During the nineteenth century, they came into contact as Russia expanded its Far Eastern domains and Japan expanded to the north. Eventually, they clashed in the Russo-Japanese War of 1904–1905. Japan won that conflict and consequently expanded its territories and influence at Russia's expense. Russia exacted its revenge when the USSR declared war against Japan in August 1945 at the very end of World War II. Russia had come under Communist rule in 1917, whereas Japan's government in the period up to and including the Pacific war had been increasingly dominated by the military.

After 1945, the paths of the two countries continued to diverge. Japan was democratized under U.S. tutelage and integrated into the Western alliance. The USSR continued under Communist rule, albeit a more moderate version in the post-Stalin period. The USSR was now one of the major poles of world politics as the Cold War antagonist of the United States. Because Japan played an integral role in the Western alliance in the Asia Pacific region, its relationship with the USSR continued to be tense. The Cold War accentuated the historical antagonism that existed between the two countries.

As long as these antagonisms remained, the potential for developing the economic relationship between the two countries was unfulfilled. The USSR was a supplier of raw materials but needed capital, equipment, and skills to develop its vast Siberian territories. Japan could provide these items and could also make use of raw materials produced by the USSR. An economic relationship was developed, but not to the extent that might have been possible in more propitious political circumstances. Between 1957 and 1981, overall trade between the two countries grew from U.S. $21 million to U.S. $5.2 billion. By the 1970s, Japan was the USSR's single most important trading partner, though the Soviet share of Japanese trade remained less than 3 percent.[2]

The postwar territorial issue emerged when the Soviets entered the Pacific war in August 1945. The Kurils, the chain of islands running northeast from Hokkaido to Kamchatka, were part of the contested frontier zone between Japan and Russia in the mid-nineteenth century.[3] Under the Shimoda Treaty in 1855, the Russo-Japanese frontier in the Kurils was placed between the islands of Etorofu and Urup. This was superseded by the Treaty of St. Petersburg in 1875, whereby the entire chain came under Japanese rule.

The Kurils remained under Japanese control until the Soviet occupation in August–September 1945. The USSR occupied not just the islands relinquished to Japan in 1875, but also Etorofu and Kunashiri (sometimes referred to as the southern Kurils) and Shikotan and the Habomais, which were considered part of Hokkaido (though the Russians call them the "Little Kurils"). The Soviets believed the occupation of the islands was in accordance with the Yalta Conference agreements of February 1945, whereby they were to enter the Pacific war after the defeat of Germany.

Japan contemplated conceding the islands from Urup northward to Russia as a means of preserving the 1941 Soviet-Japanese neutrality pact[4] but regarded the Northern Territories of Etorofu, Kunashiri, Shikotan, and the Habomais as integral parts of Japan; they did not come under the 1943 Cairo Declaration's definition of territories "taken by violence and greed." Japan argues that both the Shimoda and St. Petersburg treaties exclude Etorofu and Kunashiri from the definition of the Kurils.[5] In the 1951 Japanese peace treaty, Prime Minister Shigeru Yoshida renounced all claim to the Kurils, though it was subsequently argued he meant only the islands acquired in 1875.[6]

The USSR was not a party to the 1951 treaty. In 1956, when its diplomatic relations with Japan were resumed, the USSR said that it would return Shikotan and the Habomais upon the conclusion of a Soviet-Japanese peace treaty. This gesture might have provided the basis for an eventual compromise, but there was no movement on the issue for the next thirty years. If anything, the Soviet position became more uncompromising:

In 1960 the USSR stated that all U.S. forces would have to be removed from Japan before the Habomais and Shikotan were returned. Japan's rapprochement with China, and particularly the "anti-hegemony" clause in the 1978 Sino-Japanese Treaty of Peace and Friendship, also made the USSR less inclined to compromise. Retrocession of any of the Kurils was seen as weakening the Soviet defensive bastion centered on Vladivostok and the Sea of Okhotsk. Under Leonid Brezhnev and Foreign Minister Andrei Gromyko, the USSR was inclined to deny the recognition of any territorial dispute.

The Gorbachev Period

Although Japan was initially more skeptical than most Western countries, the onset of the Gorbachev period brought signs of some improvement in Soviet-Japanese relations. Gorbachev himself was hopeful that Soviet-Japanese relations could be improved. In his Vladivostok speech of July 1986, he referred to the prospects for economic cooperation with Japan, which he saw as "a power of front-rank significance . . . [with] . . . striking accomplishments in industry and trade, education, science and technology."[7] Economic cooperation with Japan would bring obvious gains to the USSR, including the economic development of Siberia and the Soviet Far East. After falling to U.S. $3.9 billion in 1984, total Soviet-Japanese trade reached U.S. $5.9 billion in 1990; much of this growth, however, was due to the stronger yen.[8]

From Japan's perspective, the problem with establishing stronger economic ties was the continuing territorial issue. Gorbachev did not indicate that he would concede on that issue, and Japan was reluctant to embark on schemes of cooperation without such concessions. The Japanese position reflected the dominant role of the foreign ministry in formulating policy toward the USSR: It insisted "on linkage between economics and politics to pressure Moscow to return the islands."[9] This approach is also described as "entrance theory," as opposed to the "exit theory" favored by the USSR. Entrance theory says that the territorial issue must be resolved before a general improvement in relations can occur. Exit theory says that a general improvement in relations will facilitate a territorial settlement.[10]

Despite Japanese caution, a dialogue between the two countries did begin. Even before Gorbachev's Vladivostok speech, Soviet foreign minister Eduard Shevardnadze had visited Tokyo in January 1986; Japanese foreign minister Shintaro Abe reciprocated with a visit to Moscow in May 1986.[11] Some low-level cooperation was agreed to as a result of these visits, but the territorial issue was not resolved.

Broader strategic issues became prominent in the Soviet-Japanese relationship at this time. The USSR urged Japan not to participate in Ronald Reagan's Strategic Defense Initiative (SDI). Japan was concerned about Soviet plans to deploy SS-20 missiles in Asia after Gorbachev had agreed to the elimination of INF (intermediate-range nuclear forces) in Europe. In July 1987, Gorbachev agreed that the elimination of INF should be global; in September 1986, the Japanese government had committed itself to participate in SDI.[12]

Another development that affected Soviet-Japanese relations at this time was the Toshiba affair. In 1987 it was revealed that the Toshiba Corporation, in violation of COCOM controls (Coordinating Committee on Multilateral Export Controls), had exported sensitive equipment to the USSR that enabled it to develop much quieter nuclear-armed submarines. Since these submarines were more difficult to detect, the advantage in detection previously held by the United States was reduced. As a result of this episode, Japan found itself being pressured to assume a more active role in defense "burden sharing."

As Soviet-U.S. relations improved, the Cold War rationale for Japan's adversarial relationship with the USSR was weakened. Japanese-U.S. conflicts over economic issues might have led Japan to assume a more flexible approach to the USSR, but this was not the case.

By 1988–1989, however, Japan was beginning to accept that a permanent change was under way in the USSR, and this provided the basis for new policy directions to emerge. On the Soviet side, Gorbachev returned to the question of Asia Pacific policy in his Krasnoyarsk speech of 16 September 1988. Gorbachev argued that his recent discussions with former prime minister Yasuhiro Nakasone (in July 1988) had convinced him that there was "both a foundation and a mutual desire for the dynamization of our relations on the basis of a balance of bilateral and regional interests." Although "the Japanese seem to have proved that in today's world the status of a great power can be attained without relying on militarism," Gorbachev was concerned about "the persistent buildup of its military potential in the framework of 'burden-sharing' with the United States of America."[13]

Between 1988 and 1991, there were some signs of change in Soviet-Japanese relations. Japan was now even more convinced that irreversible changes were occurring in the USSR. However, in the absence of any compromise on the territorial issue, Soviet-Japanese relations could not be improved significantly. Japan was also reluctant to commit any major aid to the USSR under these circumstances. It was not until April 1991 that Gorbachev visited Japan. Although that visit was important, the development of the Soviet-Japanese relationship can also be charted in other visits that took place during these years.

Following Gorbachev's Krasnoyarsk speech, Eduard Shevardnadze visited Tokyo in December 1988 for talks with Foreign Minister Sosuke

Uno and Prime Minister Noboru Takeshita.[14] No major breakthrough occurred, but it was agreed to set up working groups to consider issues (including the territorial issue) relevant to the conclusion of a peace treaty.[15] During a visit to Moscow in May 1989, Foreign Minister Uno advocated a policy of "balanced expansion" whereby negotiations could occur on a range of bilateral issues pending a resolution of the territorial issue.[16] There was an indication of some flexibility on the Soviet side when Politburo member Alexander Yakovlev led a delegation to Japan in November 1989. Without specifying details, Yakovlev referred to the possibility of a "third way" as the basis for settling the territorial issue.[17] Nevertheless, when delegations led by Deputy Foreign Ministers Igor Rogachev and Hisashi Owada met in Tokyo on 18 December 1989, no progress was made; the Soviet side called on Japan to accept the "results of World War II regarding Soviet-held lands off Hokkaido."[18] After a meeting with Gorbachev in Moscow on 15 January 1990, Shintaro Abe, former Japanese foreign minister and secretary-general of the Liberal Democratic Party (LDP), claimed Gorbachev had said that Japan, "as a sovereign nation," had a right to express its territorial claim. However, both Soviet and Japanese sources denied that there had been any Soviet acceptance of the Japanese claim.[19]

Soviet foreign minister Shevardnadze again visited Japan from 4 to 7 September 1990. At this stage, there were signs of increased flexibility on the Soviet side. Shevardnadze's position appeared to be that the territorial issue could be dealt with in the context of a broader range of issues. There could be "amendment" of frontiers through "negotiations based on rational dialogue."[20] He also implied that, in the present circumstances, Japan would be at a disadvantage in undertaking entrepreneurial activities in the "vast tracts of the Russian republic" that were about to be opened up.[21] Shevardnadze also proposed Soviet-Japanese "confidence-building measures," as well as a regional security conference for 1993.[22]

Shevardnadze's economic proposals might have been designed to appeal to key economic groups in Japan as a means of weakening the foreign ministry's stance on the territorial issue. Prime Minister Toshiki Kaifu seemed cautious in his response. While he rejected the "optimistic view" of Soviet-Japanese relations, he acknowledged that the relationship could play a key role in the development of post–Cold War thinking in Asia Pacific: "If the [Soviet] new thinking which put an end to East-West confrontation and overcame Cold War–era thinking is also to prevail in Asia and the Pacific region, the first thing to do is to establish relations of true friendship between Japan and the Soviet Union."[23]

In an article for *Foreign Policy,* Kaifu spoke of "pursuing a more normal relationship with the Soviet Union, expanding our ties in a balanced manner while devoting our utmost energies to settlement of the issue of Japan's Northern Territories." He hoped that "Gorbachev's visit to Japan in

1991 will mark the start of a new era of improved Japanese-Soviet relations."[24] But Kaifu's high hopes for the April 1991 summit meeting were not to be realized. In the best of circumstances, it would have been difficult for Gorbachev to make significant concessions to Japan, both because of the strategic value placed on the islands in terms of their relationship to the USSR's military bastion in the Sea of Okhotsk and because of the emotional attachment to the islands among Russian nationalists.[25] In late 1990 and early 1991, the USSR was experiencing a significant swing to the right as a consequence of the perceived loss of Eastern Europe and the growth of ethnic nationalism, and in December 1990, Shevardnadze resigned as foreign minister.

In view of these circumstances, the main achievement of Gorbachev's visit was that it had occurred at all. To prepare for the visit, LDP secretary-general Ichiro Ozawa visited Moscow in late March 1991, a trip followed shortly by Soviet foreign minister Alexander Bessmertnykh's visit to Tokyo. It was reported that Ozawa offered a package of aid and loans worth up to U.S. $28 billion for the return of the islands.[26] However, talk of a "grand deal" during Gorbachev's visit to Japan from 16 to 19 April 1991 came to nothing. An exchange of land for money would have been offensive to Russian nationalists, to say the least. Some fifteen agreements on relatively low-level matters were signed, and Gorbachev agreed that all four islands—Shikotan, the Habomais, Etorofu, and Kunashiri—could be the subject of discussion and that Soviet military presence on the islands would be reduced.[27] The USSR did not receive from Japan any aid in addition to the U.S. $100 million emergency food aid that had been announced in the previous December.[28] Japan did not respond favorably to Gorbachev's proposals for a new regional security order to be developed either from "trilateral Soviet-Japanese-US consultations" or from a conference with China and India in addition to the three other powers.[29]

In general, Japan had been reluctant to extend large-scale bilateral aid to the USSR. This unwillingness was based not just on the territorial issue but on the argument that aid would be wasted unless there was more far-reaching economic reform in the USSR. When Kaifu visited Europe in January 1990, he announced an aid package of U.S. $1.2 billion for Hungary and Poland. Aid was not extended to other Eastern European countries, however, on the grounds that a commitment to economic and political transformation was lacking, and hence, in the words of Kaifu's spokesman Shigeo Takenaka, "money could be wasted."[30] At the G7 (Group of Seven) summit meeting in London in July 1991, Kaifu made similar arguments in regard to aid to the USSR. He also asserted that before the Soviet Union received any aid there should be a stronger Soviet commitment to democratization and human rights, improved relations between the union and the republics, and an easing of tensions in Asia Pacific (referring to the territorial dispute and Soviet force levels).[31]

At the time of the attempted conservative coup against Gorbachev in August 1991, Japan came under fire for its cautious response. On 21 August, Kaifu simply described the crisis as an "abnormal situation with a high possibility of violating the [Soviet] constitution," although a more unambiguous denunciation was issued the following day.[32] Japan generally put more emphasis on "effective control" as the criterion for recognizing a government and less emphasis on human rights than did most Western governments. However, there was also the argument that Japan would be in a strong position in relation to a new Soviet government if that government were ostracized by Western powers. This would in turn enhance Japan's bargaining position over issues such as the Northern Territories.[33]

Japan did follow the lead of the major Western powers in condemning the coup. With the collapse of the coup, Japan looked more favorably at extending economic aid to the USSR. In early September, it was reported that Japan was modifying the linkage between a settlement of the territorial dispute and the provision of aid, and in October a U.S. $2.5 billion aid package was announced.[34] The failure of the coup also meant that Japan had to take account of the strengthened position of Yeltsin and the weakening of Gorbachev and the Soviet government.

Relations with Russia Under Yeltsin

Boris Yeltsin had visited Japan in January 1990 as leader of the reformist opposition to Gorbachev. On that occasion, he put forward a five-point plan for the resolution of the territorial dispute. The plan was based on a series of steps involving the recognition of the dispute and the education of the Soviet public about it (the first two to three years), the establishment of a free economic zone (the next three to five years), demilitarization (a further five to seven years), and the conclusion of a peace treaty. After fifteen to twenty years, the next generation would be in a position to seek "an original, unorthodox solution."[35] By the time Gorbachev visited Japan in April 1991, the balance between the Soviet and Russian governments had shifted to the point where Gorbachev felt constrained to include Foreign Minister Andrei Kozyrev and four other Russian officials in his delegation.[36] At this point, however, Yeltsin's January 1990 proposal appeared more conservative than what Gorbachev and Kaifu were able to agree to.[37]

After the coup Russian deputy foreign minister Georgii Kunadze supported a compromise that would have involved the return of Shikotan and the Habomais in the context of a peace treaty with Japan.[38] In line with this thinking, a delegation led by Ruslan Khasbulatov, acting chairman of the Russian parliament, visited Japan in early September 1991 with a proposal that Japan provide up to U.S. $15 billion in aid in return for a favorable settlement of the territorial dispute.[39] Kunadze also visited the

Kurils in late September to prepare the local population for the anticipated changes.[40]

Japan adopted a dual approach that attempted to balance relations with the USSR and Russia. Among Foreign Minister Taro Nakayama's five principles for guiding Japan's relations with the USSR and Russia, which were announced in late September 1991, were "setting up aid for Soviet reform" and "strengthening cooperation with the Russian Federation."[41] In any event, the "Kunadze option" was overtaken by the nationalist reaction in Russia, and Kiichi Miyazawa, who became prime minister in November 1991, was not prepared to take the political risks involved in modifying the Japanese position to accept that option.[42]

With the collapse of the USSR in December 1991, Japan's dual approach was no longer relevant. Japan extended diplomatic recognition to the Russian Republic amid calls for Russia to return the disputed islands to Japan.[43] In this context, Russian foreign minister Kozyrev stated on 28 December: "The Russian government recognises the legality of the 1956 Japan-Soviet Joint Declaration, including an item concerning the return to Japan of the Habomai islands and Shikotan on the conclusion of a peace treaty."[44]

During 1992, the Russian government moved toward settlement of the territorial issue on Japanese terms but then found itself constrained by the force of the nationalist reaction. Miyazawa and Yeltsin met each other in New York in late January 1992, and a vice-ministerial working group resumed discussions on a peace treaty in February. Kozyrev and Japanese foreign minister Michio Watanabe had also met in Moscow on 27 January. Subsequently, Kozyrev visited Japan from 19 to 22 March 1992, and Watanabe again visited Moscow in both April and early May of that year.[45] During the April visit, Watanabe suggested that although Japan had sought the immediate return of Shikotan and the Habomais, it was prepared to be flexible about the return of Etorofu and Kunashiri provided Japan's residual sovereignty was recognized.[46]

However, it might be argued that rather than showing greater flexibility, Japan was attempting to move too rapidly and was insensitive to Yeltsin's domestic situation. Watanabe's proposal went well beyond the Kunadze option, which was difficult enough for Russian nationalists to accept.[47] Japan also took a strong line against aid to Russia at the G7 summit meeting in Munich in July 1992 and successfully argued for the inclusion of a reference to the territorial dispute in the summit's political declaration. This reference stated: "We welcome Russia's commitment to a foreign policy based on law and justice. We believe that this represents a basis for full normalization of the Russian-Japanese relationship through resolving the territorial issue."[48] Yeltsin reacted angrily by warning against linkage between aid and the territorial issue and claiming that Japan had not invested "one cent, one half-dollar, one half-yen" in Russia.[49]

With the deterioration of Russo-Japanese relations and Yeltsin's domestic difficulties, it was not surprising in the end that Yeltsin canceled his proposed visit to Japan in September 1992.[50] It appeared that Japan, which had refused his demand that there be no linkage between aid and a settlement of the territorial issue, did not fully appreciate the impact of Russian domestic politics on Yeltsin's position. Japan seemed to think that Russia was already committed to the Kunadze option, and it proceeded to formulate proposals that would have linked economic cooperation to Russian acceptance of Japanese sovereignty over all four of the Northern Territories.[51] In the absence of a settlement of the Kurils dispute, Japan had not advanced the U.S. $2.5 billion in economic aid promised to the USSR in October 1991. Its main contributions had been U.S. $25 million to upgrade safety standards at nuclear power stations and U.S. $20 million to help pay the salaries of nuclear scientists in Russia and Ukraine.[52]

During 1993 the question of linkage between economic aid and the territorial issue continued to dominate Russo-Japanese relations. Japan was pressured to modify its position, beginning with a visit by Chancellor Helmut Kohl of Germany in February.[53] Pressure by France was instrumental in convening a G7 summit in Tokyo in April instead of the scheduled date of July, and the United States also expressed concern about the need to support Yeltsin.[54] In the interests of maintaining solidarity with the major Western powers, Foreign Minister Kabun Muto stated on 13 April that the aid and territorial issues would no longer be linked. At the summit a Japanese aid package of U.S. $1.8 billion was announced. After the meeting, however, Muto modified the Japanese position: Although aid given in an international context would not be linked to the territorial issue, bilateral aid would.[55]

When Russian foreign minister Kozyrev met Japanese prime minister Miyazawa at the G7 summit, he said that Yeltsin hoped to visit Tokyo the following month.[56] When it became clear, however, that linkage was tied to bilateral aid, the visit was postponed.[57] Yeltsin did visit Tokyo in July 1993, but that trip was to attend the "G7 plus one" meeting. On that occasion, Yeltsin agreed that he would visit Tokyo the following October to discuss bilateral issues; Yeltsin considered "balanced expansion" of relations the most appropriate course to follow.[58] The problems facing Yeltsin in dealing with the linkage issue were indicated by Prime Minister Viktor Chernomyrdin, who said during a visit to the Russian Far East in August: "As long as the present [Russian] Cabinet exists, we will never hand over any part of our territory." Moreover, a spokesman for Yeltsin said that the 1956 Soviet-Japanese declaration on the return of Shikotan and the Habomais had become "unrealistic" to implement. Yeltsin himself said that Chernomyrdin's stance was one of many positions being considered by the Russian government.[59]

Yeltsin visited Japan from 11 to 13 October 1993, soon after the quelling of the parliamentary uprising in Moscow. His political position remained vulnerable, and the Hosokawa government appeared more sensitive to the vagaries of Russian politics than it had earlier. Yeltsin gained approval by apologizing for the treatment of 600,000 Japanese prisoners of war kept in Siberia after World War II (60,000 of whom died in captivity). He attributed the treatment to a "remnant of totalitarianism" in the Soviet system.[60] On the question of the disputed islands, Yeltsin said to Hosokawa that the "issue exists and must be resolved some day," but he did not make any commitments about their return.[61] Yeltsin promised to complete the demilitarization of the disputed islands and to "execute the agreements and treaties that were concluded between Japan and the Soviet Union with respect to any issue."[62] When questioned about the 1956 declaration, Yeltsin said that this, too, would be included.[63]

The Tokyo Declaration signed by Yeltsin and Hosokawa on 13 October omitted reference to the 1956 declaration. Nevertheless, it committed the two sides to "negotiations on the issue of where Etorofu, Kunashiri, Shikotan and the Habomai islands belong" and declared that the basis for a settlement should be "historical and legal facts," together with "documents produced with the two countries' agreement" and the principles of law and justice.[64] An economic declaration committed Japan to "balanced expansion of overall bilateral ties." Only 10 percent of the U.S. $5 billion in aid promised by Japan had been distributed, but this was expected to increase as relations improved.[65]

Although no concrete promises were made, Yeltsin's visit did succeed in improving Russo-Japanese relations. Progress in resolving the territorial dispute was impeded by the nationalist gains made in the December 1993 parliamentary elections in Russia (including the Far East).[66] When Foreign Minister Tsutomu Hata visited Moscow in March 1994, Prime Minister Viktor Chernomyrdin was quoted as saying that Russia "will act without haste" in dealing with the dispute and that "one way or another we will move toward the signing of a peace treaty between our countries."[67]

Despite the lack of progress in resolving the territorial dispute, Oleg Soskovets, the third-ranking member of the Yeltsin government, was given a warm welcome when he arrived in Japan in late November 1994. Japan agreed to reschedule U.S. $280 million of government and government-guaranteed loans in addition to the U.S. $800 million rescheduled in the previous year, U.S. $500 million was promised in humanitarian aid, and talks were to resume on a U.S. $700 million loan to Russia's biggest oil company, Lukoil.[68] In the past Japan had supported, albeit with some reluctance, Western efforts to stabilize the situation in Russia through economic aid. It was suggested that on this occasion Japan might have also had another long-term purpose in mind. In the event that China emerged as a threat to Japan's position in Asia Pacific, an improved relationship with Russia might prove useful to Japan to balance that threat.[69]

There has been little progress on the territorial dispute since the Tokyo Declaration of 1993. Foreign Minister Yevgeny Primakov, in a press conference soon after taking office in December 1995, did say that the practice used in the Senkakus/Diaoyus should be followed in resolving the territorial issue; that is, it should be shelved pending resolution at some future time.[70] However, the Northern Territories are different from the Senkakus/Diaoyus in that they are inhabited. Given the way in which the latter group of islands aroused nationalist passions in Japan, China, Taiwan, and Hong Kong in 1996, this strategy is not necessarily a good example to follow. Certainly Ryutaro Hashimoto, who became Japan's prime minister in January 1996, was inclined to follow a nationalist course, and Yeltsin in Russia was also subject to nationalist pressures. An early resolution of the conflict appeared unlikely.

Notes

1. Useful overviews of the relationship include Stockwin, "Japan and the Soviet Union"; Stephan, "Japanese-Soviet Relations"; and Mendl, "Stuck in a Mould." An overview of the historical background and more recent developments in Japanese relations with the USSR and Russia up to mid-1993 is provided in Nimmo, *Japan and Russia.*
2. Stephan, "Japanese-Soviet Relations," p. 142.
3. The standard historical treatment of this issue is Stephan, *The Kuril Islands.*
4. Ibid., p. 156.
5. Mack and O'Hare, "Moscow-Tokyo and the Northern Territories Dispute," p. 383.
6. Stephan regards this argument as specious. See Stephan, *The Kuril Islands,* pp. 199–200.
7. "Text of Speech by Mikhail Gorbachev in Vladivostok, 28 July 1986," pp. 216, 220.
8. Ziegler, *Foreign Policy and East Asia,* p. 89.
9. Rozman, *Japan's Response to the Gorbachev Era, 1985–1991,* p. 27.
10. Berton, "Russia and Japan in the Post–Cold War Era," p. 30.
11. See Berton, "Soviet-Japanese Relations," pp. 1274–1280.
12. Johnson, "Japanese-Soviet Relations in the Early Gorbachev Era," pp. 1150–1151.
13. *Current Digest of the Soviet Press,* vol. 40 no. 38, 19 October 1988, p. 5.
14. *Keesing's Record of World Events,* vol. 35 (1989), p. 36620.
15. Menon, "Gorbachev's Japan Policy," p. 162.
16. Berton, "Russia and Japan in the Post–Cold War Era." p. 31.
17. *Keesing's Record of World Events,* vol. 35 (1989), p. 37042; Ian Rodger, "Moscow May Seek to Settle Islands Dispute with Tokyo," *Financial Times,* 14 November 1989, p. 7.
18. *Keesing's Record of World Events,* vol. 36 (1990), pp. 37279–37280.
19. Ibid., p. 37279.
20. Charles Smith, "Islands for a Sum," *Far Eastern Economic Review,* 20 September 1990, p. 11.

21. David E. Sanger, "Islands Can Be Negotiated, Shevardnadze Declares in Tokyo," *International Herald Tribune*, 8–9 September 1990, p. 2.

22. Ibid.; C. Smith, "Islands for a Sum," *Far Eastern Economic Review*, 20 September 1990, p. 11.

23. *Keesing's Record of World Events*, vol. 36 (1990), p. 37715.

24. Kaifu, "Japan's Vision," p. 37.

25. Menon, "Gorbachev's Japan Policy," pp. 163–164.

26. See Sophie Quinn-Judge and Anthony Rowley, "Cash for Kuriles," *Far Eastern Economic Review*, 11 April 1991, pp. 10–11; Stefan Wagstyl, "LDP Chiefs Try to Win Back Soviet Islands," *Financial Times*, 2 April 1991, p. 6.

27. Steven R. Weisman, "Gorbachev Fails to Win Japan Aid," *International Herald Tribune*, 19 April 1991, p. 1.

28. T. R. Reid, "Gorbachev and Kaifu: Reasons to Smile," *International Herald Tribune*, 22 April 1991, p. 2.

29. *Keesing's Record of World Events*, vol. 37 (1991), p. 38148; Berton, "Russia and Japan in the Post–Cold War Era," p. 31.

30. Marc Fisher, "Japan Giving Aid to Eastern Europe," *International Herald Tribune*, 10 January 1990, p. 2.

31. James Bartholomew, "Carrots for Gorbachov," *Far Eastern Economic Review*, 25 July 1991, p. 13.

32. Robert Delfs, "Hesitant as Usual," *Far Eastern Economic Review*, 5 September 1991, pp. 12–13. See also Steven R. Weisman, "Kaifu's Inaction Is Criticized," *International Herald Tribune*, 27 August 1991, p. 4.

33. Steven Brull, "Japan Has Little at Risk in Soviet Crisis," *International Herald Tribune*, 22 August 1991, p. 9.

34. Stefan Wagstyl, "Tokyo Plays Down Territorial Dispute," *Financial Times*, 11 September 1991, p. 2; Stefan Wagstyl, "Japan to Give Soviet Union $2.5bn in Aid," *Financial Times*, 9 October 1991, p. 2.

35. Menon, "Gorbachev's Japan Policy," pp. 161–162.

36. Ziegler, *Foreign Policy and East Asia*, p. 102.

37. Hasegawa, "Japan," p. 107.

38. Ibid., p. 106.

39. "Russia Seeks $15 Billion from Japan to Settle Kuril Dispute," *International Herald Tribune*, 14–15 September 1991, p. 2.

40. Sophie Quinn-Judge, "Russia Takes the Lead," *Far Eastern Economic Review*, 10 October 1991, pp. 12–13.

41. Hasegawa, "Japan," p. 108.

42. Ibid., pp. 108–110.

43. "Japanese Recognize Russia, Cite Islands," *International Herald Tribune*, 28–29 December 1991, p. 6.

44. Quoted, Hasegawa, "Japan," p. 110.

45. *Keesing's Record of World Events*, vol. 38 (1992), pp. 38820, 38864, 38911. There is a detailed discussion of Russo-Japanese relations during 1992 in Hasegawa, "Japan," pp. 110–122.

46. Emiko Ohki, "Watanabe Hopes to Break Isle Deadlock During Visit to Russia," *Japan Times*, 25 April 1992, p. 26.

47. See Hasegawa, "Japan," p. 114.

48. Quoted, ibid., p. 115.

49. Susumu Awanohara, "Yeltsin's Yoke," *Far Eastern Economic Review*, 16 July 1992, p. 11.

50. The relevance of Russian domestic politics is discussed in Hasegawa, "Japan," pp. 116–122; Buszynski, "Russia and Japan," pp. 52–53.

51. Hasegawa, "Japan," p. 120.

52. Jonathan Friedland, "Stuck on the Rocks," *Far Eastern Economic Review,* 24 September 1992, p. 16.

53. Steven Brull, "Tokyo Still Backs Away from Assisting Moscow," *International Herald Tribune,* 26 February 1993, pp. 1, 8; "Miyazawa, Kohl Back Yeltsin: Russian Stability a Global Concern," *Japan Times* (Weekly International Edition), 8–14 March 1993, pp. 1, 5.

54. Ako Washio, "Divided over Russian Aid: Tough G-7 Road Ahead for Tokyo," *Japan Times* (Weekly International Edition), 29 March–4 April 1993, pp. 1, 5.

55. *Keesing's Record of World Events,* vol. 39 (1993), p. 39419.

56. David E. Sanger, "In a Turnabout, Yeltsin Says He Now Wants to Visit Tokyo," *International Herald Tribune,* 15 April 1993, p. 2.

57. David E. Sanger, "New Yeltsin Snub Has Japan Fuming," *International Herald Tribune,* 7 May 1993, p. 1; Robert Delfs, "Off Again," *Far Eastern Economic Review,* 20 May 1993, p. 13.

58. Ako Washio, "October Eyed for Yeltsin Visit," *Japan Times* (Weekly International Edition), 19–25 July 1993, p. 6.

59. "Dispute, What Territorial Dispute?" *Japan Times* (Weekly International Edition), 30 August–5 September 1993, p. 3.

60. David E. Sanger, "In Tokyo, Yeltsin Finesses Issue of the Kuril Islands," *International Herald Tribune,* 13 October 1993, p. 2.

61. Charles Smith, "The Bear Hug," *Far Eastern Economic Review,* 21 October 1993, p. 12.

62. David E. Sanger, "In Tokyo, Yeltsin Finesses Issue of the Kuril Islands," *International Herald Tribune,* 13 October 1993, p. 2.

63. "Yeltsin Vows to Uphold '56 Isle Accord," *Japan Times* (Weekly International Edition), 18–24 October 1993, p. 1.

64. Miu Okikawa Dieter, "Japan Is Overtly Satisfied with Yeltsin Visit," *Japan Times* (Weekly International Edition), 25–31 October 1993, p. 3.

65. Ibid.; *Keesing's Record of World Events,* vol. 39 (1993), p. 39690.

66. Ako Washio, "Russian Polls Hinder Relations with Tokyo," *Japan Times* (Weekly International Edition), 31 January–6 February 1994, p. 3; Jeffrey Lilley, "Far Eastern Satraps," *Far Eastern Economic Review,* 13 January 1994, p. 21.

67. "Hata's Russia Trip Yields Scant Progress on Islands Dispute," *Japan Times* (Weekly International Edition), 28 March–3 April 1994, p. 3.

68. "A Polite Bow," *Economist,* 3–9 December 1994, p. 34.

69. Ibid.

70. "Press Conference with Foreign Minister Yevgeny Primakov," Official Kremlin International News Broadcast, 12 December 1995.

PART IV

OTHER REGIONAL ACTORS

11

KOREA

In addition to examining the relationships among the major powers, one can obtain an insight into the international politics of post–Cold War Asia Pacific by investigating regional situations that have been the settings of conflict and other types of interactions. One important center for conflict has been the Korean peninsula.

The origins of the conflict date to the end of World War II, when Soviet forces occupied Korea north of the thirty-eighth parallel, and U.S. forces occupied Korea south of that line. This set the scene for the establishment of two rival Korean states: Communist in the north under Kim Il Sung, and anti-Communist in the south under Syngman Rhee. Both states proclaimed unification as their goal and, in June 1950, North Korea attacked South Korea. Although the United States had previously stated that Korea was not within its "vital defense perimeter" in Asia Pacific, it now took military action (under UN auspices, and supported by various allies) to stem the Communist tide. With China intervening from late 1950 in support of North Korea, the Korean War eventually stalemated close to the original dividing line. In 1953 an armistice (but not a peace treaty) was signed between China and North Korea on the one side and the United States (representing the UN) on the other.

Over the ensuing period of more than forty years, the conflict has not reverted to war, but the underlying differences between the two Koreas over the issue of unification have remained. By the 1990s, South Korea had become an economically dynamic country in which democratic norms were becoming increasingly institutionalized. North Korea survived as one of the few remaining Communist states (and the most illiberal at that). The legacy of the "great helmsman," Kim Il Sung (who died in 1994), was a totalitarian state undergoing economic decline. This decline fueled speculation that unification might be achieved through the collapse of North Korea. Such a scenario, however, would place a great burden on South Korea (even greater than that faced by post-unification Germany). This strengthened the argument for dealing with North Korea in such a way that it might achieve a soft landing. To isolate it as a pariah state could have adverse consequences not just for the people of North Korea but also for South Korea and Northeast Asia more generally.

The role played by the two Korean states will be examined not directly but from the perspective of how they have interacted with the major powers. In each case, a brief overview of the historical context from the perspective of the particular power is provided and then the post–Cold War period is examined in more detail. The United States and China have been the two most important external powers in the post–Cold War period, followed by Japan. The role played by the USSR and Russia will also be examined.

The United States

The Historical Context

Cold War perceptions were of central importance to the United States in its decision to counter the North Korean attack in June 1950. U.S. forces remained in South Korea following the Korean War to assist in the defense of the Republic of Korea (ROK). This goal was formalized in a mutual security treaty that went into effect in 1954, an agreement that complemented the continuing involvement of the UN command (dominated by the United States) in the defense of the ROK. Washington did not look favorably on the autocratic rule of Syngman Rhee, but under the circumstances, the defense commitment took priority. In 1960 Rhee was replaced briefly by a democratic government that in turn was overthrown by a military coup in May 1961 led by Park Chung Hee. This military-dominated government was slow to win U.S. support, but South Korea's participation in the Vietnam War and its normalization of relations with Japan after 1965 helped it gain acceptance.

During the 1970s, the United States focused on plans to reduce the size of its defense commitment in South Korea. In view of the Guam doctrine of 1969, it was announced in 1970 that 20,000 U.S. troops would be withdrawn from South Korea.[1] President Jimmy Carter planned to take this process further by withdrawing the remaining U.S. forces (amounting to 41,000 in 1977[2]) from South Korea but was eventually dissuaded from doing so. U.S. commitment to South Korea was strengthened at this time by the establishment of a Combined Forces Command (CFC) between the U.S. and ROK armies in 1978. The details of the CFC are complex, but a U.S. general acts as its commander-in-chief.[3] The CFC is the only combined command between the United States and an allied country outside NATO.

In October 1979, following the assassination of President Park, there was a possibility that a democratically elected government would emerge in

South Korea. This possibility was forestalled, however, by the role played by the South Korean military under General Chun Doo-Hwan, including the bloody suppression of the Kwangju uprising in May 1980. In March 1981, General Chun arranged his "election" as president, a process made easier by Ronald Reagan's assumption of the U.S. presidency at this time.[4] The strongly anti-Communist orientation of both Reagan and Chun led to a strengthening of the official relationship between the two countries. The United States supported South Korea in opposition to North Korean terrorist attacks such as the Rangoon bombing of a South Korean cabinet party in October 1983 (which narrowly missed President Chun) and the destruction of a KAL (Korean Air Lines) airliner on a flight from the Middle East in November 1987.

At the same time, U.S. support for the military regime contributed to a widespread anti-U.S. sentiment in South Korean society. There were also some frictions over trade issues: The trade balance in South Korea's favor grew to U.S. $8.6 billion by 1988,[5] and the United States felt that it was being denied access to South Korea's agricultural market. The democratic legitimacy of the South Korean government was facilitated by presidential elections held in December 1987. Although the candidate favored by the military, Roh Tae Woo, was elected, this was only because the opposition parties could not agree on a single candidate.

Post-Cold War Developments

Broadly speaking, this was the situation in U.S.-ROK relations by the late 1980s. In dealing with the Korean issue, recent U.S. administrations have been influenced by the way this relationship developed and have shown increasing concern about North Korea's role in the context of nuclear proliferation.

The Bush administration. Secretary of State James Baker gave a good indication of the Bush administration's approach to Korea in a 1991 article for *Foreign Affairs*.[6] Baker saw South Korea's growing economic strength as the basis for "transforming what has been primarily a military alliance into a more equal political, defense and economic partnership." At the same time, he viewed the nuclear proliferation issue as serious, arguing that "the very real danger of nuclear proliferation on the Korean peninsula is now the number one threat to stability in the Asia-Pacific community." Baker believed that to counter this threat it was necessary to have "a credible agreement by both Seoul and Pyongyang to abstain from the production or acquisition of any weapons-grade nuclear material on the Korean peninsula." At the same time, Baker recognized that "the key to reducing tensions on the peninsula . . . is an active North-South dialogue." If North Korea responded favorably, the United States was "prepared to enhance [its] deal-

ings with Pyongyang." Baker also suggested that as the dialogue pro-
gressed it might be appropriate to organize a forum involving the two
Koreas and the four major powers in Northeast Asia (the United States,
China, Japan, and the USSR).

Roh Tae Woo specifically rejected the idea of "two plus four" talks on
the grounds that the involvement of the great powers would detract from
the direct North-South dialogue.[7] The issues Baker referred to were, however, the basis of the United States' relationship with Korea during the
Bush administration. Although security concerns were foremost in the U.S.
approach, economic issues were also important in the relationship with the
ROK. Thus, when George Bush made his first official visit to Seoul on 27
February 1989, his address to the South Korean National Assembly focused
on the need to reduce the barriers restricting U.S. imports.[8] Defense burden
sharing was also an issue; many members of the U.S. Congress argued that
the growth in the South Korean economy meant that the United States
should be able to reduce the size of its defense commitment to the ROK.[9]
When Roh visited the United States in October 1989, he promised that
South Korea would contribute more to its own defense. Bush stated that
U.S. forces would remain in South Korea while the need continued.[10]

Despite Bush's reassurance, plans were subsequently put in motion to
reduce the number of U.S. troops in South Korea as part of the post–Cold
War modifications in U.S. strategy in Asia Pacific. As a result of U.S.-ROK
talks in December 1989 and January 1990, it was expected that by 1992
2,000 U.S. troops would be withdrawn and three air force bases closed.[11]
As it turned out, the United States withdrew nearly 7,000 military personnel from South Korea between 1990 and 1992 (5,000 army; 1,987 air
force). Plans to withdraw a further 6,500 in the 1992–1995 period were
deferred because of the perceived North Korean threat.[12]

In the aftermath of the Cold War, the United States also had to adjust to
the broadening of South Korea's diplomatic relations. A significant development was Roh's meeting with Mikhail Gorbachev in San Francisco on 4
June 1990; formal diplomatic relations between the USSR and the ROK
were subsequently established in December 1990. During the Gulf War,
South Korea gave limited support to the United States (in the form of med-
ical personnel and a financial contribution) but did not attract U.S. criticism
the way that Japan did.[13]

The possibility of North Korea (the Democratic People's Republic of
Korea, or DPRK) acquiring nuclear weapons was of increasing concern to
the Bush administration. While the United States had been developing low-
level contacts with North Korea (mainly through the U.S. embassy in
Beijing), it also wished to see North Korea conclude an inspection agreement with the International Atomic Energy Agency (IAEA) as a means of
substantiating North Korea's adherence to the Nuclear Nonproliferation
Treaty (or NPT, which had been signed in 1985). When Roh visited the

United States in July 1991, he and Bush issued a call to North Korea to agree to the international inspection of its nuclear facilities. Secretary of State Baker, however, appeared to reject suggestions that the United States should change its own deployment of nuclear weapons in South Korea to encourage such agreement from North Korea.[14] Nevertheless, in October 1991, the United States announced that it would withdraw all tactical nuclear weapons from South Korea. On 8 November, Roh said South Korea would "not manufacture, possess, store, deploy or use nuclear weapons" or develop nuclear reprocessing or enrichment facilities.[15]

From North Korea's perspective, these changes were not significant, because South Korea remained under the U.S. nuclear umbrella. Nevertheless, on 25 November 1991, North Korea did propose international inspection of its nuclear facilities if the United States began the withdrawal of its nuclear weapons from South Korea; negotiations between North Korea and the United States on both matters would be necessary.[16] Prior to this proposal, U.S. secretary of defense Richard Cheney had said that the United States would not proceed with plans to withdraw further troops from South Korea by 1995; Patriot missiles would be supplied to South Korea and joint military exercises would be held in 1992.[17]

Relations between the two Koreas appeared to have improved when an Agreement on Reconciliation, Non-aggression, and Exchanges and Cooperation Between the South and the North was signed in December 1991.[18] In January 1992, another agreement was signed in which the two states committed themselves not to "test, produce, receive, possess, store, deploy or use nuclear weapons."[19] Denuclearization would be verified by the South and the North conducting "inspection[s] of objects chosen by the other side and agreed to by both parties."[20] Once the accord was signed by North Korea in January 1992, the United States took steps to upgrade the level of its contacts. Suspicions subsequently arose that North Korea was prevaricating over the implementation of the accord.[21] This issue continued to be a major concern for the Clinton administration.

The Clinton administration. On 31 March 1993, Winston Lord, in his nomination hearing as assistant secretary of state for East Asian and Pacific Affairs, set forth ten goals for U.S. policy in Asia Pacific. Korea featured as an important issue, specifically "erasing the nuclear threat and moving toward peaceful reconciliation on the Korean Peninsula."[22] Lord spoke approvingly of the ROK's economic growth and diplomatic broadening, as well as its move toward democratization with the recent election of Kim Young Sam (previously an opposition figure). The United States planned to work with the ROK toward "greater economic cooperation and reforms on intellectual property rights, financial liberalization, the investment climate, and market access."

Lord saw "the threat from the North [as] the most perilous legacy of the Cold War." He referred specifically to North Korea reneging on its commitment to nuclear inspection and its intention to withdraw from the NPT (North Korea had announced this plan on 12 March 1993). Under these circumstances, the United States would "maintain significant military forces in South Korea as long as Americans and Koreans believe they are needed for deterrence and regional stability" and would also support "the IAEA and other international bodies to eliminate the North Korean nuclear threat." Although the future of the Korean peninsula depended primarily on "direct South-North negotiations," the United States stood ready "to enhance this process through close consultation with our South Korean ally and multilateral diplomacy." Relations with North Korea could be improved "if it cooperates on fundamental issues."[23]

The possible development of a nuclear weapons capability by North Korea remained a major focus for the Clinton administration. In June 1993 talks between North Korea and the United States in New York resulted in North Korea suspending its notice of withdrawal from the NPT (though not terminating it altogether). Nevertheless, the question of inspection arrangements remained unresolved.[24] The United States' commitment to the ROK was underlined when Clinton visited South Korea in July 1993. During an inspection of U.S. forces in the vicinity of the demilitarized zone separating North and South Korea, he declared that it would be "pointless" for North Korea to acquire nuclear weapons because "if they ever use them it will be the end of their country."[25]

IAEA inspectors were admitted to North Korea between 3 and 10 August 1993 but were not permitted to inspect the two sites in the Yongbyon nuclear complex where it was believed there was evidence of weapons-grade nuclear material being acquired.[26] Another crisis came at the end of October 1993, when North Korea refused to allow the IAEA to replace the batteries and film in the surveillance cameras at North Korea's declared nuclear sites.[27] During talks between the United States and North Korea on 3 December 1993, North Korea offered to open its five declared nuclear facilities to inspection. Because the proposal did not include the suspected Yongbyon facilities, the United States did not accept the offer.[28] In January 1994 it was reported that North Korea would allow IAEA inspection of seven nuclear facilities but would reject "challenge" inspections of suspected sites.[29] This proposal was unacceptable to both the United States and the IAEA,[30] and the issue then moved to the UN Security Council, which had the power to impose sanctions on North Korea. In the face of Chinese opposition to sanctions, the Security Council, on 31 March 1994, simply issued an appeal to North Korea to allow IAEA inspections.[31] At this stage, Secretary of Defense William Perry warned that the United States was prepared to risk war rather than see North Korea develop "a substantial arsenal of nuclear weapons."[32]

Having reached the brink, the Clinton administration subsequently moved to consider more positive measures as a means of encouraging North Korea to comply with the nuclear nonproliferation regime. By the end of April 1994, it was reported that these measures might include diplomatic normalization between North Korea and the United States and Japan, the cessation of joint ROK-U.S. military exercises, and encouragement for Japan to pay war reparations to North Korea.[33] However, when the IAEA announced that North Korea had definitely broken nuclear safeguards, Clinton made it clear that economic sanctions would need to be considered. At the same time he said, "The door is still open for them to become part of the world's community and that's what we want."[34] Although North Korea proceeded to withdraw from the IAEA, the suggestion by Clinton that accommodation was still possible may have facilitated an attempt at mediation by former president Jimmy Carter during a visit to North Korea in late June.[35]

North Korea was clearly using the nuclear issue to enhance its bargaining position in various respects, a situation that the death of Kim Il Sung in July 1994 did not change. Following talks between U.S. and North Korean representatives in Geneva, a draft agreement was signed on 13 August 1994. In return for not reprocessing the 8,000 spent nuclear fuel rods from its Yongbyon reactor, North Korea would receive a supply of new light-water reactors—arranged by the United States at an estimated cost of U.S. $4 billion—that would not produce weapons-grade plutonium. Questions such as the inspection of North Korea's existing facilities by the IAEA and the arrangements for the supply of the new reactors remained to be resolved.[36]

Some of these issues were resolved in the agreement between North Korea and the United States announced on 17 October 1994.[37] The United States would be responsible for organizing an international consortium including South Korea and Japan to build two 1,000-megawatt light-water reactors for North Korea. Since the building of these reactors was expected to take until 2003, the United States would supply crude oil to North Korea for energy purposes as an interim measure. North Korea would cease building new graphite-type reactors and would suspend operation of its Yongbyon reactor. North Korea's reprocessing facility would also be closed, and the 8,000 spent nuclear fuel rods from Yongbyon would be available for IAEA inspection. The IAEA could inspect all nuclear facilities in North Korea, but not until one of the light-water reactors was completed (which was expected to take five years). North Korea and the United States would work toward reducing trade barriers and establishing liaison offices; intra-Korean dialogue would also be resumed.

The major weakness in the agreement was the provision that full IAEA inspection of North Korean nuclear facilities would not occur until at least one light-water reactor was operational. The measure was criticized by Republicans both in the U.S. Congress and during the 1996 presidential election campaign. Clinton attempted to minimize congressional involvement by arranging for Japan and South Korea to pay most of the cost of the new reactors.[38]

During 1995, North Korea's objections to South Korea's direct involvement in the supply of the planned nuclear reactors was an obstacle to implementing the agreement. Negotiations broke down on 21 April in Berlin. Subsequently, an agreement was signed by the United States and North Korea in Kuala Lumpur on 13 June whereby the reactors would be supplied by an international consortium known as the Korea Peninsula Energy Development Organization (KEDO).[39] Although KEDO consisted of representatives from the United States, Japan, and South Korea, South Korea would not be referred to in the agreement for the supply of the reactors. North Korea's desire to deal directly with the United States to the exclusion of South Korea was likely to cause further problems in the future. The United States attempted to reassure South Korea that it would not make concessions to North Korea on this point. When Kim Young Sam visited Washington, D.C., in late July 1995, Clinton assured him that "the US regards North Korea's commitment to resume dialogue with the South as an integral component" of the October 1994 agreement.[40]

The widely reported food crisis in North Korea was one factor that pressured Pyongyang to deal directly with Seoul. The World Food Programme estimated that in 1996 grain production in North Korea would fall short by 1 million tonnes, or one-seventh of what would normally be produced.[41] Secret talks were held between the two Koreas in Beijing in late May 1996; Seoul considered direct negotiations on the future of the peninsula its price for agreeing to provide food aid to the North. In late May 1996, Democratic congressman Bill Richardson from New Mexico traveled to Pyongyang to persuade North Korea to accept the proposal for four-party talks (North Korea, South Korea, the United States, and China) made the previous month by Clinton and Kim Young Sam.[42]

In September 1996, North Korea was responsible for the intrusion of a submarine and the landing of a commando team near Kangnung, on South Korea's east coast. In the ensuing conflict, most of the commandos lost their lives, either at the hands of South Korean forces or through execution by their own leaders to avoid capture. The United States did not want this episode to undermine the general direction of its Korean diplomacy, but Kim Young Sam insisted that there be an explicit apology from North Korea. In the meantime, the implementation of the 1994 Geneva Accord was held up, raising fears that North Korea would resume its own nuclear program. Eventually, an acceptable apology was agreed to on 28 December 1996, but as the outcome of negotiations between U.S. and North Korean officials in New York.[43] North Korea expressed its "deep regret" and promised to "work with others for peace and stability on the Korean peninsula." The apology enabled food aid to North Korea from the United States and South Korea to resume and allowed KEDO to proceed with its plans. It remained unclear as to whether four-party talks on Korea would commence; North Korea's clear preference was to negotiate directly with the United States.

China

The Historical Context

Turning next to China, we find that Korea has traditionally played an important role in Chinese security perceptions. Korea has often been portrayed as the "lips" to China's "teeth." Because Korea adjoins northeastern China, the political situation in the peninsula can affect China's security. This was most clearly illustrated when Korea was under Japanese colonial rule between 1910 and 1945. Korea formed a base from which Japan was able to extend its control to Manchuria in 1931, and from there to extend war to China as a whole after 1937. This perception of Korea's role continued during the postwar period.

In the Cold War years, Korea's significance to China's security was demonstrated most dramatically during the Korean War (1950–1953). Rival Communist and anti-Communist states were emerging on the peninsula in the late 1940s, and the potential for a conflict that would affect China's security was always present. Following the outbreak of the war, the major threat to China emerged when UN forces (predominantly from the United States) entered North Korea in late 1950. To protect China's security, Chinese "volunteers" were committed to the conflict; the war eventually stalemated along a line very close to the previous division between North and South.

Following the 1953 armistice, China maintained its commitment to North Korea while remaining hostile to South Korea. South Korea was on friendly terms with Taiwan and looked to the United States as the guarantor of its security; hence the Chinese view that South Korea was like a U.S. aircraft carrier anchored off its shores. China's attitude to South Korea was reciprocated: South Korea had no contact with the Communist world. North Korea, however, was seen as a friendly Communist state whose model of development in many respects followed that of China. China's relationship with North Korea was formalized in a security treaty in 1961.

China's relationship with North Korea was affected by the onset of the Sino-Soviet conflict.[44] The Korean War had contributed to tensions between China and the USSR. China saw North Korea as being mainly under Soviet influence and believed that the USSR had not acted to restrain North Korea from engaging in a conflict that threatened China's security. China was left to take action on its own, while Soviet involvement in the conflict was cautious at best. During the Sino-Soviet conflict, North Korea attempted to maintain a position of equidistance to both Communist powers. It wished to retain support from both powers while alienating neither. Although culturally and politically North Korea was closer to China, both China and the USSR supported North Korea's position on Korean reunification, that is, that North and South should be reunited on the basis of a confederation. The South Korean view has generally favored reunification on the basis of free elections (Syngman Rhee, in the 1950s, foresaw reunification on the basis of military force).

During the 1970s and 1980s, China's position in relation to Korea was affected by various changes. The polarization in East Asia was undermined by the conclusion of the Sino-U.S. rapprochement in 1972. South Korea began to modify its rigidly anti-Communist stance. In 1971 it announced that it was willing to establish diplomatic relations with China and the USSR under certain conditions and in 1973 said that it would support UN membership for both Koreas.[45] Following Mao Tse-tung's death in 1976 and the emergence of Deng Xiaoping as leader, China emphasized achieving economic growth through a policy that combined economic liberalization and political authoritarianism. At the same time, South Korea was achieving remarkable economic growth through its policy of export-oriented industrialization. China could see economic benefits in developing closer economic relations with South Korea. For both economic and strategic reasons China was also developing closer relations with both the United States and Japan in the late 1970s and early 1980s.

North Korea began to view the USSR as the more orthodox of the two Communist powers, and this led to some distancing in its relationship with China.[46] North Korea's ability to play the two Communist powers against each other was weakened by the development of a Sino-Soviet rapprochement, particularly during the Gorbachev era. China and the USSR clearly viewed their relationship with each other as more important than their respective relationships with North Korea.

China also began to move toward improving relations with South Korea. Economically, this was reflected in its expansion of trade and investment relations during the 1980s. By 1989 China's trade with South Korea was more than ten times its trade with North Korea; direct South Korean investment in China by 1991 was approximately U.S. $125 million.[47] By 1992 South Korea was China's eighth most important trading partner.[48] Politically, China established official contact with South Korea in May 1983, when a Chinese aircraft was hijacked to South Korea.[49] Subsequently, the main point of contact was through the South Korean consulate and the representatives of the New China News Agency in Hong Kong. China continued to provide military aid to North Korea and gave at least formal support to the North Korean position on reunification. In practice, however, China appeared to view the U.S. military presence in South Korea as a stabilizing force[50] and reunification as impracticable.[51]

Developments Since the Late 1980s: Nordpolitik and After

The general direction of its policy during the 1980s made China receptive to South Korea's Nordpolitik, or Northern Policy, as announced by President Roh Tae Woo on 7 July 1988.[52] Nordpolitik was an extension of South Korea's attempts to improve relations with the Communist countries since the early 1970s, and it also proposed ways of improving relations with North Korea specifically. Not only was South Korea "willing to cooperate with North Korea in its efforts to improve relations with countries friendly to us including the U.S. and Japan," but it also sought "improved relations with the Soviet Union, China and other socialist countries."[53] (Cross-recognition, of course, would have tended to formalize and stabilize the division of the peninsula, which was contrary to the confederal proposals of the North.) Among other things, by developing South Korea's links with North Korea's ostensible allies, Nordpolitik would have put more pressure on the North to accept the South's proposals. South Korea established diplomatic relations with a number of Eastern European countries: Hungary (February 1989); Poland and Yugoslavia (November 1989); Czechoslovakia (January 1990); and Bulgaria (February 1990). Mongolia followed in March 1990.[54] Although changes had been occurring before Nordpolitik was adopted, its announcement did give a new momentum to these changes.

In the post–Cold War era, a major issue was whether diplomatic normalization would occur between South Korea and the two major Communist powers. In the case of the USSR, this was achieved in September 1990; in China's case, August 1992. An examination of the most significant developments since 1989 can bring insight into China's changing relationship with Korea. Such an examination should study not just China's relationship with the two Koreas but also its stance on issues affecting the peninsula as a whole. While moving toward normalization with South Korea, China has attempted to preserve its relationship with North Korea. Its position on issues relating to the entire peninsula has been governed primarily by a concern to protect its own security and economic interests.

Roh's interest in improving relations with China had been signaled during the presidential election campaign in South Korea in December 1987.[55] China's attitude at this stage was revealed by General Secretary Zhao Ziyang, who stated on 27 February 1988 that improving relations with South Korea "would be too early for the time being, but we are carefully avoiding any statements which would dampen movements on the

South Korean side and undermine hope for the future."[56] This statement indicated that China would be receptive to the formal announcement of Roh's Nordpolitik, but during 1989, it was North Korea that received the most official Chinese attention.

The first occasion for affirming ties between China and North Korea was Zhao Ziyang's visit to North Korea in April 1989. It was reported that Zhao had "reaffirmed China's firm support for the Korean people's just cause for the independent and peaceful reunification of their country" and also supported dialogue between North Korea and the United States.[57] The second occasion was Kim Il Sung's visit to China in November 1989, which was partly in response to the success of South Korea's diplomatic offensive in Eastern Europe. In the aftermath of the Beijing massacre and the changes sweeping the rest of the Communist world, it was also an occasion for both countries to stand firm against reformism.[58]

South Korea's commitment to improving relations with China was clearly indicated in the policy of "nonreaction" it adopted at the time of the Beijing massacre. Roh commented on 26 June 1989 that "the incident is regrettable and a cause for concern. We hope that this tragedy will be overcome quickly and stability restored. If China recovers its stability, we would like to continue economic exchanges."[59] However, there was no rescheduling of a Sino–South Korean joint venture that had been planned to commence on 17 June.[60] From the Chinese perspective, the Beijing massacre meant a setback for the policy of developing a more pragmatic relationship with South Korea. The conservative elements who were strengthened as a result of the massacre tended to favor the traditional policy of giving priority to the relationship with North Korea.[61]

During 1990 there were signs of tensions in Chinese policy between an ideological commitment to North Korea and the pragmatic benefits to be gained from developing relations with South Korea. Official visits continued between China and North Korea. Most significant to the Chinese side was the visit by General Secretary Jiang Zemin to North Korea in March 1990, during which he expressed support for North Korea's "unremitting efforts to ease tension in the area and in realizing the independent and peaceful reunification of the country." Jiang also supported a withdrawal of U.S. troops and military installations from South Korea, as well as talks between the two Koreas and the United States "to explore a *reasonable* solution to the Korean issue."[62]

At this stage relations between China and South Korea focused mainly on improving economic relations rather than pursuing diplomatic normalization. In early 1990, it was reported that China had suspended negotiations with South Korea to establish trade missions; South Korea had wanted such missions to have consular functions, whereas China believed that diplomatic functions should be excluded.[63] In the aftermath of the Roh-

Gorbachev summit meeting in San Francisco in June 1990, one of China's concerns was that North Korea would be further isolated.[64] Following diplomatic normalization between South Korea and the USSR in September 1990, China was even more unwilling to consider a similar step.[65] A reported visit by Kim Il Sung to China in September 1990 to discuss Soviet–South Korean relations suggested increased North Korean dependence on China.[66]

Even though diplomatic relations had not been normalized, Chinese–South Korean relations continued to develop on a pragmatic basis. The Asian Games in Beijing (22 September–7 October 1990) provided a context in which the development of the relationship was discussed.[67] Later in October, an agreement was signed to allow each country to establish a trade office with limited consular functions in the capital of the other.[68]

In the period leading up to diplomatic normalization between China and South Korea in August 1992, China continued to give attention to its relationship with North Korea but did not allow North Korea to exert undue influence over the direction of Chinese policy. During a visit to North Korea in May 1991, Premier Li Peng again affirmed China's support for North Korea's policy on reunification. This was not unqualified support, however; Li Peng stated that China valued "every *reasonable* suggestion on peaceful reunification put forward by the Korean Party and government" and that "Korea's reunification should be accomplished under the condition of non-interference from the outside and through *dialogue and consultation* between the two sides of Korea."[69] During this visit, Li Peng also told North Korea that China would not veto Seoul's application for separate membership in the UN (North Korea's position, in line with its policy on reunification, was that there should be a single Korean seat). Rather than being humiliated by this issue, North Korea announced on 28 May 1991 that it, too, would seek separate membership in the UN.[70] In October 1991, following the admission of the two Koreas to UN membership in September, Kim Il Sung visited China. Amid reports of increased Sino–South Korean contact, there was speculation that Kim was likely to ask China to delay diplomatic normalization with South Korea until Japan extended recognition to North Korea.[71] Chinese president Yang Shangkun also visited North Korea in April 1992 for Kim Il Sung's eightieth birthday.[72]

Ultimately, however, a desire to maintain the Sino–North Korean relationship did not stand in the way of Sino–South Korean diplomatic normalization. In the joint communiqué establishing diplomatic relations as of 24 August 1992, South Korea recognized the People's Republic of China as "the sole legal government of China, and respect[ed] the Chinese position that there is but one China and Taiwan is part of China" (point 3). China supported the proposition that "the Korean Peninsula shall be peacefully reunified by the Korean people" (point 5).[73] For South Korea, normalization was the culmination of Roh's Nordpolitik, and it was symbolically acknowledged by Roh's visit to China in late September 1992.[74]

South Korea believed that Sino-ROK normalization, as part of Nordpolitik, would push North Korea in the direction of South Korea's objectives for the peninsula. Both countries believed that normalization would enhance the possibilities for expanded trade and investment. For China, South Korea's severing of diplomatic ties with Taiwan was a boost for its own one-China policy. It was argued that diplomatic relations with two Koreas did not undermine that policy, because the UN had admitted both states but had affirmed that there could be membership for only one China.[75] It could be argued that, diplomatically, normalization placed China at an advantage to a number of its rivals for influence in the peninsula. Although the USSR (and subsequently Russia) also had diplomatic relations with both Korean states, its earlier recognition of South Korea had been at the expense of the relationship with North Korea. China and South Korea also have a mutual interest in guarding against excessive Japanese influence in the region. They might also be able to use the relationship to advance their respective interests in relation to the United States.[76]

In May 1991 both China and the USSR urged the two Koreas "to refrain from taking any acts that might impede detente on the peninsula and a peaceful reunification of Korea."[77] Although its recognition of South Korea was contrary to North Korean wishes, China has sought to maintain its influence with North Korea. This intention was evident most recently in China's reaction to North Korea's possible acquisition of nuclear weapons: China warned other nations against isolating North Korea and opposed the imposition of sanctions, believing that the issue should be resolved through discussions and negotiations. As a commentary in *Beijing Review* concluded, "The Chinese government has expressed its hope that the nuclear issue of the DPRK can be solved through sincere dialogues by all those concerned, and believes that sanctions and direct confrontation will only aggravate the tense situation on the Korean Peninsula."[78] China was not directly involved in the settlement of the nuclear issue between the United States and North Korea in October 1994.

Increasing tensions in Sino-U.S. relations meant that China did not play a significant role in resolving the subsequent difficulties that arose in implementing the agreement. Nevertheless, China has continued to insist that it have a major role in determining the future of the peninsula. Although it was included as one of the four parties (in addition to South Korea, North Korea, and the United States) in the negotiating framework proposed by Bill Clinton and Kim Young Sam in April 1996, China has not been a major advocate for this proposal, largely because it was not involved in its initial formulation. It has, however, played a role in facilitating contact between the two Koreas, a good example of which was allowing secret talks to be held in Beijing in late May 1996.[79]

Although China's influence over North Korea is greater than that of other states, it is still limited. China would prefer that North Korea embark on a program of economic modernization comparable to its own, because conflict on the peninsula is more likely to occur while North Korea is so much weaker economically than the South. Economic modernization would also open the North to outside influences and hence reduce its sense of isolation. With greater economic equality between North and South, the prospects for peaceful reunification are likely to be enhanced. Whether reunification would be in China's long-term interests is open to debate. A reunified and economically strong Korea would be a strong competitor and could possibly challenge China politically in the way that a reunified Vietnam has done. A divided but peaceful Korea, with both states on good terms with China, might be more in China's interests.

Japan

The Historical Context

Geographical proximity is a factor that has affected the relationship between Japan and Korea. Korea has often been described as "a dagger pointed at the heart of Japan." For this reason, developments on the Korean peninsula have an inevitable effect on Japan.

In the long sweep of history, both Japan and Korea have been influenced a great deal by Chinese culture. However, Korea was generally regarded as having assimilated that culture more thoroughly and as occupying a more elevated position within the hierarchically organized area of Chinese culture. In the late nineteenth century, Japan embarked on a program of Westernization so that it would survive and succeed in the modern world. As the "Hermit Kingdom," Korea continued to resist outside influence at the very time when external powers sought involvement in the affairs of the peninsula. In the early twentieth century, Japan and Russia were the main powers vying for influence in Korea. After the Russo-Japanese War of 1904–1905, Korea became a Japanese protectorate and then a colony from 1910 to 1945. Given their previous attitude of cultural superiority, this was a deeply humiliating experience for the Koreans, and it has continued to color Japanese-Korean relations ever since.

When Korea was divided into North and South as a consequence of World War II, both Japan and South Korea ended up within the U.S. security orbit. Before 1950, Japan had been regarded as more central to U.S. security purposes. With the outbreak of the Korean War in June 1950 and the United States' decision to support South Korea, the defense of South

Korea was also defined as a key security objective for the United States. Both Japan and South Korea developed their own separate security relationships with the United States. There was no security treaty between Japan and the ROK, and the two countries did not even have diplomatic relations until 1965. Syngman Rhee (president of South Korea from 1948 to 1961) found it difficult to forgive Japan for its treatment of Korea in the past, and accommodation proved elusive.

Nevertheless, with encouragement from the United States and a greater political commitment by both South Korea (led by Park Chung Hee after 1961) and Japan (particularly under Eisaku Sato, prime minister from 1964 to 1972), a normalization treaty was signed in 1965. In the Nixon-Sato joint communiqué of 21 November 1969, Sato stated that "the security of the Republic of Korea is essential to Japan's own security."[80] Although Sato was firmly committed to the ROK as the basis for Japan's approach to Korean affairs, some modification occurred under his successor, Kakuei Tanaka (prime minister from July 1972 to December 1974). In August 1974, Foreign Minister Toshio Kimura stated that it was not "the peace and security of South Korea," but "the peace and security of the entire Korean peninsula" that was "vital to Japan's own security."[81] Kimura's statement suggested that Japan would also improve its relations with North Korea. Subsequent governments made clear that Japan's prior commitment was to the ROK but that it was in Japan's interests to see peace maintained on the peninsula as a whole.

Japan's relations with the ROK were disrupted from time to time by incidents such as the kidnapping of Korean opposition leader Kim Dae Jung in Tokyo by South Korean agents in August 1973 and the killing of Park Chung Hee's wife in August 1974 by a Korean living in Japan. In the long term, however, these incidents did not undermine the relationship. Both Japan and the ROK opposed Jimmy Carter's plan to withdraw U.S. troops from South Korea. Such a development would have strengthened the case for a more direct security relationship between Japan and the ROK, but it would have been politically difficult for both countries. In January 1983, Yasuhiro Nakasone became the first Japanese prime minister to visit Seoul, and the gesture was reciprocated in September 1984, when Chun Doo-Hwan became the first South Korean leader to visit Tokyo. On the latter occasion, both leaders declared: "The maintenance of peace and stability on the Korean peninsula is essential to those of East Asia, including Japan."[82]

Following the Tanaka government, there was a reaffirmation of Japan's commitment to the ROK. At the same time, a commitment remained to improving relations with the DPRK. Japan was always conscious, however, that in improving relations with Pyongyang, it should take care not to offend Seoul. Diplomatic recognition of North Korea would be difficult without prior or concurrent recognition by the United States and approval by South Korea. Japan's policy was influenced by its own domestic politics: There was a vocal minority in Japan that favored giving priority to North Korea. This group included the Japanese Socialist Party (JSP) and, to a lesser extent, the Japanese Communist Party (JCP). North Korea also had significant influence among the Korean minority of over 600,000 in Japan, a vestige of Japanese colonial rule in the peninsula. The trend toward improved Japanese relations with North Korea was disrupted by incidents such as the North Korean–orchestrated bombing of the South Korean cabinet delegation in Rangoon in October 1983. In general, however, Japan appeared committed to a de facto "two Koreas" policy.

The strengthening relationship with both South Korea and North Korea was supported by economic developments, particularly in the case of South Korea. Total trade between South Korea and Japan rose from U.S. $210 million in 1965 to more than U.S. $12 billion in 1984.[83] Japan is South Korea's main source of imports and second only to the United States as a destination for its exports; in 1989 South Korea was the second leading source of imports for Japan and also second as a destination for exports.[84] The large trade surplus in Japan's favor, amounting to U.S. $5.9 billion in 1990, was a major problem in Japanese-ROK trade relations.[85] Machinery and equipment constituted the largest category of Japanese exports to South Korea; textiles were the single most important category of South Korean exports to Japan, followed by machinery and equipment.[86] Japanese investment was second only to that of the United States in the development of South Korea's industrial base. In terms of Japan's total overseas investment, however, the proportion going to South Korea was low; for 1951–1989, it amounted to less than U.S. $3.9 billion, or 1.5 percent of total overseas Japanese investment during this period.[87]

In the case of North Korea, there was little economic reason for Japan to develop the relationship, and hence political considerations were more overtly important than they were in Japanese-ROK relations. Japan saw the development of economic relations with the DPRK as a way of contributing to economic development in the North and helping stabilize the political situation in the peninsula as a whole. Its trade with North Korea rose from nearly U.S. $9 million in 1961 to an annual figure between U.S. $400 million and U.S. $500 million during the 1980s; Japan was North Korea's most important non-Communist trading partner.[88] Exchanges of delegations encouraged this trade, though North Korea's reputation for not paying its debts on time had a negative effect.[89] Since the early 1970s, the trade balance has invariably been in Japan's favor.

Developments Since the Late 1980s: Nordpolitik and After

The pursuit of Nordpolitik by Roh Tae Woo after his election as South Korea's president in December 1987 made it easier for Japan to pursue its own objective of contributing to stability in the peninsula on the basis of recognizing existing power realities. Roh's policy of developing relations with the Communist powers and encouraging North Korea to become a "normal" member of the international community was consistent with Japan's own approach. The development of Japan's post–Cold War relationship with Korea has been similar to its historical relationship.[90] That is, Japan has attempted to consolidate its relationship with South Korea and simultaneously improve its relationship with North Korea. The latter objective has been complicated by the dispute concerning North Korea's nuclear status. Japan has sought to harmonize its policy on this matter not only with South Korea but also with the United States and China, the other major powers with a significant interest in the situation.[91]

In his proclamation of 7 July 1988, Roh Tae Woo declared South Korean willingness to facilitate North Korean attempts to improve relations with such countries as the United States and Japan.[92] Japan, which did not wish an improvement in its relations with North Korea to harm its relationship with South Korea, took Roh's statement as approval for a policy of rapprochement.[93] Japan had been working toward improved relations with North Korea since the early 1970s, but there had been various obstacles along the way. At the time of Roh's declaration, for example, Japan had imposed sanctions on North Korea in response to the destruction of a Korean Air Lines aircraft off the coast of Burma in November 1987, which resulted in the loss of 115 lives. Another obstacle was North Korea's detention of two Japanese seamen for their alleged role in assisting a North Korean stowaway in 1983. North Korea rejected a Japanese proposal for bilateral negotiations based on prior release of the seamen; in January 1989, it also rejected negotiations without preconditions.[94] On the basis of suggestions made by JSP secretary general Tsuruo Yamaguchi after his visit to Pyongyang in September 1988, the Japanese government lifted its sanctions against North Korea and also allowed a visit to Japan by a delegation from the North Korean Workers' Party in January 1989.[95]

Prime Minister Noboru Takeshita also assisted the process of rapprochement when he said in the Diet on 30 March 1989 that Japan had "inflicted great suffering on the peoples of nearby lands. . . . On this occasion, when the situation surrounding the Korean Peninsula is entering upon a new era, I would like to express toward all the people of the peninsula our deep remorse and regret for the unfortunate past."[96] Takeshita's statement was also notable for referring to North Korea by its official name, the Democratic People's Republic of Korea, and for not raising the issue of the Japanese seamen.[97]

The emphasis placed on a bilateral relationship with South Korea was reflected in Roh's visit to Japan in May 1990. Although the trade deficit and Japan's treatment of its Korean minority were particular concerns for South Korea, the question of Japan expressing contrition for its treatment of Korea under the colonial regime was the main issue.[98] As Roh said when he addressed the Diet on 25 May: "The perceptions and emotions of the Korean and Japanese peoples about past mistakes are yet to be sorted out. The negative vestiges of the past era continue to hamper the development of bilateral ties. There must be true understanding between our two peoples on the basis of truth so that a bright future can be ensured for our bilateral relationship."[99]

Japan went much further than it had previously in expressing regret for its past treatment of Korea. Emperor Akihito said: "I think of the suffering your people underwent during this unfortunate period, which was brought about by my country, and I cannot but feel the deepest regret."[100] Prime Minister Toshiki Kaifu expressed his "sincere remorse and honest apologies for the fact that there was a period in our history in which Japanese actions inflicted unbearable suffering and sorrow on the people of the Korean peninsula."[101]

North Korea. One thing Roh did not do on his May 1990 visit to Tokyo was inform the Japanese government of the changes occurring in Soviet-ROK relations (which led to full diplomatic normalization in September 1990). Japan consequently felt it had not been taken fully into Seoul's confidence. North Korea became more open to Japanese overtures and on 15 June 1990, Kaifu spoke in the Diet of his desire for "contact with North Korea without any precondition attached."[102]

All of these circumstances prepared the way for a delegation from the LDP (Liberal Democratic Party) and JSP to visit Pyongyang in September 1990. The delegation was led by Shin Kanemaru, an LDP leader and former deputy prime minister. The visit succeeded in facilitating moves toward rapprochement between Japan and North Korea but subsequently attracted criticism in both Japan and South Korea that too much had been conceded to North Korea. Upon his arrival, Kanemaru apologized for the "intolerable sufferings and hardships" inflicted on the Korean people under Japanese rule and also carried a letter from Kaifu (as LDP leader) to Kim Il Sung to the same effect. Kanemaru also conceded that "Japan is responsible for solving the compensation issue whether or not the two nations have diplomatic relations."[103] The visit resulted in a joint declaration agreed to by the LDP and JSP delegations and the Korean Workers' Party.[104] The declaration urged an apology by Japan "for the unhappiness and suffering caused to the Korean people during the 36 years of colonial rule." It also suggested that Japan should compensate North Korea not just for the period of colonial rule but also for the "losses suffered by the Korean people in the 45 years" following World War II. Peaceful reunification between North and South was supported on the basis of the proposition that "there is only one Korea." Talks were to begin in November 1990 with a view to establishing diplomatic relations as soon as possible. The two Japanese seamen detained by North Korea were released in October 1990.

Roh met Kanemaru on 8 October and asked that Japan take into account five principles in developing relations with North Korea.[105] They were consulting with South Korea, urging North Korea to sign a nuclear safeguards agreement with the International Atomic Energy Agency, taking heed of the dialogue between North Korea and South Korea, withholding compensation or aid to North Korea until diplomatic relations were established, and supporting openness and reform in North Korea. Roh reiterated these principles when Kaifu visited Seoul from 9 to 10 January 1991.[106]

In December 1990, Japan and North Korea agreed to begin negotiations on the normalization of diplomatic relations.[107] Talks between the two sides continued over the next two years but eventually collapsed in November 1992.[108] Key issues included the question of compensation to North Korea for Japan's colonial rule and for the adverse effects of Korea's division in the postwar period. (Japan refused to accept responsibility for the latter.) The issue of North Korea's jurisdiction on the Korean peninsula was also important. Japan wanted the territorial limits of that jurisdiction specified, whereas North Korea argued that it was an internal affair between North and South. Another issue that divided the parties was Japan's requirement that North Korea agree to nuclear inspections under the auspices of the IAEA before normalization could be achieved. Although North Korea indicated in June 1991 its willingness to sign a nuclear safeguards agreement, Japan remained wary of its intentions on this issue.

Negotiations were facilitated by such developments as the joint entry of North Korea and South Korea into the UN in September 1991; the North-South agreement on reconciliation, nonaggression, and exchanges and cooperation (December 1991); and the North-South agreement on denuclearization of the Korean peninsula (January 1992). Nevertheless, disagreements over the nuclear issue and compensation in particular (some reports suggested that North Korea was claiming up to U.S. $10 billion, compared with the U.S. $500 million paid to South Korea in 1965[109]) remained major obstacles. The talks collapsed in November 1992 over the Japanese allegation that North Korea had abducted a Japanese woman ("Li Un-hye") in 1978 and was still holding her, but the arguments over the more general issues continued.

Kiichi Miyazawa's emergence as Japanese prime minister in November 1991 may have made the conclusion of a normalization agreement more difficult. Miyazawa was more experienced in foreign affairs and was regarded as stronger politically than Kaifu. He was less inclined to heed the advice of people such as Kanemaru, who favored a conciliatory approach to North Korea for the sake of achieving an agreement. Miyazawa was also viewed as more sensitive to the concerns of the United States and South Korea on this issue.[110]

The question of Japanese relations with North Korea was an important aspect of Japanese–South Korean discussions during Miyazawa's term as prime minister. Miyazawa's first official visit to South Korea was in January 1992, when he told Roh that North Korea must "sign the nuclear safeguards accord and agree to international inspection of its nuclear facilities" as a condition of normalizing relations with Japan.[111] South Korea continued to press for action to reduce its trade deficit with Japan and was also concerned about Japanese legislation that would enable Japanese forces to take part in peacekeeping missions. The past continued to weigh heavily on the bilateral relationship; there were reports about "comfort women" (most of them Korean) being forcibly recruited by the Japanese army between 1931 and 1945. Miyazawa apologized for Japanese colonial rule: "We Japanese . . . recall the truth of that tragic period when Japanese actions inflicted suffering and sorrow upon your people and we will never forget our feelings of remorse."[112]

One aim of Roh's November 1992 visit to Japan was to emphasize the continued importance of the bilateral relationship in the aftermath of Sino-ROK diplomatic normalization (August 1992) and Yeltsin's visit to Seoul in November 1992 (even though the Russian leader's planned visit to Tokyo two months earlier had been canceled). Japan again made clear that the normalization of relations with North Korea would be dependent on a resolution of the nuclear issue.[113] When South Korean foreign minister Han Sung Joo visited Japan in April 1993, Miyazawa said that North Korea's withdrawal from the Nuclear Nonproliferation Treaty (announced the previous month) was "a great security threat" to Japan and South Korea. Nevertheless, Japanese foreign minister Michio Watanabe believed that diplomatic pressure rather than economic sanctions were the appropriate instrument to use to persuade North Korea to reverse its decision.

The nuclear issue continued to be a major preoccupation in Japan's relations with both Koreas during 1993 and 1994. From Japan's perspective, the prospect of North Korea developing nuclear weapons was not only an obstacle to diplomatic normalization but also a direct threat to its own security. The succession of governments in office in Japan after August 1993 did not result in fundamental changes in this underlying approach, but it did weaken Japan's ability to act decisively.

In June 1993, Japan welcomed North Korea's decision to suspend its withdrawal from the Nuclear Nonproliferation Treaty, also saying that it would counter the development of North Korean missiles with the capacity to attack Japan.[114] In late May, North Korea had tested a Rodong I missile with a reported range of up to 600 miles. As the 1993 Japanese Defense Paper made clear, "If the development program [for the Rodong I] is completed successfully, the missile could not only hit part of western Japan but also cover much of Japan, depending on its deployment sites."[115]

Coalition governments in Japan. An interesting issue in the Hosokawa coalition government, which was established in August 1993, was the position of the Social Democratic Party of Japan (SDPJ) on Korean affairs. As the JSP, this party was very sympathetic toward North Korea, but it was now a major partner in the coalition. As such, the party took steps to put its relations with South Korea on a new footing. In September 1993 Sadao Yamahana, the chairman of the SDPJ, made an official visit to Seoul, where he met President Kim Young Sam. Kim was reported to have told Yamahana: "Until now, the Social Democratic Party of Japan had been thought to stand only on the side of North Korea. I appreciate the changing of your party policy toward the Republic of Korea."[116] Yamahana apologized for Japan's treatment of Korea during the colonial period and also said the issue of the "comfort women" should be settled from "Japan's moral point of view." The SDPJ would continue to urge North Korea both to remain within the NPT and to allow international inspection of its nuclear facilities.[117]

Hosokawa himself visited South Korea in November 1993. On this occasion he went further than previous Japanese leaders had by expressing "heartfelt remorse" for Japanese colonial rule in Korea and by describing Japanese forces at the time as "assailants."[118] Hosokawa's statements helped clear the psychological obstacles that had hindered greater cooperation between Japan and South Korea. He and Kim agreed that they should coordinate their policies for dealing with suspected nuclear developments in North Korea.[119]

This objective remained important when Kim Young Sam visited Japan in March 1994. Because North Korea continued to refuse IAEA inspection of its nuclear facilities, there was a stronger possibility of international sanctions being imposed. Japan was likely to be pressured to restrict remittances, estimated between U.S. $600 million and U.S. $1.6 billion, that were sent by pro-DPRK Koreans to North Korea each year. Hosokawa counseled caution but said Japan would support sanctions "within the limit of the constitution." Kim and Hosokawa supported "a united, resolute stand" by the international community on the nuclear inspection issue, but they also wanted to maintain "windows of dialogue" with North Korea.[120]

Japan continued to take a cautious approach to the North Korean nuclear issue during the short-lived Hata government (April–June 1994), even though Ichiro Ozawa (co-leader with Hata of the Japan Renewal Party) favored a firmer stance.[121] With the IAEA announcement in June 1994 that North Korea was not adhering to nuclear safeguards, pressure for international action had intensified. Japan, South Korea, and the United States supported a statement that the UN Security Council "urgently consider an appropriate response" to this situation, "including sanctions."[122] Nevertheless, Japan preferred that the crisis be resolved through diplomatic means. Hata declared that it was Japan's position "not to seek an immediate punishment" of North Korea.[123] Foreign Minister Koji Kakizawa said: "It is important for Japan, South Korea and China—as Pyongyang's neighbours—to send North Korea the right message together"; the aim was not to punish North Korea but to have it work within the international nuclear regime.[124] It was reported that the Japanese foreign ministry favored a "sub-regional dialogue" on North Korea with participation by the United States, China, South Korea, Russia, and Japan.[125] The issues of Japan-DPRK diplomatic normalization and Japanese compensation payments to North Korea could play a role in the search for a diplomatic solution.[126] On 19 June Kakizawa said Japan could help North Korea replace its nuclear facilities with light-water reactors if the issue were considered in the context of talks on normalization.[127]

When an LDP-SDPJ coalition led by Socialist Tomiichi Murayama took office in late June 1994, one of its first moves was to consolidate the relationship with South Korea. Given the traditional Socialist alignment with North Korea, there was concern in Seoul that Japan's relationship with South Korea would be downgraded. Murayama attempted to put such fears to rest when he visited South Korea on 23–24 July. Following the example of Hosokawa and Hata, Murayama stated: "The Japanese need to recognize anew, as the 50th anniversary of the end of World War II arrives next year, that Japan's past wrongdoing caused unbearable suffering and sorrow for many people on the peninsula."[128]

On the North Korean nuclear issue, Kim Young Sam and Murayama agreed that their countries should act together in seeking a solution, but no specific initiative was forthcoming. Among the new developments affecting the situation were the commencement of North Korean–U.S. talks in Geneva and the death of Kim Il Sung, both in early July. In this context, Japan had been considering the resumption of its own normalization talks with North Korea.[129] At the Geneva talks in August 1994 the United States had agreed that North Korea should be supplied with light-water reactors (which, unlike its graphite reactors, would not produce weapons-grade plutonium) in return for closing its reprocessing facility and placing it under the supervision of the IAEA. Although there was argument about how the agreement should be implemented, it was reported that the United States had asked Japan to pay U.S. $1 billion of the expected U.S. $4 billion cost; Foreign Minister Yohei Kono indicated on 22 September that Japan was willing to be involved.[130] Following the signing of the agreement between the United States and North Korea on 21 October 1994, Japan agreed to pay about 20 percent of the cost, and South Korea about 70 percent.[131] In subsequent negotiations between the United States and North Korea, Japan's participation was through the international consortium known as KEDO. In response to the food crisis that emerged in North Korea during 1996, Japan, along with the United States and South Korea, provided food aid to the North.

These latest developments were consistent with Japanese policy toward Korea as it had evolved since the 1970s. While there had been variations in the way that policy was implemented—depending on factors such as Japanese domestic politics, the situation in North Korea and South Korea, and the general international situation—there had also been some constancy of purpose. Whatever support was given in principle to peaceful reunification of the peninsula, in practice Japan was inclined to base its policy on the realities of the situation. Japan thus accepted the division of Korea for the indefinite future. Japan gave priority to consolidating its often difficult relationship with South Korea, but in the long term, it hoped to normalize its relationship with North Korea. This aim persisted even when it became clear that North Korea was failing economically and becoming increasingly isolated politically. Japan believed that supporting economic renovation in North Korea was preferable to seeing its political collapse. Although such a collapse might lead to reunification, it could also be accompanied by much instability, which could have repercussions in the wider region, including Japan. There was also the argument that a reunified Korea might, in the long term, be an economic and political challenge to Japan. Japan, along with other powers, could have more influence if Korea remained divided.[132]

The USSR and Russia

During the Cold War, the USSR had a major influence on the Korean peninsula and, together with China, played an important role in North Korea. Its role became more fluid during the late 1980s, which saw the emergence of Mikhail Gorbachev as the leader of the USSR and the pursuit of Nordpolitik by South Korea. Since 1991, the Russian Federation has assumed the role previously played by the USSR, but its influence has been less.

Historical Context

Having been instrumental in the emergence of North Korea as a separate state, the USSR was probably aware of North Korea's long-term plans but was not directly responsible for the attack by the North on the South in 1950. Its failure to provide full backing to the North became a source of contention between China and the USSR; China felt compelled to intervene in the conflict from late 1950. This set the scene for China and the USSR to vie for influence in North Korea. In 1961 both Communist powers signed mutual security treaties with the DPRK. North Korea was able to use the Sino-Soviet conflict to its advantage. Pyongyang may have felt closer ideologically to Beijing, but it was able to obtain important economic and military advantages from its relationship with Moscow.

Despite the emphasis on self-reliance in Kim Il Sung's Juche ideology,

North Korea relied heavily on Soviet economic assistance. North Korea was not very important as a trading partner for the USSR, but the USSR was important to North Korea. From 1955 to 1984, the proportion of North Korea's total trade with the USSR decreased from 80 percent to 30 percent, but the latter amount was still a significant figure.[133] Similarly, while North Korea may have preferred to be more militarily self-reliant, the aid it received from the USSR was crucial to its military power. Even though the USSR was frequently less forthcoming than North Korea would have preferred, a Sino-Soviet rapprochement would have made North Korea less significant to the two Communist powers and would probably have resulted in a reduced level of assistance.

The USSR gave general support to the North Korean position on reunification but was disinclined to take any steps to promote that goal. For this reason, the USSR did not respond to President Park Chung Hee's declaration of 23 June 1973 that South Korea was interested in establishing diplomatic relations with the Communist states. Some low-level contacts did develop between the USSR and South Korea in such areas as trade and sport. Even these contacts were jeopardized when Korean Air Lines flight 007 was shot down by a Soviet fighter aircraft in September 1983 and all 269 people aboard were killed.

The Gorbachev Era and South Korea's Nordpolitik

After Gorbachev emerged as leader of the USSR in 1985, he announced the approach he favored in Asia Pacific in a speech in Vladivostok in July 1986. There was little indication in this speech of significant change in the Soviet view of the Korean situation. Gorbachev appeared to support North Korea, maintaining that there were "no rational grounds for rejecting the serious dialogue being proposed by the DPRK" and seeing value in "the DPRK proposal for the creation of a nuclear-free zone on the Korean peninsula."[134]

By 1988, however, the situation appeared much more fluid. Improving relations with the USSR was one of the main objectives of Roh Tae Woo's Nordpolitik, which was announced on 7 July 1988. In a speech in Krasnoyarsk on 16 September 1988, Gorbachev appeared to support a corresponding relationship with South Korea. He referred to "movement toward a dialogue between the North and the South" and proposed multilateral discussions to reduce the level of air and naval forces in the region where the coasts of the USSR, China, Japan, and the two Koreas meet. Furthermore, he stated: "In the context of the general improvement of the situation on the Korean Peninsula, possibilities may open up for establishing economic ties with South Korea."[135] Roh responded to Gorbachev's proposal for multilateral discussions by suggesting at the UN General Assembly in October that there should be a six-power conference involving the two Koreas, the United States, the USSR, China, and Japan.[136] Soviet participation in the 1988 Olympics in Seoul also helped improve relations between the USSR and South Korea. Trade between the two countries was growing rapidly: South Korean exports to the USSR rose from U.S. $26 million in 1988 to almost U.S. $642 million in 1991; South Korean imports over the same period grew from more than U.S. $178 million to more than U.S. $581 million.[137]

The improving political and economic relationship between the USSR and South Korea was taken one step further with the establishment of diplomatic relations on 30 September 1990. This event had been preceded by a summit meeting between Roh and Gorbachev in San Francisco on 5 June 1990 and was followed by another summit meeting between the two leaders in Moscow in December 1990. The latter meeting resulted in the Moscow Declaration, which provided a broad political framework for the relationship between the USSR and South Korea.[138] In April 1991, Gorbachev met Roh on the South Korean island of Cheju en route to Moscow after a visit to Japan. Because Gorbachev had never visited North Korea, his visit to South Korea indicated the much greater priority the USSR now placed on relations with that country.[139]

Soviet relations with North Korea during the later Gorbachev period were ambivalent. North Korea was widely seen in the USSR as a Stalinist remnant, and North Korea regarded the Soviet recognition of South Korea as a betrayal. Nevertheless, the USSR was not prepared to cut off North Korea completely. The 1961 treaty remained in force, and the USSR believed that it could exert some influence on North Korea to facilitate an accommodation on the peninsula or at least reduce the risk of international conflict. Moscow made known its concerns about North Korea moving to develop its nuclear weapons capability.

From 1991 on, Soviet exports to members of the former socialist bloc were to be paid for in hard currency, a measure that had major implications for North Korea. Oil imports from the USSR doubled in price, although Moscow finally decided to continue providing some oil to North Korea on a concessional basis.[140] North Korean imports from the USSR fell to U.S. $11 million in the first six months of 1991, compared with U.S. $887 million in January–July 1990.[141]

Another consideration affecting Gorbachev's policy toward North Korea was the support the regime still had among conservative circles in the USSR. It was no surprise that Pyongyang (unlike Seoul) looked favorably on the attempted conservative coup in Moscow in August 1991.

How do we explain the shift in Soviet policy toward South Korea and away from North Korea? Economic factors were of great importance. Gorbachev believed that developing closer relations with the dynamic economies of Asia Pacific would help the USSR's own economic situation, and South Korea provided economic opportunities. North Korea was more of an economic burden to the USSR. The changing strategic situation in Northeast Asia also influenced Soviet policy. With the Sino-Soviet rapprochement, China and the USSR had less reason to compete for influence in North Korea. The general improvement in relations with other major powers in the region, such as the United States and even Japan, also reduced North Korea's strategic significance to the USSR. At the same time, the USSR believed that by maintaining some links with North Korea, it was in a good position to play a mediating role on the Korean peninsula. Keeping these ties would also disarm Gorbachev's conservative critics at home.

Roh's Nordpolitik meant that there was a coincidence of interests between South Korea and the USSR. The changing configuration of circumstances affecting the USSR was reflected in South Korea's desire to improve its own diplomatic position and in its perception that economic benefits might flow from an improved relationship with the USSR.

Russia

The factors that affected Soviet policy toward Korea during the latter part of the Gorbachev era also applied broadly to Russian policy as it developed under Boris Yeltsin. That is, Russia emphasized the relationship with South Korea but also attempted to maintain a state-to-state relationship with North Korea. In general, however, Russian influence on the Korean situation has tended to decline.

Yeltsin visited Seoul in November 1992 and used his address to South Korea's National Assembly to promote "the formation of a mechanism for multilateral talks in the Asian-Pacific region, to work out a system of crisis settlement in order to prevent an increase in military tension in this region."[142] A broad framework for the bilateral relationship was established with the signing of a Treaty on Basic Relations.[143] Kim Young Sam's visit to Moscow in June 1994 further developed the relationship between the two countries. Among the points of agreement on this occasion were that Russia would support South Korea's bid for a nonpermanent seat on the UN Security Council for 1996–1997 and that South Korea would support Russian membership in APEC (Asia-Pacific Economic Cooperation).[144]

The priority Russia accorded to South Korea was clear, but the relationship was not without difficulties. Because Russia had no major bilateral disputes with South Korea (unlike its relationship with Japan), it had assumed that the development of the relationship with South Korea held out great economic promise. Following the establishment of diplomatic relations, the USSR had been promised loans worth U.S. $3 billion by South Korea, and by the end of 1991, U.S. $1.47 billion had been provided.[145] However, a dispute arose over Russia's repayment of Soviet debts of U.S. $400 million: Moscow wanted to provide arms to settle the debt, but this plan was unacceptable to Seoul. In April 1995, Seoul finally agreed to accept arms and raw materials in repayment of the debt.[146] South Korean investment in Russia has not met Russian expectations. The political and economic problems in Russia have been a disincentive to South Korea; China has emerged as the preferred destination for South Korean investment.[147]

Russia has retained state-to-state relations with North Korea. The 1961 mutual security treaty has remained in force at least formally, even though it has complicated Russia's relations with South Korea. Article 1 of that treaty, requiring Soviet assistance in the event of an attack on North Korea, has been particularly problematical. On his trip to Seoul in November 1992, Yeltsin spoke of abolishing this article,[148] but in practice, Russia has tried to reinterpret it. Thus, earlier in 1992, Deputy Foreign Minister Georgii Kunadze had said that Article 1 applied only in the event of unprovoked aggression against North Korea.[149] The treaty was automatically renewed in 1991 and would again come up for renewal in 1996. Russia preferred revision since it would preserve some Russian influence and avoid isolating North Korea too much.[150] Russia was unable to conclude a revised treaty with North Korea in 1996, but was hopeful that such a treaty would eventuate in 1997.[151]

The treaty's relevance to the Korean situation became clear during the crisis over North Korea's nuclear program in 1994. Although the USSR had provided assistance to North Korea in the development of this program, it had also been an important influence in North Korea joining the International Atomic Energy Agency (1977) and the Nuclear Nonproliferation Treaty (1985). When allegations arose that North Korea was developing nuclear weapons, Russia urged it to renounce any such intention. On 29 March 1994, Deputy Foreign Minister Alexander Panov said that Russia would assist North Korea under the 1961 treaty if North Korea suffered unprovoked aggression. However, other Russian sources subsequently indicated that military action against North Korea would not come under the heading of "unprovoked aggression" because of its development of nuclear weapons.[152] Russia's pressure on North Korea over the nuclear issue further reduced Russian influence in that country. For example, Russia felt that it had not been consulted sufficiently in the negotiations that led to the accord between the United States and North Korea in October 1994. Russia was also disappointed that the light-water reactors to be provided to North Korea under these accords were to come from South Korea, not from Russia.[153]

The United States and China have tended to be the most important external powers on the issue of Korean reunification. When diplomatic relations between China and South Korea were established in August 1992, China joined Russia in having diplomatic relations with both Koreas. China's economic importance to both North Korea and South Korea is far greater than Russia's. In opposition to the "two plus two" approach favored by the United States and China (involving the two Koreas, China, and the United States) to deal with the Korean reunification issue, Russia has argued for a "two plus four" approach based on the involvement also of Russia and Japan.[154] This proposal has not proceeded very far, a measure of Russia's declining influence on the Korean peninsula.

Notes

1. Nam, *America's Commitment to South Korea,* p. 78.

2. Ibid., p. 148.

3. For a summary of the arrangements for the CFC, see McLaurin and Moon, *The United States and the Defense of the Pacific,* p. 143. It has been argued that the U.S. Army has a strong institutional interest in maintaining the military status quo in South Korea since it gives the Army an important role in U.S. military strategy in Asia Pacific, where the Navy, supported by the Air Force, is otherwise dominant. See Martin, "Security Relations: A U.S. View," p. 194.

4. Olsen, *U.S. Policy and the Two Koreas,* p. 12.

5. Kihl, "The Politics of U.S.-Korean Economic Relations," p. 219.

6. Baker, "America in Asia," pp. 11–13.

7. *Keesing's Record of World Events,* vol. 37 (1991), p. 38576.

8. Ibid., vol. 35 (1989), p. 36455.

9. See "Korean President Warns Hill Against Troop Cutback," *Congressional Quarterly Weekly Report,* 21 October 1989, p. 2819.

10. Susumu Awanohara and Mark Clifford, "Security Blanket Slips," *Far Eastern Economic Review,* 2 November 1989, p. 38.

11. *Keesing's Record of World Events,* vol. 36 (1990), p. 37282. These reductions were incorporated in Cheney's statement of 23 February 1990, which applied also to Japan and the Philippines (ibid., p. 37409).

12. *A Strategic Framework for the Asian Pacific Rim: Report to Congress 1992,* p. 22.

13. Anthony Rowley and Shim Jae Hoon, "Paying for Time," *Far Eastern Economic Review,* 24 January 1991, p. 12.

14. *Keesing's Record of World Events,* vol. 37 (1991), p. 38341.

15. Ibid., p. 38576.

16. Ibid.

17. Ibid.

18. Ibid., p. 38660.

19. "Joint Declaration for a Non-Nuclear Korean Peninsula," January 20, 1992, *Foreign Policy Bulletin,* vol. 2 nos. 4–5 (January–April 1992), p. 110.

20. Ibid.

21. *Keesing's Record of World Events,* vol. 38 (1992), pp. 38721–38722, 38818–38819.

22. Lord, "A New Pacific Community," p. 49.

23. Ibid., p. 50.

24. *Keesing's Record of World Events,* vol. 39 (1993), p. 39509.

25. Ibid., p. 39557.

26. Ibid., p. 39597.

27. See Nayan Chanda, "Bomb Cradle," *Far Eastern Economic Review,* 28 October 1993, p. 20.

28. *Keesing's Record of World Events,* vol. 39 (1993), p. 39776.

29. Nayan Chanda and Shim Jae Hoon, "Devil in the Details," *Far Eastern Economic Review,* 13 January 1994, p. 14.

30. See Nayan Chanda, "Bomb and Bombast," *Far Eastern Economic Review,* 10 February 1994, pp. 16–18.

31. Julia Preston, "U.N. Bows to China, Issues Mild Call to N. Korea to Permit Nuclear Checks," *Washington Post,* 1 April 1994, p. A27.

32. R. Jeffrey Smith, "Perry Sharply Warns North Korea," *Washington Post,* 31 March 1994, p. A1.

33. Nayan Chanda, "Forgive and Forget?" *Far Eastern Economic Review,* 12 May 1994, p. 15.

34. Nayan Chanda, "No Soft Options," *Far Eastern Economic Review,* 16 June 1994, p. 15.

35. Nayan Chanda, "Enough Is Enough," *Far Eastern Economic Review,* 23 June 1994, pp. 14–15.

36. Nigel Holloway and Shim Jae Hoon, "The Price of Peace," *Far Eastern Economic Review,* 25 August 1994, pp. 14–15.

37. Shim Jae Hoon, "Give and Take," *Far Eastern Economic Review,* 27 October 1994, p. 15.

38. See Shim Jae Hoon and Nigel Holloway, "Hold the Champagne," *Far Eastern Economic Review,* 27 October 1994, pp. 14–15; Nigel Holloway and Melana K. Zyla, "Collision Course," *Far Eastern Economic Review,* 19 January 1995, pp. 14–15.

39. Nayan Chanda, "Sounds Familiar," *Far Eastern Economic Review,* 4 May 1995, p. 17; Shim Jae Hoon and Nigel Holloway, "Pyongyang Two-Step," *Far Eastern Economic Review,* 29 June 1995, pp. 22–23.

40. Nigel Holloway, "Fast Friends," *Far Eastern Economic Review,* 10 August 1995, p. 22.

41. Nigel Holloway, "Appointment in Beijing," *Far Eastern Economic Review,* 13 June 1996, p. 14.

42. Ibid., p. 15.

43. Shim Jae Hoon and Nigel Holloway, "Forced Apology," *Far Eastern Economic Review,* 9 January 1997, pp. 15–16.

44. See Chung, *Pyongyang Between Peking and Moscow.*

45. Clough, *Embattled Korea,* p. 330.

46. See Williams, "North Korea: Tilting Towards Moscow?"

47. Lee, "China and the Two Koreas," p. 105.

48. Hao and Qubing, "China's Policy Toward the Korean Peninsula," p. 1146.

49. Opitz, "Changing Alliances," p. 252.

50. See Lee, "China's Policy Toward North Korea," p. 209.

51. See the comments in 1984 by Chinese prime minister Zhao Ziyang to visiting Australian prime minister Bob Hawke as reported in Levin, "Evolving Chinese and Soviet Policies Toward the Korean Peninsula," p. 191

52. Ahn, "South Korea's New *Nordpolitik,*" pp. 694–695. See also Armstrong, "South Korea's 'Northern Policy.'"

53. Ahn, "South Korea's New *Nordpolitik,*" p. 695.

54. Opitz, "Changing Alliances," pp. 247–248.

55. John McBeth, "A Bridge to China," *Far Eastern Economic Review,* 7 January 1988, pp. 15–16.

56. Quoted in Izumi and Kohari, "Sino–South Korean Relations Under the Roh Administration," p. 17.

57. "Zhao Re-visits DPRK," *Beijing Review,* 8–14 May 1989, p. 6.

58. *Keesing's Record of World Events,* vol. 35 (1989), p. 37041.

59. Quoted in Izumi and Kohari, "Sino–South Korean Relations Under the Roh Administration," p. 18.

60. "Quarterly Chronicle and Documentation (April–June 1989)," *China Quarterly,* no. 119 (September 1989), p. 697.

61. See Hakjoon, "China's Korea Policy Since the Tiananmen Square Incident," pp. 110–112.

62. "Jiang, Kim Renew Sino-Korean Ties," *Beijing Review,* 26 March–1 April 1990, p. 8. Emphasis added.

63. "Quarterly Chronicle and Documentation (January–March 1990)," *China Quarterly,* no. 122 (June 1990), p. 370.

64. "Quarterly Chronicle and Documentation (April–June 1990)," *China Quarterly,* no. 123 (September 1990), p. 591.

65. "Quarterly Chronicle and Documentation (July–September 1990)," *China Quarterly,* no. 124 (December 1990), p. 779.

66. Ibid., p. 776.

67. Shim Jae Hoon, "Diplomatic Games," *Far Eastern Economic Review,* 4 October 1990, p. 26.

68. *Keesing's Record of World Events,* vol. 37 (1991), p. 38623.

69. "China Backs DPRK Reunification Efforts," *Beijing Review,* 20–26 May 1991, p. 7. Emphases added.

70. Shim Jae Hoon, "Reluctant Choice," and Tai Ming Cheung, "More Advice than Aid," *Far Eastern Economic Review,* 6 June 1991, p. 15.

71. *Keesing's Record of World Events,* vol. 37 (1991), p. 38530; Shim Jae Hoon, "The Pace Quickens," *Far Eastern Economic Review,* 1 August 1991, pp. 22–23.

72. "Yang's Visit Braces Sino-DPRK Ties," *Beijing Review,* 27 April–3 May 1992, pp. 4–5.

73. "Text of Joint Communique," *Korea News Review,* 29 August 1992, p. 5.

74. See Lincoln Kaye and Susumu Awanohara, "Peking Pilgrimage," *Far Eastern Economic Review,* 8 October 1992, pp. 10–11; "Sino-ROK Ties Praised," *Beijing Review,* 12–18 October 1992, p. 4.

75. Liu, "The Sino–South Korean Normalization," p. 1088.

76. In ibid., pp. 1083–1094, Hong Liu examines the perceived advantages of normalization for China in terms of its position in five triangles: China-USSR–North Korea; China-USSR–United States; China–North Korea–South Korea; China–South Korea–Taiwan; and China-Japan–South Korea.

77. Sino-Soviet communiqué as quoted in Hao and Qubing, "China's Policy Toward the Korean Peninsula," p. 1148.

78. Wang Dajun and Jiang Ye, "The Nuclear Issue of the DPRK," *Beijing Review,* 4–10 July 1994, p. 17. See also Michael Richardson, "China Holds a Key in North Korea Rift," *International Herald Tribune,* 21 December 1993, p. 6; "Making Haste Slowly," *Far Eastern Economic Review,* 7 April 1994, p. 16.

79. Nigel Holloway, "Appointment in Beijing," *Far Eastern Economic Review,* 13 June 1996, p. 15.

80. Quoted, Kim, "Japan's Policy Toward the Korean Peninsula Since 1965," p. 307.

81. Quoted, ibid., p. 308.

82. Quoted, Clough, *Embattled Korea,* p. 226.

83. Ibid., pp. 227–228.

84. Hoon and Clifford, "South Korea: So Near, Yet So Far," p. 28.

85. Ibid.

86. Ibid., p. 34.

87. Ibid., p. 32; Clough, *Embattled Korea,* p. 228.

88. Ibid., p. 356; Lee, *Japan and Korea,* p. 78; Olsen, "Japan and Korea," p. 177.

89. Clough, *Embattled Korea,* pp. 355–356.

90. For a good overview of the major themes in Japanese-Korean relations in the post–Cold War era, see Bridges, *Japan and Korea in the 1990s.*

91. Japan has placed less emphasis on its relationship with the USSR (and subsequently Russia) in the development of its Korean policy. In any event, as indicated below, Soviet (and Russian) influence in Korean affairs has tended to decline in the post–Cold War era.

92. Ahn, "South Korea's New *Nordpolitik,*" p. 695.

93. Useful discussions of developments in Japanese–North Korean relations in the late 1980s and early 1990s are Kim, "The Normalization of North Korean–Japanese Diplomatic Relations" and "Japan and North Korea."

94. Kim, "The Normalization of North Korean–Japanese Diplomatic Relations," p. 654.

95. Ibid.; Charles Smith, "All at Sea," *Far Eastern Economic Review,* 9 February 1989, p. 19.

96. Steven R. Weisman, "Tokyo Apology to Pyongyang," *International Herald Tribune,* 31 March 1989, p. 4.

97. Charles Smith, "Bow to the North," *Far Eastern Economic Review,* 13 April 1989, p. 30.

98. See John Ridding and Ian Rodger, "Emotions Still Rule Korean-Japanese Relationship," *Financial Times,* 24 May 1990, p. 6.

99. "Let's Work Together for Future, Roh Proposes in Address to Diet," *Japan Times,* 26 May 1990, p. 10.

100. *Keesing's Record of World Events,* vol. 36 (1990), p. 37457.

101. Ibid.

102. Quoted, Kim, "Japan and North Korea," p. 115.

103. Quoted, Kim, "The Normalization of North Korean–Japanese Diplomatic Relations," p. 659.

104. Ibid., p. 660. Japanese and South Korean criticism of the declaration is discussed in ibid., pp. 662–666.

105. Ibid., p. 667.

106. *Keesing's Record of World Events,* vol. 37 (1991), p. 37960.

107. Takeshi Uemura, "Japan, North Korea Agree to Hold Full-Scale Talks," *Daily Yomiuri,* 18 December 1990, p. 22.

108. See Kim, "Japan and North Korea," pp. 118–125; *Keesing's Record of World Events,* vol. 37 (1991), pp. 38098, 38191, 38437, 38576; vol. 38 (1992), pp. 38722, 38911, 39004, 39191.

109. Louise do Rosario, "Playing for Time," *Far Eastern Economic Review,* 14 February 1991, pp. 20–21. This same report claimed that Japan was willing to offer U.S. $3–$4 billion in aid.

110. Kim, "Japan and North Korea," p. 122.

111. "Japan Apologizes for 'Suffering' It Inflicted on Korea," *International Herald Tribune,* 17 January 1992, p. 8.

112. Ibid.

113. John Burton, "South Korea and Japan Seek Thaw in Relations," *Financial Times,* 9 November 1992, p. 4.

114. "Muto Vows 'Countermeasures' Against N. Korean Missile," *Japan Times* (Weekly International Edition), 21–27 June 1993, p. 3.

115. Quoted in Takahiko Ueda, "Defense White Paper Takes Aim at Arms Programs," *Japan Times* (Weekly International Edition), 9–15 August 1993, p. 3.

116. "Seoul Welcomes Shift in SDPJ's Policy Toward Korea," *Japan Times* (Weekly International Edition), 13–19 September 1993, p. 1.

117. Ibid., p. 5.

118. Robert Thomson, "Japan Makes Wartime Apology," *Financial Times,* 8 November 1993, p. 5.

119. "Hosokawa, Kim Vow to Establish Partnership," *Japan Times* (Weekly International Edition), 15–21 November 1993, p. 5.

120. "Making Haste Slowly," *Far Eastern Economic Review,* 7 April 1994, p. 16. See also William Dawkins, "Japan Looks at Options for Pyongyang Sanctions," *Financial Times,* 23 March 1994, p. 6; John Burton, "Hosokawa Reassures Kim over N. Korea," *Financial Times,* 25 March 1994, p. 7; Michiyo Nakamoto, "North Korean Threat Tests Japan's Resolve," *Financial Times,* 21 April 1994, p. 4.

121. Charles Smith, "Ifs and Buts of Sanctions," *Far Eastern Economic Review,* 16 June 1994, p. 16.

122. Nayan Chanda, "No Soft Options," *Far Eastern Economic Review,* pp. 14–15.

123. "Tokyo Seeks Peaceful Solution," *Japan Times* (Weekly International Edition), 20–26 June 1994, p. 1.

124. Ako Washio, "Hata Seeks Diplomatic Solution to N. Korea Crisis," *Japan Times* (Weekly International Edition), 13–19 June 1994, p. 5.

125. Charles Smith, "Ifs and Buts of Sanctions," *Far Eastern Economic Review,* 16 June 1994, p. 16.

126. Nayan Chanda, "Forgive and Forget?" *Far Eastern Economic Review,* 12 May 1994, p. 15.

127. "Japan Welcomes Pyongyang's Overture but with Reserve," *Japan Times* (Weekly International Edition), 27 June–3 July 1994, p. 6.

128. "South Korean Fears About SDPJ Eased," *Japan Times* (Weekly International Edition), 1–7 August 1994, p. 6. Murayama's "heartfelt apologies" on 15 August 1995 for Japan's wartime aggression were also welcomed by Kim Young Sam. See Emily Thornton, "Final Mea Culpa?" *Far Eastern Economic Review,* 24 August 1995, p. 18.

129. "Tokyo Considers Resumption of Talks with North Korea," *Japan Times* (Weekly International Edition), 4–10 July 1994, p. 1.

130. Miu Oikawa Dieter, "Tokyo Ready to Join Program to Replace Pyongyang Reactors," *Japan Times* (Weekly International Edition), 3–9 October 1994, p. 3.

131. "Japan to Cover 20% of New Reactors' Costs in N. Korea," *Japan Times* (Weekly International Edition), 31 October–6 November 1994, pp. 1, 6.

132. See Olsen, "Japan and Korea," pp. 181–182.

133. Clough, *Embattled Korea,* p. 246.

134. "Text of Speech by Mikhail Gorbachev in Vladivostok," p. 224.

135. "Gorbachev Offers New Bids on Asian Policy," *Current Digest of the Soviet Press,* vol. 40 no. 38 (19 October 1988), pp. 5–7.

136. Meyer, "Gorbachev and Post-Gorbachev Policy Toward the Korean Peninsula," pp. 759–760.

137. Kim, "The Soviet Union/Russia and Korea," p. 88.

138. See *Korea and World Affairs,* vol. 15 no. 1 (Spring 1991), pp. 131–133.

139. Meyer, "Gorbachev and Post-Gorbachev Policy Toward the Korean Peninsula," p. 762.

140. Ibid., p. 766.

141. Ziegler, *Foreign Policy and East Asia,* p. 122.

142. "Yeltsin in South Korea, Pushes Rapprochement," *Current Digest of the Post-Soviet Press,* vol. 44 no. 46 (16 December 1992), p. 15.

143. For the text of this treaty, see "Treaty on Basic Relations Between the Republic of Korea and the Russian Federation" in *Korea and World Affairs,* vol. 16 no. 4 (Winter 1992), pp. 744–748.

144. "Full Text of Joint Declaration at Moscow Summit," *Korea Observer,* vol. 25 (Autumn 1994), pp. 434–435.

145. Joo, "Russian Policy on Korean Unification in the Post–Cold War Era," p. 37.

146. Ibid.

147. Buszynski, *Russian Foreign Policy After the Cold War,* p. 206.

148. "Yeltsin in South Korea, Pushes Rapprochement," *Current Digest of the Post-Soviet Press,* vol. 44 no. 46 (16 December 1992), p. 16.

149. Buszynski, *Russian Foreign Policy After the Cold War,* p. 204.

150. See Rubinstein, "Russia and North Korea," pp. 499–507.

151. Sophie Quinn-Judge, "Fancy Footwork," *Far Eastern Economic Review,* 27 February 1997, p. 23.

152. Rubinstein, "Russia and North Korea," p. 487.

153. Joo, "Russian Policy on Korean Unification," p. 45.

154. Shim Jae Hoon, "Silent Partner," *Far Eastern Economic Review,* 29 December 1994 and 5 January 1995, p. 15.

12

INDOCHINA

During the post–Cold War era, Indochina has been important to the United States, China, and Japan. This chapter examines the relationship of the three powers with Indochina during this period and studies the Cambodian peace process and the development of relations with Vietnam in particular.[1] The chapter also looks at the involvement of the USSR and subsequently Russia in the region. For each power, a brief survey of the development of the post-1945 relationship is presented before the post–Cold War period is examined in more detail.

The United States

In the early postwar period, the United States became increasingly involved in Southeast Asia as a result of its Cold War containment strategy. Its initial focus was the war being fought in Vietnam between France and the Communist-led Vietminh. Despite U.S. support for France, especially in the early 1950s, the war came to an end in 1954 with a modified victory for the Vietminh. The victory was modified in the sense that the Vietminh controlled Vietnam only north of the seventeenth parallel (North Vietnam), whereas South Vietnam was ruled by a U.S.-supported anti-Communist government. Because of its fear that communism would spread, the United States became increasingly involved in shoring up the Saigon government, especially from the early 1960s on. Full-scale U.S. intervention occurred in 1965.

Military involvement in Vietnam proved to be a disaster for the United States. Following the election of Richard Nixon as president in 1968, the United States was increasingly intent on extricating itself from Vietnam, but in a way that would avoid the immediate collapse of the Saigon government. The Guam doctrine of 1969, which was announced by Nixon, indicated that the United States would not become involved in ground conflicts in the region in the future. "Vietnamization" was an attempt to put this doctrine into practice in Vietnam, with the Saigon forces doing most of the ground fighting. The Paris Accords of 1973 provided for U.S. withdrawal from South Vietnam. Without strong U.S. backing, the Saigon government had collapsed by 1975 and Vietnamese unification under Communist auspices was achieved soon after.

Following the collapse of the Saigon government, the United States still faced important issues in Indochina. These included not only the question of the normalization of relations with Vietnam but also the radical revolution being undertaken in Cambodia (or Kampuchea, as it was renamed) by the Khmer Rouge under Pol Pot. Reports of genocide caused an outcry in the United States and other countries, but this opposition did not lead to support for Vietnam when it intervened in Cambodia in late 1978 and installed a pro-Vietnamese government. In general, the United States supported the position taken by the Association of Southeast Asian Nations (ASEAN) and China that Vietnam should cease its intervention in Cambodia; at the same time, the United States was opposed to any return to power by the Khmer Rouge. Vietnamese withdrawal from Cambodia was one of the major preconditions for the normalization of relations with the United States.

The Bush Administration

The issues that were important in the United States' relations with Indochina in the late 1970s were still important when George Bush came to office in 1989 as the first post–Cold War president. Secretary of State James Baker's 1991 *Foreign Affairs* article on U.S. policy in Asia referred to Indochina among other issues. Baker argued that cooperative efforts with ASEAN were central "to the successful conclusion of a comprehensive agreement to end the conflict in Cambodia."[2] Once the Cambodian peace process was worked through with "free and fair elections [and] the installation of a legitimate government in Phnom Penh," and assuming "substantial resolution of our POW/MIA concerns," the United States would be in a position "to normalize relations with Vietnam, Cambodia and Laos."[3]

The Cambodian issue. The Bush administration had a number of objectives in Cambodia.[4] During the Reagan administration, the United States had followed the lead of ASEAN and China in opposing Vietnamese intervention and the Vietnamese-backed government in Cambodia. It was also opposed to the return to power of the Khmer Rouge,[5] preferring a settlement in which the non-Communist factions led by Prince Norodom Sihanouk and Son Sann would be dominant. Between 1985 and 1988, the United States provided over U.S. $3 million of overt nonlethal aid annually to these factions.[6] The problem was that in prosecuting the war against the pro-Vietnamese government led by Hun Sen, the Sihanoukist and Son Sann factions were aligned with the Khmer Rouge. Although China believed the Khmer Rouge played a useful role in restraining Vietnam, and ASEAN was at least ambivalent about the matter, Washington could not brook any settlement that returned power to this group. The United States contemplated giving lethal aid to the non-Communist factions[7] and increased the level of overt nonlethal aid from U.S. $5 million in 1989 to U.S. $7 million in 1990.[8] When Vietnam announced that it would withdraw its forces from Cambodia by the end of September 1989, the prospects for achieving a settlement were improved. However, the announcement also meant that the relative power of the different groups in Cambodia would become a crucial issue.

The essence of the U.S. approach to this situation was set out by James Baker in his comments to the ASEAN postministerial conference on 7 July 1989:

> First, there should be a comprehensive solution encompassing a ceasefire, measures to control the Khmer Rouge effectively, transitional power-sharing arrangements, and then free elections to enable the Cambodians to determine their own future. . . . Second, there should be an interim coalition government in which Prince Sihanouk plays the leading role. . . . Third, these arrangements should be supervised by an international control mechanism organized by the United Nations.[9]

There was some hint of the United States' willingness to compromise in Baker's statement at the international conference on Cambodia in Paris on 30 July 1989. Thus, said Baker, while "the United States strongly believes that the Khmer Rouge should play no role in Cambodia's future . . . [it is] prepared . . . to support Prince Sihanouk should he deem it necessary to accept the inclusion of all Khmer factions in an interim coalition or an interim authority." Similarly, Baker continued, although "we also cannot accept a continuation of the present regime in Phnom Penh, which was established through Vietnamese aggression [we] recognize . . . that elements of that regime are likely to be included in any transitional coalition."[10]

Following the failure of the Paris conference to achieve a settlement, Richard Solomon (assistant secretary of state for East Asian and Pacific Affairs), in an address on 8 September 1989, emphasized the limited role the United States could play in Cambodia.[11] It was an issue of conscience for the international community "to ensure that there [were] no more Cambodian killing fields." Hence, Solomon said, "the United States will play an active role in pursuit of these objectives, but it must be recognized that we have neither the political position nor the resources to do the job on our own." Strategically, the United States' interest was "in seeing Indochina freed of the rivalries of the great powers." Solomon envisaged U.S. diplomatic activity occurring at three levels: through the five permanent members of the UN Security Council, by supporting ASEAN, and by backing the non-Communist resistance with "Prince Sihanouk as the political center of a process of national reconciliation."

In January 1990, with the United States taking a leading role, the five permanent members of the Security Council agreed to the principles that should underlie a Cambodian settlement; a more detailed framework agreement was announced in August 1990.[12] The council envisaged vesting Cambodian sovereignty in a Supreme National Council (SNC, upon which all Cambodian parties would be represented), pending elections under UN auspices to determine a future government. It was proposed that the SNC transfer effective authority to the UN, which would also run key government ministries.[13]

The Cambodian parties agreed in principle to this plan, but it took more than a year to work out a more detailed agreement. In the meantime, the United States also attempted to distance itself further from the Khmer Rouge. The United States was concerned that the non-Communist factions it supported were in coalition with the Khmer Rouge. Congress was also concerned that this support could strengthen the Khmer Rouge and that the Hun Sen government (known as the State of Cambodia, or SOC) was in a better position to check the Khmer Rouge.[14] Partly in response to these pressures, Baker announced on 18 July 1990 that the United States would discontinue support for the seating of the anti–Hun Sen coalition (the Coalition Government of Democratic Kampuchea, or CGDK) in the UN.[15] The United States would engage Vietnam in dialogue on the Cambodian issue and was prepared to consider humanitarian assistance to the SOC. Both China and ASEAN saw the United States' move as weakening the solution they sought to the Cambodian conflict. As Nayan Chanda wrote: "The switch on Indochina without consulting Asean has ended a decade-long situation that gave Asean—and by extension China—an effective veto over US policy on the issue."[16]

Following this shift in policy, the United States concentrated on diplomacy aimed to win support for the Security Council plan. This involved dialogue with all of the key players, including Vietnam. In March 1991, Richard Solomon visited China, Japan, Indonesia, and Thailand as part of this diplomatic effort; in China he was able to meet Soviet deputy foreign minister Igor Rogachev.[17] In April 1991, it was revealed that the U.S. $20 million package for humanitarian and nonlethal military aid to the non-Communist Cambodian factions had been suspended in response to reports of "tactical military cooperation" between those factions and the Khmer Rouge. Although the U.S. State Department was opposed to the move, the suspension was necessary because of the provision in the 1991 foreign aid bill proscribing aid to any group "cooperating, tactically or strategically, with the Khmer Rouge."[18]

In October 1991, a detailed plan to implement the framework agreement was finally approved at the Paris Conference on Cambodia. The

Supreme National Council, representing the four Cambodian groups, would play a largely symbolic role; the UN, through the UN Transitional Authority in Cambodia (UNTAC), would supervise the arrangements needed for free elections to take place. It remained to be seen how the agreement would be implemented in practice. Baker's statement of 23 October 1991 suggested a certain optimism: "We welcome the Supreme National Council's acceptance of a multiparty liberal democratic order, and we look to the United Nations to ensure that the elections it is charged to organize will be free and fair."[19]

Solomon was more realistic in drawing attention to the importance of China and Vietnam resolving their differences and of Sihanouk becoming actively involved in the negotiations, factors that would contribute to the final settlement.[20] Solomon's judgment was that the Khmer Rouge would do worse in elections than they would on the battlefield: "The settlement agreement obliges the Khmer Rouge to turn from the battlefield, where they have particular strengths and experience, to the ballot box, where they can be held accountable by the Cambodian people for their bloody record."[21]

Relations with Vietnam. Closely connected to U.S. involvement in the Cambodian peace process was the question of U.S. relations with Vietnam. The POW/MIA issue had been one factor impeding the normalization of relations between Vietnam and the United States; Vietnamese intervention in Cambodia had been the major consideration in the United States' broader regional policies. When Vietnamese forces withdrew from Cambodia and Vietnam seemingly cooperated in achieving a settlement, one major obstacle to improved Vietnamese-U.S. relations was removed.

In the latter part of the Reagan administration, there were attempts to improve U.S.-Vietnamese relations. In August 1987, General John Vessey, a former chairman of the Joint Chiefs of Staff, visited Hanoi as a special envoy for President Reagan to discuss the MIA and other humanitarian issues.[22] General Vessey made subsequent visits to Vietnam during the Bush administration, and in April 1991, it was announced that the United States would open a POW/MIA office in Hanoi.[23]

A significant development at the broader political level was Baker's announcement on 18 July 1990 that U.S. policy toward the Cambodian issue had been revised. Among other things, Baker said that the United States proposed to discuss the issue directly with Vietnam: "We want to talk to Vietnam because we think they have influence over the Cambodian government and could use this to help us construct conditions permitting free elections."[24] Talks were held in New York on 6 August 1991 between Kenneth Quinn, deputy assistant secretary of state for East Asian and Pacific Affairs, and Vietnam's ambassador to the UN, Trinh Xuan Lang, and on 29 September 1991 between Baker and Vietnam's foreign minister, Nguyen Co Thach.[25]

A further development occurred on 9 April 1991, when Richard Solomon proposed to Trinh Xuan Lang at a meeting in New York that the United States would normalize relations with Vietnam on the basis of four phases, beginning with the signing of the Cambodian peace plan and ending with the election of a Cambodian government under this plan. The first phase would involve the commencement of normalization discussions and approval by the United States of visits to Vietnam by veterans' and business groups. Once the UN was established in Cambodia, the United States would partially lift its trade embargo. After the UN had been in Cambodia for six months, the United States and Vietnam could establish diplomatic offices in each other's capital, the U.S. trade embargo would be lifted, and the United States would relax its opposition to international banks lending to Vietnam. Following the completion of the peace process in Cambodia, there could be full diplomatic and economic relations and support for international bank lending. Progress on the MIA issue would also be necessary in conjunction with this process.[26]

When the Cambodian peace plan was signed in Paris in October 1991, Baker indicated that preliminary discussions on normalization could occur. Restrictions on U.S. citizens traveling to Vietnam and on Vietnamese diplomats at the UN were removed, but on 15 October the United States blocked the provision of International Monetary Fund (IMF) assistance to Vietnam.[27] Subsequently, Solomon and Vietnamese vice foreign minister Le Mai met in New York on 21 November 1991 to begin discussions on normalization, and further talks were also held in Hanoi on 5 March 1992.[28] In line with the phases previously outlined by Solomon, the United States in April 1992 eased some of the restrictions on links with Vietnam, including bans concerning telecommunications and the activities of humanitarian groups and some aspects of humanitarian trade.[29]

The Clinton Administration

The first major statement of policy by Winston Lord, assistant secretary of state for East Asian and Pacific Affairs in the Clinton administration, gave some attention to Vietnam and Cambodia.[30] On the Vietnam issue, Lord saw the MIA problem as a continuing concern but at the same time argued that Vietnam could "play an important political and economic role"; with the necessary groundwork, regional stability could be strengthened. Lord also sought some modification of the "repressive communist political system." Vietnam's continued support for the peace process in Cambodia was important, but that process also had broader implications as "a crucial test of multilateral peacekeeping by the international community." While the problems were many, Lord argued, "the United States must support the process of free and fair elections and assist the government that emerges."

In practice, the issue of normalizing relations with Vietnam has been the biggest concern for the Clinton administration.[31] In the UN-sponsored Cambodian elections in May 1993, the Clinton administration essentially followed Bush's policy of supporting the UN and excluding the Khmer Rouge as much as possible. Bill Clinton moved slowly on normalizing relations with Vietnam, particularly compared with the steps taken by the previous administration under the phases proposed by Solomon in April 1991. More rapid progress was impeded by the failure to resolve the MIA issue to U.S. satisfaction and the pressure that the MIA lobby in the United States could bring to bear against normalization. Pressure for normalization came mainly from U.S. business interests who saw prospects for expansion in Vietnam. Clinton took some steps that gradually moved the relationship toward normalization. On 2 July 1993, he announced that the United States would no longer prevent the IMF from providing assistance to Vietnam to clear its U.S. $140 million debt to that organization.[32] As a result of a visit by Winston Lord to Vietnam from 15 to 17 July, agreement was reached that three U.S. State Department officials could be stationed in Vietnam to provide assistance to U.S. visitors.[33] On 13 September, the United States announced that U.S. companies could bid for projects in Vietnam financed by bodies such as the IMF, the World Bank, and the Asian Development Bank.[34] Finally, on 4 February 1994, Clinton lifted the trade embargo, mainly in response to pressure from U.S. businesses. U.S. companies could now compete openly with companies from other countries, but Vietnam, which had not been granted most-favored-nation (MFN) status, would be restricted in its ability to export to the United States.[35] Clinton's sensitivity to domestic pressure on the MIA issue slowed further progress toward full normalization.[36]

During 1995 Clinton decided that, despite the continued relevance of the MIA issue, it was time to improve U.S. relations with Vietnam. On 28 January, it was announced that the United States and Vietnam would establish liaison offices in Hanoi and Washington, D.C., respectively.[37] On 11 July, Clinton announced that full diplomatic recognition would be extended to Vietnam.[38] Granting MFN status to Vietnam remained as an issue to be considered in the future, but the ability of U.S. business interests to compete in Vietnam was enhanced. Because there were tensions in both Sino-Vietnamese and Sino-U.S. relations, the normalization of relations between the United States and Vietnam also had implicit strategic advantages.

Vietnam's New Role

These developments in U.S.-Vietnamese relations should be examined in the context of Vietnam's developing international role in the 1990s.[39] Although the situation in Cambodia was an international preoccupation during the early years of the decade, in the long term, Vietnam's international role was much more significant. As far as Vietnam was concerned, its role was affected by two considerations in particular: its domestic situation and the changing international environment.

The domestic situation led Vietnam to place more emphasis on economic matters in the conduct of its foreign policy. Traditionally, the country had been governed by a centralized Leninist system that had features distinctive to Vietnam. The importance of popular mobilization during Vietnam's wars of liberation meant that the party could not simply be oblivious to the views of the masses. The position of the south, with its decades-long experience of capitalism, made it more difficult to absorb that region into the command economy.[40]

Whatever the distinctive features of Leninism in Vietnam, it was clear by the mid-1980s that the system was failing to deliver economic progress to the country. This led to the institution of a process known as *doi moi* (renovation), similar to perestroika in the USSR. One significant change was the decollectivization of agriculture in 1988, in which agriculture came essentially under private control. Production was boosted as a result, and Vietnam became the world's third largest exporter of rice.[41] Although a large state sector remained, there was a significant expansion of the private sector and foreign investment was encouraged.

At the political level, there was an attempt to distinguish more clearly between the party and the state. Although the party retained overall control, its involvement in administrative matters was reduced. Any suggestion that Vietnam would undergo a process of political liberalization based on "peaceful evolution" was denied. Despite its aspirations to become an "Asian tiger," Vietnam remained poor. With a population of 75,690,000 (1996), Vietnam's gross domestic product (GDP) in 1995 was U.S. $21.3 billion and its per capita GDP an estimated U.S. $1,000.[42] The foreign policy implications of the stronger focus on economic issues were that Vietnam needed to look at countries that could assist it economically. In terms of investment, the most significant countries for Vietnam in January–September 1996 were (in order) Taiwan, South Korea, Singapore, Japan, Hong Kong, Thailand, and Indonesia.[43] In 1995, Vietnam's leading trade partners were (in order) Japan, Germany, Singapore, and China for exports and Singapore, South Korea, Taiwan, and Japan for imports.[44]

The strategic dimension of Vietnam's foreign policy also remained important. Vietnam was clearly the most significant of the three Indochinese countries. Although it no longer dominated Cambodia and Laos the way it did during the 1980s, it still sought to protect its interests in those countries. Within Southeast Asia more generally, Vietnam's entry into ASEAN in 1995 was consistent with its economic interests but was also indicative of its perceptions of the changing strategic environment. Without the Cambodian conflict, it seemed feasible for Vietnam to make common cause with other Southeast Asian countries on some issues, such as the South China Sea, and, through ASEAN, provide a counterbalance to China.

(However, there are differences of emphasis among the ASEAN countries. Thailand, for example, tends to be on good terms with China but is more suspicious of Vietnam.)

Now that Vietnam is part of ASEAN, it has more scope for joining the other Southeast Asian countries. Vietnam would also like to join APEC (the Asia-Pacific Economic Cooperation), a move it believes would be beneficial both economically and strategically. The relationships between Vietnam and the major Asia Pacific powers have both an economic and a strategic dimension, even though the balance between the two varies according to each relationship. The major focus in Vietnam's relationship with Japan is economic, whereas the strategic domain is more important in its relationship with China. It has been argued that, strategically, China constitutes the main threat to Vietnam. Vietnam's efforts to improve relations with the United States and the ASEAN countries are useful in countering that threat, but significant obstacles remain. India has also had a difficult relationship with China, and although it is geographically distant from the context of Sino-Vietnamese relations, it could possibly provide a diversion in the event of a direct Sino-Vietnamese conflict.[45] The significance of the relationship between China and Vietnam will be discussed in more detail in the next section of this chapter.

China

The Historical Context

Following the proclamation of the People's Republic of China in 1949, the most important security issue in Southeast Asia for the new government was the situation in Indochina. In the struggle between the Vietminh and France, China's sympathies clearly lay with the former. This support was expressed not just in political terms but in the provision of military assistance. Nevertheless, China's support was not necessarily absolute. When Sino-Vietnamese relations were at their nadir during the 1970s and 1980s, Vietnam alleged that Chinese pressure had been important in persuading the Vietminh to accept in 1954 a compromise settlement that involved the partition of the country.[46] China wished to avoid a major involvement by the United States in Indochina, and its security requirements were satisfied by having Communist power consolidated on its immediate borders.

However, when the United States undertook a massive military intervention in Vietnam during the Vietnam War, China gave support (mainly military aid) to North Vietnam. Since this war was occurring at the same time as the Sino-Soviet conflict, China's support was tied to its competition with the USSR for influence over North Vietnam. The seemingly close relationship between China and North Vietnam obscured the underlying political and cultural tensions that had resulted from the long history of Chinese attempts to dominate Vietnam. These tensions came to the surface again after the Sino-U.S. rapprochement of 1972. The rapprochement indicated that China placed more importance on its relationship with the United States than on the success of its erstwhile allies in Vietnam. The rapprochement was one factor leading North Vietnam (and subsequently the reunified Vietnam) to develop a close alliance with the USSR.

China also gave support to the Khmer Rouge government that emerged in Cambodia after 1975. From China's perspective, tensions between this government and Vietnam were a means of restraining Vietnam (and also of limiting Soviet influence). When Vietnam invaded Cambodia in late 1978 and installed a pro-Vietnamese government, this was seen as a challenge to China itself.[47] In the border war of early 1979, China unsuccessfully attempted to teach Vietnam a lesson.

China was a leading player in the coalition of forces, which included the ASEAN countries and the United States, attempting to end Vietnamese intervention. China was most active in supporting the Khmer Rouge resistance to the pro-Vietnamese government. (Although the resistance also included Sihanoukist and rightist elements, the Khmer Rouge was seen as the most effective force.) ASEAN and the United States wanted to end Vietnamese intervention but favored a solution that would also preclude a return to power of the Khmer Rouge. Despite these differences, the external coalition and the internal resistance were effective in preventing the legitimation and consolidation of power by the pro-Vietnamese Hun Sen government during the 1980s.

The Cambodian Settlement and Beyond

By the late 1980s, China's stance on Cambodia was beginning to change as Vietnam's position was weakening and the prospect of a settlement was thus becoming more likely. The change in Vietnam's position on Cambodia was strongly influenced by the USSR, although it was also clear to Vietnam that it could not continue its Cambodian strategy on a long-term basis. Under Mikhail Gorbachev, the USSR had indicated that it wished to accelerate the process of Sino-Soviet détente. Vietnam thus came under pressure from the Soviet Union because the Cambodian issue was regarded by the Chinese as one of the three obstacles to be overcome if Sino-Soviet relations were to improve. An early sign that Vietnam would no longer receive wholehearted Soviet support occurred in March 1988, during the Sino-Vietnamese clashes in the South China Sea.

Vietnam was becoming increasingly isolated and therefore had to think seriously about achieving an accommodation with China. A settlement of the Cambodian conflict would also help Vietnam address its economic problems. Vietnam began to show that it was willing to withdraw from

Cambodia and to facilitate a settlement of the conflict.[48] China began to show some flexibility in terms of discussing issues before a Vietnamese withdrawal and modifying its support for the Khmer Rouge.[49] The essence of China's position was conveyed in a foreign ministry statement of 1 July 1988.[50] China envisaged "complete withdrawal by Viet Nam of its troops from Kampuchea at the earliest possible date" and the establishment of "a provisional quadripartite coalition government" pending the holding of "free elections." The Vietnamese withdrawal, the maintenance of peace, and the conduct of elections should be under "effective international supervision."

The movement toward a settlement in Cambodia was given a push in January 1989, when Vietnam announced that its forces would be withdrawn from Cambodia by the following September. When Dinh Nho Liem, the Vietnamese first deputy foreign minister, visited China from 14 to 20 January, it was the first direct contact between the two countries in ten years.[51] As discussed in Chapter 9, China and the USSR attempted to resolve their differences on the Cambodian issue during Eduard Shevardnadze's visit to Beijing in February 1989. Although differences remained on the question of the transitional regime in Cambodia, most issues were resolved before Gorbachev's visit to Beijing in May 1989. It was clear that the USSR was now giving priority to Sino-Soviet détente over any previous commitment to Vietnam.

Prior to the Sino-Soviet summit, Dinh Nho Liem had visited China for talks with Chinese foreign minister Qian Qichen. While the Hanoi news service announced that the talks had led to "basic agreement on some points concerning the international aspect of the Kampuchean issue," differences remained on "the Pol Pot genocide and the settlement of Kampuchea's internal affairs."[52] China was more pessimistic in its assessment of the outcome. On 31 July 1989 at the International Conference on Cambodia in Paris, Qian continued to press for Vietnamese withdrawal under international supervision and for the establishment of a provisional quadripartite government.[53] In late September, China rejected Vietnamese claims that military withdrawal had been accomplished; UN supervision and verification was necessary to substantiate such claims.[54]

The circumstances and aftermath of the uprising at Tiananmen Square might be regarded as advantageous to Vietnam.[55] China was more preoccupied with domestic issues and therefore weakened in its ability to pursue its goals in Indochina. From a broader perspective, however, the events of June 1989 might be viewed as part of a process that brought the two countries closer together. Vietnam and China would soon be among the much reduced number of Communist countries remaining in the world, and they would have a common interest in defending the Communist system.

Contacts between China and Vietnam over the Cambodian issue continued during 1990. When Dinh Nho Liem visited China in early May, it was agreed for the first time that "internal" aspects of the issue could be discussed.[56] Subsequently, Xu Dunxin, the Chinese deputy foreign minister, visited Vietnam from 9 to 15 June for further discussions. The two sides remained divided over the role of the Supreme National Council. China believed that the SNC should hold "temporary legislative power and administrative authority in the transitional period" and that the UN should be authorized by the SNC to conduct the administration during this time. Vietnam opposed the granting of these powers to the SNC and the conduct of administration by the UN. It believed that the Phnom Penh government should remain in place and that the SNC should simply play "a co-ordinating role between the two existing governments."[57] China's concern not to strengthen the position of the Hun Sen government was also reflected in its opposition to the U.S. move to withdraw support from the Coalition Government of Democratic Kampuchea (representing the three resistance groups, including the Khmer Rouge) as the official Cambodian representative in the UN.[58]

Despite the apparent impasse in Sino-Vietnamese relations, it seemed that China was toning down its anti-Vietnamese criticisms. This change might have reflected a concern not to undermine the Communist system in Vietnam.[59] A breakthrough came at a secret meeting of Chinese and Vietnamese leaders held in China from 3 to 4 September 1990. Both sides agreed to pressure their respective Cambodian allies to accept the settlement plans being devised under the auspices of the UN Security Council. The main concession came from Hanoi, which was now prepared to accept substantial UN involvement in Cambodian affairs. The agreement led to progress on the settlement, including a meeting of the four Cambodian factions in Djakarta later in September.[60] A sign that Sino-Vietnamese relations had improved was the arrival of Vietnamese vice premier Vo Nguyen Giap in Beijing on 17 September for the opening of the Asian Games.[61] On 22 November, China stated that it was no longer providing military assistance to the Cambodian resistance.[62] In his National Day speech on 1 October, Premier Li Peng had linked "gradual" normalization of Sino-Vietnamese relations to a settlement of the Cambodian issue and had urged Vietnam to take "positive measures."[63]

During 1991, the process of resolving the Cambodian conflict continued, and Sino-Vietnamese normalization was achieved. Despite the inability of the Cambodian parties to achieve a settlement at their meeting in Djakarta,[64] China and Vietnam moved closer in their approach to the issue. This, in turn, became a factor that facilitated agreement among the Cambodian groups.

Changes at Vietnam's party congress in June 1991 also encouraged rapprochement between Hanoi and Beijing.[65] Foreign Minister Nguyen Co Thach, who was regarded as hostile to China, lost his position on the politburo and later his portfolio. Interior Minister Mai Chi Tho, whom China blamed for the expulsion of ethnic Chinese in the late 1970s, suffered a similar fate. In addition, the congress declared that the party would retain political power while liberalizing the economy. China saw this as an attempt to emulate the Chinese model. In late July, at China's invitation, General Le Duc Anh, the second-ranking member of the Vietnamese polit-buro, visited Beijing to report on the party congress. In early August, Vice Foreign Minister Nguyen Dy Nien had talks in Beijing with his counter-part, Xu Dunxin, on the Cambodian settlement and Sino-Vietnamese nor-malization.[66]

Nguyen Manh Cam, the new Vietnamese foreign minister, visited China from 9 to 14 September. In his meeting with the Vietnamese minis-ter, Premier Li Peng noted that with progress toward a Cambodian settle-ment, "the normalization of Sino-Vietnamese relations has been put on the agenda." On the issue of Cambodia, the joint communiqué stated: "The two sides were convinced that the improvement of Sino-Vietnamese relations could contribute to spurring a comprehensive political solution."[67] With the signing of the Agreement on a Comprehensive Political Settlement of the Cambodian Conflict at the Paris Conference on Cambodia on 23 October 1991, the way was clear for normalization of relations between China and Vietnam.[68] Normalization was achieved during talks in China between 5 and 10 November among Vo Van Kiet, prime minister of Vietnam, General Secretary Do Muoi of the Vietnamese Communist Party, and their Chinese counterparts, Li Peng, and Jiang Zemin.[69]

The impending collapse of the USSR was also a factor encouraging greater harmony between China and Vietnam. The communiqué issued at this time expressed support for the Cambodian settlement but also commit-ted the two sides "to settle the boundary and other territorial issues peace-fully through negotiations" (point 5) and "to solve in a proper manner the question concerning their nationals residing in each other's country at an appropriate time through friendly consultations" (point 6).[70]

As Robert Ross argues, "The Comprehensive Political Settlement [on Cambodia] reflects considerable Chinese success. The Phnom Penh gov-ernment has been legally dissolved and the SNC is recognized as the 'unique legitimate body and source of authority in which . . . the sovereign-ty, independence and unity of Cambodia are enshrined.'"[71] In practice, the situation was more difficult because the Hun Sen government remained in place, and though it had to share power with the SNC and the UN, it was able to resist the weakening of its position. This situation contributed to the announcement by the Khmer Rouge in November 1992 that it would not participate in the UN-supervised elections scheduled for May 1993. Those elections gave a plurality to the Sihanoukist FUNCINPEC over the Cambodian People's Party (CPP) of Hun Sen. The coalition government that subsequently emerged reflected the electoral popularity of the

Sihanoukists and the fact that the CPP had been able to retain effective control over a number of levers of power in Cambodia. A low-level guerrilla conflict with the Khmer Rouge continued.

Having achieved its strategic objectives in Indochina, China appears to be willing to accept the new situation. There remain conflicts between Vietnam and China on a number of issues, but China now sees Vietnam as giving priority to its accommodation with China rather than seeking primacy in Indochina.[72] The new Cambodian government also maintains a good relationship with China, a major factor affecting its own security.

In the context of the Paris Agreement, Chinese foreign minister Qian Qichen visited Phnom Penh on 11–12 February 1992.[73] The visit was a clear indication of China's support for the implementation of the agreement. Norodom Sihanouk and an SNC delegation from Cambodia visited China from 7 to 15 April 1992. China saw Sihanouk as playing a key role in the agreement. In the words of the communiqué: "The Chinese side expressed appreciation for the efforts and important contributions made by Samdech Sihanouk since his glorious return to Cambodia five months ago in leading the SNC to implement the Agreement in co-operation with UNAMIC and UNTAC. It highly assessed the unique role of Samdech Sihanouk in achieving peace, national solidarity and unification in Cambodia."[74] China and the SNC delegation both saw the Paris Agreement as "an important basis for national reconciliation, unification, peace, stability and free and fair general elections in Cambodia and a basic guarantee for a new Cambodia which would be independent, sovereign, neutral, non-aligned, democratic and progressive."[75]

With this kind of commitment, it is not surprising that China attempted to dissuade the Khmer Rouge from withdrawing from the peace process. One such attempt was made by Xu Dunxin, Chinese vice minister of foreign affairs, when he held discussions with Khmer Rouge leader Khieu Samphan in Cambodia in September 1992.[76] China was clearly unsuccessful in this regard but did not modify its commitment to the peace process. Following the elections in May 1993, China gave priority to developing a relationship with the new coalition government. A Cambodian government delegation led by Hun Sen and Prince Norodom Ranariddh visited China in January 1994.[77]

Since diplomatic normalization in November 1991, Sino-Vietnamese relations have focused mainly on bilateral issues. The expansion of trade has been important, but so have security issues, such as disputes over the land border and the South China Sea. Qian Qichen visited Vietnam in February 1992, and Premier Li Peng from 30 November to 4 December. Among other things, Qian's visit resulted in an agreement to have a meeting of experts to consider the territorial disputes.[78] Li used his visit to assert that "China will never seek hegemony nor practice expansionism." Agreement was reached to use the Sino-French treaties of 1887 and 1895 as the basis for determining the Sino-Vietnamese land border, but Vietnam was perturbed by China's refusal to compromise over the South China Sea issue.[79] Border talks were held in Beijing from 24 to 30 August 1993, and a preliminary agreement was signed on 19 October 1993.[80]

The new relationship was further confirmed when Chinese president Jiang Zemin visited Vietnam in November 1994.[81] The visit's emphasis was on economic cooperation, but the two sides also announced the appointment of a committee of experts to consider their differences over the South China Sea. With Vietnam joining ASEAN in July 1995, some modification in the emerging Sino-Vietnamese relationship could be expected. As previously noted, from a strategic perspective, this development could strengthen Vietnam if its relationship with China were to deteriorate. Nevertheless, divisions within Southeast Asia could also make such support problematical.

Japan

In the postwar period, Japan's relations with Southeast Asia focused mainly on the ASEAN countries and, to a lesser extent, Indochina. Japan did not directly support U.S. intervention in Vietnam in the 1960s, though Okinawa (still under U.S. rule at the time) was used as a base for bombing raids.

In the aftermath of the fall of the Saigon government in 1975, Japan followed a policy of promoting normalization with Vietnam (reunified in 1976) and assisting in the country's economic reconstruction.[82] This policy was based on the assumption that isolating Vietnam and depriving it of economic assistance would simply make it more dependent on the Communist powers, particularly the USSR. Japan believed it could function as a bridge between Vietnam and both the United States and the ASEAN countries. After a close alignment between Vietnam and the USSR was established in the 1970s and Vietnam intervened in Cambodia in late 1978, this policy proved difficult to maintain. Japan was unable to fulfill the function it aspired to and sided with the United States and ASEAN over the Cambodian conflict. However, it was not until January 1980 that Japan decided to suspend its aid to Vietnam.[83] Japan remained willing to help facilitate a settlement of the Cambodian conflict. Its position in favor of compromise was closer to that of Malaysia and Indonesia than the hard-line position of Thailand and Singapore.

Developments in Indochina in 1989 signaled the end of the Cold War in Southeast Asia. Although the region had been affected by the changes in the Soviet-U.S. and Sino-Soviet relationships, the most direct manifestation of the changing international situation in Southeast Asia was Vietnam's statement in January 1989 that it would withdraw its forces from Cambodia by the following September. This move laid the groundwork for the resolution of the conflict between Vietnam and ASEAN and thus enabled Japan to resume the role to which it had aspired in the late 1970s.

The Cambodian Peace Process

Changes in ASEAN's position toward the Cambodian conflict prepared the way for Japan to modify its policy and to become more actively involved in efforts to resolve the issue. Perhaps the clearest sign of the changes occurring within ASEAN was the statement in August 1988 by Thailand's prime minister, Chatichai Choonhavan, that Indochina should be transformed "from a battlefield to a trading market."[84] Thailand, as the ASEAN state most affected by developments in Indochina, had previously taken the lead in formulating ASEAN's hard-line policy. The Sino-Soviet normalization, symbolized by Gorbachev's visit to Beijing in May 1989, and the withdrawal of Vietnamese forces from Cambodia during 1989 were further signs that the international situation was becoming more favorable to a Cambodian settlement. The main problem was to reconcile the different Cambodian factions. Japan saw a role for itself in facilitating this reconciliation and in contributing to postwar reconstruction.

During 1988 Japan made a number of contributions to the Cambodian peace process. In July, at the Jakarta Informal Meeting of the various Cambodian groups, Vietnam, and ASEAN, Japan had offered financial and material contributions to facilitate a ceasefire and the holding of elections.[85] Sihanouk himself was invited to Japan for discussions in August 1988.[86] As a further indication of Japan's commitment, Prime Minister Noboru Takeshita stated during his visit to the ASEAN countries in May 1989 that Japan was willing to assist ASEAN in resolving the Cambodian conflict: It could "extend financial cooperation, despatch personnel and provide non-military materials to assist the introduction of an effective control mechanism to facilitate the peace process."[87] Japan co-chaired a committee on reconstruction and refugee relief at the first meeting of the International Conference on Cambodia in July 1989.[88]

Perhaps Japan's most significant contribution to the negotiations for a Cambodian peace settlement was the hosting of a meeting of Cambodian leaders in Tokyo in June 1990. The meeting had been proposed by Chatichai Choonhavan when he visited Tokyo in April 1990, and Thailand played an important diplomatic role in negotiations leading up to the meeting. Leaders of all four Cambodian groups attended, including Sihanouk and Hun Sen (the leader of the pro-Vietnamese government). However, Khieu Samphan of the Khmer Rouge withdrew when it became clear that the meeting would focus not just on the issue of a cease-fire but also on the formation of a Supreme National Council. The Khmer Rouge wanted all four groups to have equal representation on such a body, rather than the equal numbers for the Hun Sen government and the resistance coalition as provided for in the final communiqué. Because the declaration was not supported by the Khmer Rouge, the Tokyo meeting was described as a "half success" by Sihanouk. However, Japanese foreign minister Taro Nakayama believed the declaration had "important points leading to peace in Cambodia."[89] The meeting is probably best seen as part of the process of negotiations that led ultimately to a Cambodian peace agreement in October 1991.

Japan participated at other stages of the process as well. For example, it was active in suggesting amendments to the draft Cambodian agreement prepared under the auspices of the five permanent members of the UN Security Council and released in November 1990.[90] As Japanese prime minister Toshiki Kaifu wrote in a *Foreign Policy* article in Fall 1990: "It is essential to keep up a mutually complementary process of direct talks among the Cambodians, aided by the efforts of other countries in the region and by the moves of the international community as a whole."[91] Similarly, in a speech in Singapore on 3 May 1991, Kaifu indicated Japan's continued commitment to the Cambodian peace process.[92]

When the Cambodian peace agreement was signed in October 1991, the issue for Japan became how it could best contribute to the implementation of the accord. Three main methods were employed: political support for the process of reconciliation within Cambodia; financial assistance; and a contribution of personnel to the UN peacekeeping force in Cambodia (UNTAC). Japan was among the first countries to recognize Cambodia's Supreme National Council in November 1991.[93] In a visit to Japan on 11 March 1992, Yasushi Akashi, the head of UNTAC, said that the Japanese government should contribute one-third of UNTAC's total estimated cost of U.S. $1.9 billion, even though it was only assessed at 12.5 percent under current UN contribution rates. Foreign Minister Michio Watanabe said that the government was prepared to contribute more for refugee resettlement and economic reconstruction.[94]

Japan's role in economic reconstruction was highlighted by the convening of a Ministerial Conference on the Rehabilitation and Reconstruction of Cambodia, which met in Tokyo on 22 June 1992. Aid worth U.S. $880 million was promised; Japan and the United States were the most important donors. Two statements were adopted at the conference. The Tokyo Declaration on Rehabilitation and Reconstruction of Cambodia emphasized the importance of aid and established an International Committee on the Reconstruction of Cambodia to oversee the aid program. The Tokyo Declaration on the Cambodian Peace Process was a call for all the Cambodian parties to respect the peace agreement; it pointedly referred to "the refusal of one party" (i.e., the Khmer Rouge) to do so.[95] Japan's commitment to economic reconstruction was further underlined in Prime Minister Kiichi Miyazawa's speech in Bangkok on 16 January 1993, in which he called for the establishment of a Forum for the Comprehensive

Development of Indochina, including not just Cambodia but also Vietnam and Laos.[96]

Within Japan, the most controversial aspect of Japanese support for the Cambodian peace process was the dispatch in September 1993 of the first Self-Defense Force to participate in the UN peacekeeping operation, about 1,730 personnel overall.[97] This was the first peacekeeping operation involving Japan since the passage of legislation in June 1992 approving Japanese participation in such operations. Growing instability in Cambodia resulted in calls within Japan for its peacekeeping force to be withdrawn, particularly after the deaths of a Japanese election official in April 1993 and a civilian police officer in May 1993, but these calls were not heeded by the government.[98]

Following the May 1993 elections in Cambodia and the establishment of a government based on the Sihanoukist and Hun Sen forces, Japan's focus shifted to giving political and economic support to the new government. Foreign Minister Tsutomu Hata promised to continue Japanese aid to Cambodia, where Japan was the largest single donor, during a visit to that country in September 1993. Japan also chaired the International Committee on the Reconstruction of Cambodia, which had an important role in fostering and coordinating international efforts to assist Cambodia.[99]

Relations with Vietnam

The process of achieving a settlement in Cambodia also prepared the way for Japan to renew its relationship with Vietnam. As we have seen, in the late 1970s, Japan adopted a conciliatory policy toward Vietnam but aligned itself with the ASEAN and U.S. positions following Vietnam's intervention in Cambodia in late 1978. The new situation in Indochina enabled Japan to return to the course that it had earlier favored. Japan's new policy was partly motivated by a desire to facilitate the Cambodian peace process, but its relationship with Vietnam was also significant in its own right. A visit by Vietnamese foreign minister Nguyen Co Thach to Japan in October 1990 was reciprocated when Japanese foreign minister Taro Nakayama visited Vietnam in June 1991.[100]

With the implementation of the Cambodian peace agreement, the focus in Japanese-Vietnamese relations shifted to the resumption of economic aid. In developing relations with Vietnam, Japan had to take into account not only the position of ASEAN but also the views of countries such as China and the United States. Given the importance of the Japanese-U.S. relationship, Japan took steps to urge Vietnam to cooperate fully with the United States over the MIA issue.[101] In November 1992, Japan resumed aid to Vietnam when it announced a concessional loan worth U.S. $380 million.[102] One year later, in November 1993, Japan promised further loans and other aid worth U.S. $500 million.[103] Further steps consolidating the relationship were visits by Vietnamese prime minister Vo Van Kiet to Japan in March 1993 and by Japanese prime minister Tomiichi Murayama to Vietnam in August 1994.[104]

The USSR and Russia

The involvement of the USSR and Russia in Indochina in the post–Cold War period has been far less significant than that of the three other powers. Let us look at some of the salient features of the USSR's previous involvement in the region before focusing on the Cambodian peace process and the development of relations with Vietnam during the 1990s.

The Historical Context

The USSR became involved in Indochina mainly because of the imperatives of world politics and less because of the region's importance in its own right. When conflict developed between France and the Communist-dominated Vietminh in the late 1940s, the USSR was more concerned about the situation in France than about the situation in Vietnam. So as not to undermine the position of the French Communist Party, the USSR did not give a high priority to supporting the Vietminh. With the division of Vietnam after the 1954 Geneva Agreement, the USSR was aligned with North Vietnam (Democratic Republic of Vietnam), but the alignment was not a major feature of Soviet foreign policy. The Soviet commitment to North Vietnam became more significant during the Vietnam War of the 1960s and early 1970s (Second Indochina War). When the United States became the major supporter of the Saigon government in South Vietnam, the war was viewed as an important issue in world politics. Under these circumstances, the USSR provided military assistance to North Vietnam; however, it never matched the massive U.S. intervention in support of South Vietnam. Since the USSR and China were engaged in conflict at this time, there was also competition between the two Communist powers to win influence in Hanoi.

This dimension of Soviet involvement became even more important in the next phase of conflict in Indochina. Following the Communist victories in all three Indochinese states in 1975, Vietnam aligned itself with the USSR, whereas Cambodia, under Pol Pot, was closer to China. (Laos tended to be under the influence of Vietnam.) Vietnam's alignment with the USSR was formalized in 1978 when it became a member of the Soviet-dominated Council for Mutual Economic Assistance (COMECON) and subsequently signed a treaty of friendship with the USSR. At the end of that year, Vietnamese forces invaded Cambodia and installed a pro-

Vietnamese government. The Khmer Rouge, backed by China, then mounted a guerrilla war against Vietnam and its Cambodian allies. The Third Indochina War, which continued throughout the 1980s, might be viewed as an aspect of the Sino-Soviet conflict.

The Cambodian Peace Process

As previously discussed, the process of Sino-Soviet rapprochement, culminating in Mikhail Gorbachev's visit to Beijing in May 1989, prepared the way for the 1991 Cambodian peace settlement. The USSR was involved in the settlement negotiations mainly because of its role as one of the five permanent members of the UN Security Council and its relationship with Vietnam and the Hun Sen government in Phnom Penh. The USSR was more willing to accept a significant UN role in Cambodia as a means of facilitating a settlement than were Vietnam and the Hun Sen government. These two were not necessarily opposed to UN involvement, but if possible, they wanted to secure UN recognition for the Hun Sen government.[105] By this point, the USSR did not see the issue as strategically significant to itself; it was more interested in making a constructive contribution to its resolution. At the same time, the USSR's approach was influenced by links to its erstwhile allies in Hanoi and Phnom Penh. Even its diplomatic contributions diminished as the USSR was increasingly overtaken by its own problems. Eduard Shevardnadze's resignation as Soviet foreign minister in December 1990 effectively ended Soviet efforts to contribute to the settlement of the Cambodian problem.[106]

Following the signing of the Cambodian peace settlement in October 1991, the USSR cut all military ties with the Phnom Penh government.[107] From the beginning of 1991 technical aid had ended, and Soviet trade with Cambodia was to be based on world market prices.[108] The Russian Federation, which succeeded to the USSR's position on the UN Security Council, supported the implementation of the Cambodian settlement under the auspices of UNTAC. However, UNTAC was not a high priority for Russia. In 1992, it was reported that half the salaries of Russian helicopter pilots stationed in Cambodia as part of the transition were being paid by the government there. Similarly, Russia did not play a significant role in international efforts to facilitate economic reconstruction in Cambodia.[109]

Relations with Vietnam

The conclusion of the Cambodian peace settlement occurred shortly before the disintegration of the USSR itself. The period leading up to the settlement had witnessed a downgrading in Soviet relations with Vietnam, a process that continued subsequently in relations between Russia and Vietnam. With the Sino-Soviet rapprochement, the USSR did not need to use Vietnam as a means of putting pressure on China. Under Boris Yeltsin, Russia has developed a pragmatic relationship with China. Russia has made important arms sales to China, and it has been suggested that there might be a political alignment between the two states. These developments add to the strategic difficulties Vietnam faces in the 1990s.

Both Russia and Vietnam have given some attention to developing their state-to-state relationship. Prime Minister Vo visited Moscow in June 1994 and signed a treaty to replace the 1978 friendship treaty.[110] Significantly, Vo signed the treaty with Prime Minister Viktor Chernomyrdin, not with Yeltsin himself. Russian foreign minister Andrei Kozyrev visited Vietnam in July 1995.[111] Differences remained over issues such as the repayment of Vietnam's debt to Russia and the treatment of Vietnamese workers in Russia.[112] Although Russia is far less significant economically to Vietnam than the USSR was, it is important as a supplier of arms.

Russia also remains present at Cam Ranh Bay, the former U.S. base on the coast of central Vietnam that was taken over by the USSR in the late 1970s. Although the number of naval personnel at the base was down to 500 in 1995 and ships only occasionally call there,[113] Russia is entitled to stay until 2003 and shows no signs of withdrawing early. Although the base does not have great military significance, it may symbolize Russia's aspirations to play a wider Asia Pacific role. From Vietnam's point of view, the base may have some value in reducing its sense of strategic isolation.

The involvement of the United States, China, Japan, and the USSR and Russia in Indochina since 1989 has focused primarily on the Cambodian peace process and the development of relations with Vietnam. Changes in China's policies were of particular significance in facilitating the Cambodian peace process, and they also led to a degree of accommodation between China and Vietnam.

The policies pursued by the United States also contributed to the achievement of a settlement in Cambodia, though the United States' role was less significant than China's. The United States found it difficult to establish a rapprochement with Vietnam largely because of difficulties remaining from the Vietnam War. Nevertheless, by the mid-1990s, steady progress was being made on this issue.

Japan's diplomatic involvement in Indochina has been less significant than that of either the United States or China, but its economic involvement has been particularly important. Japan also sees the possibility of developing a diplomatic role in the region.

For the USSR and Russia, Indochina has been another context indicating the declining significance of the Soviet state and its successor as a major power in Asia Pacific. Gorbachev certainly facilitated the achievement of a Cambodian settlement, but the role subsequently played by the USSR and Russia has been relatively minor.

Notes

1. Vietnam became a member of ASEAN in July 1995. For the purposes of this book, however, Vietnam is treated as the major country of Indochina rather than as one of the ASEAN countries, which are the focus of Chapter 13.

2. Baker, "America in Asia," pp. 13–14.

3. Ibid., p. 14.

4. Issues concerning U.S. policy in Indochina at the start of the Bush administration are canvassed in Brown, *Second Chance,* and Indochina Policy Forum, *Recommendations for the New Administration on United States Policy Toward Indochina.*

5. Michael Haas argues that the United States was effectively supporting the Khmer Rouge. For a discussion of the contradictions in U.S. policy, see his *Cambodia, Pol Pot and the United States.*

6. Sutter, *East Asia and the Pacific,* p. 109.

7. See Nayan Chanda, "Smoke and Mirrors," *Far Eastern Economic Review,* 4 May 1989, p. 30, and Susumu Awanohara, "Spreading the Bets," *Far Eastern Economic Review,* 28 September 1989, p. 24.

8. Sutter, *East Asia and the Pacific,* p. 109.

9. James Baker, "ASEAN: Challenges and Opportunities," *Current Policy,* no. 1190, p. 3.

10. James Baker, "International Efforts for a Peaceful Cambodia," *Current Policy,* no. 1202, p. 2.

11. Richard H. Solomon, "Cambodia and Vietnam: Trapped in an Eddy of History?" *Current Policy,* no. 1206, p. 4.

12. Sutter, *East Asia and the Pacific,* p. 109.

13. *Keesing's Record of World Events,* vol. 36 (1990), p. 37654.

14. Sutter, *East Asia and the Pacific,* p. 110; Carroll J. Doherty, "Bush Team Rethinking Aid as Hill Wariness Grows," *Congressional Quarterly Weekly Report,* 14 July 1990, pp. 2232–2233.

15. *Keesing's Record of World Events,* vol. 36 (1990), p. 37598.

16. Nayan Chanda, "For Reasons of State," *Far Eastern Economic Review,* 2 August 1990, p. 10.

17. *Keesing's Record of World Events,* vol. 37 (1991), p. 38100.

18. Ibid., p. 38150; Carroll J. Doherty, "U.S. Halts Aid to Cambodian Rebels . . . as Resurgent Khmer Rouge Muscles In," *Congressional Quarterly Weekly Report,* 13 April 1991, p. 926.

19. "Secretary Baker at Paris Conference on Cambodia, October 23, 1991," *Foreign Policy Bulletin,* vol. 2 no. 3 (November/December 1991), p. 30.

20. "Statement by Richard Solomon Before the Asian and Pacific Affairs Subcommittee, October 17, 1991," *Foreign Policy Bulletin,* vol. 2 no. 3 (November/December 1991), p. 31.

21. Ibid., p. 32.

22. Sutter, *East Asia and the Pacific,* p. 118.

23. Ibid.

24. *Keesing's Record of World Events,* vol. 36 (1990), p. 37598.

25. See Susumu Awanohara and Ted Morello, "Softly, Softly," *Far Eastern Economic Review,* 16 August 1990, p. 15; Susumu Awanohara, "Progress in Action," *Far Eastern Economic Review,* 11 October 1990, p. 24.

26. *Keesing's Record of World Events,* vol. 37 (1991), p. 38149; Susumu Awanohara, "Deal on My Terms," *Far Eastern Economic Review,* 18 April 1991, pp. 13–14. For an argument that the normalization of U.S. relations with Vietnam

should not be linked to the progress of the Cambodian settlement, see Richburg, "Back to Vietnam."

27. *Keesing's Record of World Events*, vol. 37 (1991), p. 38532.

28. "U.S.-Vietnam Discussions on Normalization of Relations, November 21, 1991," *Foreign Policy Bulletin*, vol. 2 nos. 4 and 5 (January–April 1992), p. 109; *Keesing's Record of World Events*, vol. 38 (1992), p. 38865.

29. *Keesing's Record of World Events*, vol. 38 (1992), pp. 38865, 38912.

30. Lord, "A New Pacific Community," pp. 51–52.

31. A useful discussion of the issues facing the Clinton administration in normalizing relations with Vietnam is Goodman, "Vietnam's Post–Cold War Diplomacy and the U.S. Response."

32. *Keesing's Record of World Events*, vol. 39 (1993), p. 39559.

33. Ibid.

34. Ibid., p. 39642.

35. Murray Hiebert and Susumu Awanohara, "Lukewarm Welcome," *Far Eastern Economic Review*, 17 February 1994, pp. 14–15.

36. Nigel Holloway, "Haunted by History," *Far Eastern Economic Review*, 20 October 1994, p. 21.

37. Adam Schwarz and Nigel Holloway, "Cool Handshake," *Far Eastern Economic Review*, 9 February 1995, p. 14.

38. Nigel Holloway, "Winning the Peace," *Far Eastern Economic Review*, 20 July 1995, p. 16.

39. See, for example, Frost, *Vietnam's Foreign Relations;* Betts, "Vietnam's Strategic Predicament."

40. See Beresford, "The Political Economy of Dismantling the 'Bureaucratic Centralism and Subsidy System' in Vietnam," pp. 215–218.

41. Thayer, "Beyond Indochina," p. 10.

42. *The Military Balance 1996/97*, p. 200.

43. Adam Schwarz, "Promises, Promises," *Far Eastern Economic Review*, 24 October 1996, p. 48.

44. *Direction of Trade Statistics Yearbook 1996*, p. 454.

45. Betts, "Vietnam's Strategic Predicament," p. 70.

46. Evans and Rowley, *Red Brotherhood at War*, p. 134.

47. For the Sino-Vietnamese dimension to this conflict, see ibid., chap. 5; and Duiker, *China and Vietnam;* Ross, *The Indochina Tangle;* Gilks, *The Breakdown of the Sino-Vietnamese Alliance, 1970–1979.*

48. Nayan Chanda, "Taking a Soft Line," *Far Eastern Economic Review*, 8 December 1988, pp. 27–28.

49. See Long, "China and Kampuchea," pp. 151–152.

50. "Foreign Ministry on Kampuchea," *Beijing Review*, 11–17 July 1988, pp. 6–7.

51. *Keesing's Record of World Events*, vol. 35 (1989), p. 36397.

52. Ibid., p. 36656.

53. McGregor, "China, Vietnam, and the Cambodian Conflict," p. 280.

54. *Keesing's Record of World Events*, vol. 35 (1989), p. 36882; "Quarterly Chronicle and Documentation (October–December 1989)," *China Quarterly*, no. 121 (March 1990), p. 183.

55. See "A Wary Eye on the Dragon," *Far Eastern Economic Review*, 22 June 1989, p. 20.

56. *Keesing's Record of World Events*, vol. 36 (1990), p. 37532.

57. "Sino-Vietnamese Talks Fruitless," *Beijing Review*, 9–15 July 1990, p. 7.

58. *Keesing's Record of World Events*, vol. 36 (1990), p. 37598.

59. Murray Hiebert, "Cambodia Discord," *Far Eastern Economic Review*, 28 June 1990, pp. 16–17.

60. Robert Delfs, Murray Hiebert, Rodney Tasker, and Susumu Awanohara, "Carrots and Sticks," *Far Eastern Economic Review*, 4 October 1990, pp. 11–13.

61. "Vo's Beijing Visit: A Sign of Thaw," *Beijing Review*, 1–7 October 1990, p. 7.

62. *Keesing's Record of World Events*, vol. 36 (1990), p. 37858.

63. Ibid., p. 37778.

64. Zhang Zhinian and Gu Zhengqiu, "Peace Talks on Cambodia End Without Progress," *Beijing Review*, 17–23 June 1991, pp. 8–9.

65. See Murray Hiebert and Tai Ming Cheung, "Comrades Again," *Far Eastern Economic Review*, 22 August 1991, pp. 8–9.

66. "Quarterly Chronicle and Documentation (July–September 1991)," *China Quarterly*, no. 128 (December 1991), p. 883.

67. *Keesing's Record of World Events*, vol. 37 (1991), p. 38436. See also "China, Viet Nam to Normalize Relations," *Beijing Review*, 23–29 September 1991, pp. 4–5.

68. Chen Jiaobao, "A New Era Begins in Sino-Vietnamese Relations," *Beijing Review*, 18–24 November 1991, p. 4.

69. *Keesing's Record of World Events*, vol. 37 (1991), p. 38574.

70. "Sino-Vietnamese Joint Communique," *Beijing Review*, 18–24 November 1991, p. 9.

71. Ross, "China and Post-Cambodia Southeast Asia," pp. 54–55.

72. For reviews of Sino-Vietnamese relations from a postnormalization perspective, see Frost, *Vietnam's Foreign Relations*, pp. 30–41; Thayer, "Vietnam: Coping with China," and "Sino-Vietnamese Relations."

73. *Keesing's Record of World Events*, vol. 38 (1992), pp. 38767–38768.

74. "Sino-Cambodian Joint Communique," *Beijing Review*, 27 April–3 May 1992, pp. 12–13.

75. Ibid., p. 13.

76. *Keesing's Record of World Events*, vol. 38 (1992), p. 39094.

77. Ibid., vol. 40 (1994), p. 39822.

78. Ibid., vol. 38 (1992), p. 38768.

79. Murray Hiebert, "Comrades Apart," *Far Eastern Economic Review*, 17 December 1992, p. 23. The South China Sea issue also involves China's relations with certain ASEAN countries and is discussed further in Chapter 13.

80. *Keesing's Record of World Events*, vol. 39 (1993), pp. 39602, 39687.

81. "Calmer Waters," *Economist*, 26 November 1994, p. 32.

82. A useful study of Japanese-Vietnamese relations is Shiraishi, *Japanese Relations with Vietnam: 1951–1987*.

83. Ibid., p. 86.

84. Tomoda, "Japan's Search for a Political Role in Asia," p. 46.

85. Hoong, "Japan and the Problem of Kampuchea," pp. 327–328.

86. Tomoda, "Japan's Search for a Political Role in Asia," p. 47.

87. Quoted, Michael Vatikiotis, "Lame Duck Talk," *Far Eastern Economic Review*, 18 May 1989, p. 38.

88. Tomoda, "Japan's Search for a Political Role in Asia," p. 47.

89. Charles Smith, "Disappointing Debut," *Far Eastern Economic Review*, 14 June 1990, p. 12. See also Sudo, "Japan and the Security of Southeast Asia," pp. 338–339; Tomoda, "Japan's Search for a Political Role in Asia," pp. 47–48, 50–53.

90. Tomoda, "Japan's Search for a Political Role in Asia," pp. 52–53.

91. Kaifu, "Japan's Vision," p. 36.

92. Michael Vatikiotis, "The Gentle Giant," *Far Eastern Economic Review,* 16 May 1991, p. 11.

93. *Keesing's Record of World Events,* vol. 37 (1991), p. 38574.

94. Ibid., vol. 38 (1992), p. 38817.

95. Ibid., p. 38964.

96. Masanori Kikuta, "Japan Proposes Development Forum for Indochina," *Japan Times* (Weekly International Edition), 25–31 January 1993, p. 3.

97. "SDF Peacekeeping Mission Dispatched to Cambodia," *Liberal Star,* 15 September 1992, p. 3.

98. See Ako Washio, "Renewed Fighting Revives PKO Debate," *Japan Times* (Weekly International Edition), 22–28 February 1993, pp. 1, 5; "Plan to Evacuate SDF from Cambodia Reportedly Drawn Up," *Japan Times* (Weekly International Edition), 21–27 June 1993, p. 3.

99. "Cambodian Leaders Urge Japanese Aid," *Japan Times* (Weekly International Edition), 27 September–3 October 1993, p. 3; Hisane Masaki, "Yen Loans to Cambodia May Resume," *Japan Times* (Weekly International Edition), 24–30 January 1994, p. 3.

100. *Keesing's Record of World Events,* vol. 36 (1990), p. 37776; vol. 37 (1991), p. 38272. See also Tim Jackson, "Japanese Press for Cambodia Peace," *Independent,* 11 June 1991, p. 11.

101. Susumu Awanohara, "Decent Interval," *Far Eastern Economic Review,* 30 April 1992, pp. 12–13.

102. *Keesing's Record of World Events,* vol. 38 (1992), p. 39196.

103. Hisane Masaki, "Japan to Extend $500 Million to Vietnam," *Japan Times* (Weekly International Edition), 8–14 November 1993, p. 3.

104. *Keesing's Record of World Events,* vol. 39 (1993), p. 39371; "Murayama Promises Hanoi More Assistance," *Japan Times* (Weekly International Edition), 5–11 September 1994, p. 3.

105. Buszynski, *Gorbachev and Southeast Asia,* pp. 183–184.

106. Ibid., p. 186.

107. Thayer, "Indochina," p. 220.

108. Ibid., p. 217.

109. Ibid., p. 218.

110. Akaha, "Russia in Asia in 1994," p. 109.

111. Official Kremlin International News Broadcast, 8 August 1995.

112. For a comprehensive discussion of the main issues in Russian-Vietnamese relations, see Thayer, "Russian Policy Toward Vietnam." See also Nayan Chanda, "Can't Say Goodbye," *Far Eastern Economic Review,* 16 March 1995, pp. 21–22.

113. Nayan Chanda, "Can't Say Goodbye," *Far Eastern Economic Review,* 16 March 1995, p. 22.

13

ASEAN

In addition to Indochina, the countries of ASEAN (Association of Southeast Asian Nations)[1] have also been important to the United States, China, and Japan. This chapter considers the relationship each power has developed with ASEAN, first studying the broad historical context up to the 1980s and then examining in more detail the post–Cold War situation. The involvement of the USSR and Russia with ASEAN, though less significant, is also considered.

ASEAN and Indonesia

It is worthwhile to consider the role of ASEAN as a regional organization. The major powers do not simply act on their own initiative in relation to the ASEAN countries; they also respond to initiatives taken by those countries. Therefore, it is important to consider the extent to which ASEAN has functioned as a coherent entity. Particular attention is given to Indonesia, the most prominent of the ASEAN countries.

ASEAN

ASEAN was established in 1967.[2] Its original members were Indonesia, Malaysia, the Philippines, Singapore, and Thailand. Brunei joined in 1984, Vietnam in 1995, and Laos and Burma in 1997. Cambodia's previously approved entry was postponed following Hun Sen's coup in July 1997 against his co-prime minister, Norodom Ranariddh. Although ASEAN is commonly referred to as a group, its unity should not be exaggerated. There are many issues on which the ASEAN countries have adopted a common position, but its individual members also have particular interests.

Singapore functions as a small, predominantly Chinese city-state with a high standard of living and an economy based on its role as an entrepôt and financial center; the manufacturing industry is also important. Brunei is essentially a mini-state; its high standard of living is based on its role as an oil producer. Malaysia and Thailand see themselves as emerging "Asian tigers." Traditionally, their economies combined subsistence agriculture and the production of cash crops and raw materials for export (rubber and tin in the case of Malaysia; tin, tungsten, and rice in the case of Thailand). Recently, both countries have developed important manufacturing sectors oriented toward export. The Philippines has experienced less economic growth than its ASEAN partners and has remained much more of a Third World country. It has a large peasant population, and the economy is dominated by agriculture—some for subsistence purposes, some for the local market (rice, maize), and some for export (sugar cane, coconuts). Some basic statistics for the countries of ASEAN are included in Table 13.1.

Table 13.1 The Enlarged ASEAN (including Cambodia)

	GDP (U.S. $bn, 1995)	Per capita GDP (U.S. $, 1995)	Population (millions, 1996)
Brunei	4.3 (1994)	6,700 (1994)	0.302
Burma	15.0	1,000	47.799
Cambodia	2.7	650	9.981
Indonesia	170.0	3,900	195.277
Laos	1.7	2,300	4.919
Malaysia	78.0	10,100	23.9
Philippines	74.1	2,800	70.821
Singapore	67.3	21,500	2.987
Thailand	157.0	7,200	61.277
Vietnam	21.3	1,000	75.69

Source: The Military Balance 1996/97.

The diversity within ASEAN is also suggested by the international roles its various members have played, from espousing nonalignment to adopting a more pro-Western orientation. In the past the Philippines and Thailand were most closely aligned with the United States. The Philippines was under U.S. rule from the turn of the twentieth century until 1946 (though it was occupied by Japan during World War II); both Thailand and the Philippines were linked to the United States through the Manila Treaty after 1954 (including SEATO—the Southeast Asia Treaty Organization—from 1954 to 1977). Historically, Malaysia, Singapore, and Brunei were linked to the United Kingdom. Malaya (which gained independence in 1957) joined Singapore and the former British territories in Borneo to form Malaysia in 1963. Although Singapore left the federation after only two years, Great Britain retained its defense links with both countries until the early 1970s. Subsequently, Britain (along with Australia and New Zealand) has been linked to Malaysia and Singapore through the Five Power Defence Arrangement (FPDA). Britain has also retained defense ties with

Brunei, independent since 1984. In practice, Malaysia has espoused non-alignment, advocating a Zone of Peace, Freedom and Neutrality (ZOPFAN) in Southeast Asia. During the 1990s, it has also promoted the formation of an East Asian Economic Grouping (later Caucus).

The formation of ASEAN in 1967 occurred in the aftermath of Indonesia's Confrontation ("Konfrontasi") campaign against Malaysia. President Sukarno had regarded Malaysia as a "neocolonialist plot" designed to perpetuate British influence in Southeast Asia; he mounted a campaign involving diplomacy and small-scale military action designed to undermine the federation. However, with Sukarno's own demise in Indonesia in 1965, Confrontation also came to an end. Although ASEAN was formed ostensibly to promote social, economic, and cultural cooperation, it also provided a framework within which members could deal peacefully with issues that might otherwise divide them. Implicitly, then, ASEAN has had a security and political role from the time of its formation.

Significant changes affecting ASEAN followed the end of the Vietnam War. The U.S. withdrawal raised the profile of ASEAN within Southeast Asia. Despite the differences of emphasis within ASEAN, its members had to decide whether they should work together to influence the general political direction of the region. Two statements were adopted at the Bali summit in 1976, both reflecting a stronger commitment by members to the organization. One was the Treaty of Amity and Cooperation in Southeast Asia, which provided the formal basis for cooperation among members and allowed for the accession of new members. The other was the Declaration of ASEAN Concord, which outlined various means for promoting cooperation.

Following the Bali summit, there was also a strengthening of ASEAN as an organization. Although the annual meeting of foreign ministers remained important, there was more provision for the involvement of heads of government and other ministers; the establishment of a secretariat also gave the organization greater coherence. ASEAN's external relations were promoted through a postministerial conference (PMC) involving consultations with designated "dialogue partners": Japan, the United States, the European Community (European Union since 1993), Canada, Australia, New Zealand, and, more recently, India and South Korea. For the most part, these countries have important economic links with ASEAN members. Although ASEAN has not advanced very far in promoting economic integration, it has had more success in promoting the economic interests of its members as a whole to external powers. For example, most of the ASEAN countries agree that the goal of improving access to the markets of the advanced industrialized countries should be pursued.

From the late 1970s, the Cambodian conflict gave ASEAN greater political coherence. Although this issue is discussed primarily in Chapter 12, its significance in the development of ASEAN should be noted. Certainly Thailand was the ASEAN country that felt most threatened by

Vietnamese intervention in Cambodia, but all other members supported Thailand's stance even if they were more open to an accommodation with Vietnam (as were Indonesia and Malaysia). During the 1980s, ASEAN, alongside China and the United States, became known for its role in opposing Vietnam's role in Cambodia. However, now that the issue has been resolved, the question has arisen as to what is likely to give coherence to ASEAN in the future. A number of points might be suggested.

In terms of economic cooperation ASEAN has attempted to move forward with the establishment in 1993 of an ASEAN Free Trade Area (AFTA). AFTA aims to bring about free trade in manufactured and processed goods among its members by 2008. However, there are many qualifications and escape clauses, suggesting that intra-ASEAN trade is not likely to move beyond the current figure of less than 20 percent of total ASEAN trade.[3] ASEAN will continue to promote the economic interests of its members to external powers, particularly through the PMC. It can also function as a caucus within a grouping such as APEC (Asia-Pacific Economic Cooperation). The loose nature of APEC is partly due to ASEAN's desire to avoid creating an organization that might overshadow itself. Although ASEAN as a whole has not been prepared to support Dr. Mahathir's goal of creating an East Asian Economic Grouping (excluding countries outside East Asia such as the United States, Canada, Australia, and New Zealand), a loose caucus within APEC has been more acceptable.

In terms of political and security cooperation, there has been no issue comparable to the Cambodian conflict to give greater coherence to the organization. It might be argued that the South China Sea issue (which is discussed later in the chapter) could have this effect. However, the issue has not become a conflict comparable to the Third Indochina War. If it were to intensify, there might be pressure on the ASEAN countries to collaborate more, but they would also need to overcome their own differences on the issue. The broadening of ASEAN's membership does suggest that it is seen as providing a useful framework for dealing with conflicts in the region. Another incentive might be to extend the economic success being experienced by most of the original ASEAN members to other countries of the region on the assumption that it promotes stability. As with the issues of economic cooperation, ASEAN might also play a role in Asia Pacific more broadly. The way in which the ASEAN Regional Forum was set up in 1994 as a security forum for Asia Pacific as a whole suggests movement in this direction. Although ASEAN, as a grouping of countries, does not have the coherence of the major powers in the region, insofar as the ASEAN members do act together, they are likely to be in a stronger position to influence developments in East Asia. This is an important consideration to keep in mind when examining the ways in which the major powers have pursued policies in the ASEAN countries.

Indonesia

Indonesia is ASEAN's most important member and the key power in Southeast Asia. How has Indonesia viewed its international role and how has that affected the dynamics of international politics in Southeast Asia? During the Sukarno period, before 1965, Indonesia espoused a radical direction in its foreign policy that had consequences for international politics. Under Suharto, a different approach has developed that has had different consequences for the rest of the region.

Nationalism has been a constant influence on Indonesian foreign policy. Indonesia conducted a war of independence against the Netherlands in the late 1940s; nonalignment thus provided a means for expressing Indonesia's anticolonial sentiments. Throughout the 1950s and early 1960s, Indonesia campaigned for the transfer of West New Guinea to its own sovereignty; the Netherlands had not withdrawn from this province at the time of Indonesian independence in 1949. The issue was resolved in 1962 when the Netherlands agreed (under U.S. pressure) that it would withdraw from West New Guinea the following year.

Indonesia's foreign policy direction under Sukarno was influenced by the balance of political forces within Indonesia; Sukarno was caught between the contending forces of the army and the Communists (PKI). Sukarno saw foreign policy as a way of diverting attention from pressing domestic issues in the interests of promoting national unity. During the early 1960s, Indonesian foreign policy became increasingly radical, perhaps suggesting that the political balance was shifting toward the left. Sukarno proclaimed Indonesia to be a leader of the New Emerging Forces (NEFOS) in opposition to the Old Established Forces (OLDEFOS), and Indonesia was linked to other radical Asian states in a Djakarta–Phnom Penh–Hanoi-Beijing-Pyongyang axis. This was also the time that Sukarno launched Konfrontasi against the newly proclaimed Malaysia.

As we have seen, Sukarno's downfall led to the establishment of ASEAN and an attempt to link Indonesia to the more pro-Western states of Southeast Asia. Nationalism was still important to Indonesia, and under Suharto it continued to see itself as one of the leading nonaligned countries.[4] Between 1992 and 1995, Indonesia served as chair of the Nonaligned Movement. As a predominantly Islamic country, Indonesia has been sympathetic to the position of other Islamic countries over issues such as Bosnia and Soviet intervention in Afghanistan, without espousing an Islamic foreign policy as such.

National unity has continued to be a priority for Indonesia. A low-level guerrilla campaign against Indonesian rule in West New Guinea (Irian Jaya province to Indonesia; West Papua to the Melanesians fighting for its independence) has continued since the 1960s. A more serious international issue has been the opposition to Indonesia's 1975 incorporation of East Timor following the collapse of Portuguese rule there. An independent East Timor ruled by the radical nationalist movement Fretilin is unacceptable to Indonesia. Fretilin has mounted a low-level campaign of opposition to Indonesian rule, with a significant degree of support from the Timorese population. The issue has been a point of contention in Indonesian relations with other countries, including members of the Nonaligned Movement and Western Europe (given Portugal's membership in the European Union). The conflict in Aceh, Sumatra, has also had implications for Indonesia's national unity. As a widely dispersed archipelagic state, Indonesia has taken a strong line against movements that threaten national unity.

The Suharto government has emphasized economic objectives, a priority that affects Indonesian foreign policy. Unlike Sukarno's Indonesia, the New Order government has given high priority to the achievement of economic growth. In 1965, per capita income in Indonesia was only U.S. $190;[5] by 1995 (see Table 13.1) the comparable figure was U.S. $3,900. Traditionally, the economy was based on a combination of subsistence agriculture and the export of resources such as rubber and oil; during the Suharto period, the development of the manufacturing industry for export has proceeded apace. Despite the immense wealth of certain individuals, such as Suharto and his family, the incidence of poverty has decreased. According to the Indonesian statistical service, the proportion of the population living in poverty declined from 40.1 percent in 1976 to 13.5 percent in 1993.[6]

The emphasis on the achievement of economic goals is reflected also in Indonesia's foreign policy, in which particular attention is given to promoting trade and investment. Japan is Indonesia's most important trading partner. Since 1966, Japan and the developing economies of East Asia have accounted for 50 to 60 percent of Indonesia's total trade, compared with 25 to 40 percent for the United States and the European Union combined.[7] Economic factors clearly indicate a strong emphasis in Indonesian foreign policy on relations with Japan, the newly industrializing countries of East Asia, the United States, and the European Union.

Although the major powers see Indonesia as the key country in their relations with ASEAN, Indonesia also has its own goals to pursue with these powers. Economically, these goals concern the promotion of trade and investment on terms favorable to Indonesia. Geopolitically, Indonesia has sought to maintain its position as the leading Southeast Asian power. It has not wanted Southeast Asia to become a region whose destiny is determined primarily by the involvement of the major powers. During the 1970s, Indonesia supported the ZOPFAN concept promoted by Malaysia; in 1983, it introduced its own proposal for a Southeast Asian Nuclear Weapons Free Zone (SEANWFZ), which was accepted by ASEAN in 1987. Within ASEAN, Indonesia is the country with the fewest formal historical links to external powers. In the 1990s, it remains the leading Southeast

Asian power that has wanted to limit external involvement. Although Indonesia benefited in the past from the strategic involvement of the United States, its perceptions of U.S. decline have led to some adjustment in its strategic thinking.[8] The expansion of ASEAN may be, among other things, an attempt to provide a check on greater Chinese power in Southeast Asia. Indonesia sees itself playing the leading role in an expanded and more coherent ASEAN.

The United States

Historical Context

Historically, Southeast Asia was not an important concern of the United States. At the turn of the twentieth century, the United States had taken over from Spain as the colonial power in the Philippines; following the Japanese occupation during World War II, formal independence was achieved in 1946. The onset of the Cold War led the United States to focus on conflicts involving communism in some form; the Vietnam War was the outcome of this focus. In the aftermath of the Geneva Conference of 1954, which recognized Communist rule in North Vietnam, the United States attempted, through the Manila Treaty and SEATO, to provide protection against further Communist expansionism. This protection was extended not just to Thailand and the Philippines as signatories, but also to South Vietnam, Cambodia, and Laos as protocol states. In Malaya, the suppression of the Communist uprising (known as the Emergency) was left to Britain and (after 1957) the independent Malayan government. The defense of Malaysia (formed in 1963 by the merger of Malaya, Singapore, and the Borneo states of Sabah and Sarawak; Singapore separated in 1965) was regarded by the United States as primarily a Commonwealth responsibility. Thus, during the period of Confrontation with Indonesia, Malaysia was supported mainly by the United Kingdom; Australia and New Zealand also lent their support.

With the fall of Sukarno in 1965 and the formal ending of Confrontation in 1966, one significant conflict in Southeast Asia ended. The formation of ASEAN in 1967 was the beginning of an important new phase of international politics in Southeast Asia, involving not just the member states but also external powers such as the United States. Nevertheless, at the time, the United States was preoccupied with the Vietnam War and did not immediately recognize the significance of the changes in Indonesia and the establishment of ASEAN.

Over time, this situation changed, and the United States came to see ASEAN as a significant organization. As Sheldon Simon has written: "The ASEAN states constitute precisely the kind of market-oriented, modernizing politico-economic systems that the United States hopes will come to characterize most of the Third World."[9] ASEAN had no explicit security role, but implicitly it functioned to dampen conflicts among its members.

The United States still retained its Manila Treaty links with both the Philippines and Thailand, even though SEATO as an organization had disbanded in 1977. The United States also had major military bases in the Philippines at both Clark Field and Subic Bay. Following Ferdinand Marcos's loss of power in 1986, the United States transferred its support to the government of Cory Aquino, but increasingly there were nationalist pressures on that government to modify, if not terminate, the role played by the U.S. bases.

The United States saw Indonesia as a major player in Southeast Asia.[10] Washington was broadly supportive of the anti-Communist orientation of the Suharto government, but human rights issues affected U.S. policy toward Indonesia, particularly after the Indonesian occupation of East Timor in 1975. These considerations tended to carry more weight with Democratic administrations than with Republican ones.

Beyond Southeast Asia, U.S. policy in Asia Pacific was affected by its relations with other major powers. This was most evident in the U.S. response to Chinese and Soviet policies in Indochina, particularly on the Cambodian issue. The United States urged an expanded Japanese foreign policy and defense role, but this tended to be resisted within Southeast Asia because of the memories of World War II. Resistance within ASEAN to an expanded Japanese role was often seen as an argument in favor of maintaining a U.S. presence. This argument would be significant in some security issues in Southeast Asia that arose during the Bush and Clinton administrations.

The Bush Administration

In his 1991 *Foreign Affairs* article, James Baker wrote of "the talented, industrious people and market-oriented economies of the ASEAN states setting global standards for development" and specifically referred to the Philippines and Thailand as "bilateral treaty allies."[11] The future of the U.S. bases in the Philippines was a major issue at the time, but Baker argued that, whatever the outcome, the "overriding concern [was] to sustain good relations with a democratic and economically resurgent Philippines." Furthermore, the "security engagement [of the United States] in Southeast Asia will remain undiminished, even if realized through other arrangements." To this end, Baker said, "we are exploring ways to enhance defense cooperation with our friends throughout the subregion in order to sustain an adequate security presence on a more diversified basis."[12]

The Philippines bases. U.S. policy as declared by Baker provides a good starting point for considering the way in which the U.S. relationship with the ASEAN countries developed.[13] Apart from the Cambodian issue, the most significant security issue in that relationship during the Bush administration was the future of the U.S. bases in the Philippines.[14] With some 40,000 U.S. military personnel in the Philippines, located mainly at Clark Field and Subic Bay, these bases played a vital role in U.S. strategy in Asia Pacific and beyond. The bases dated from the colonial era; in the postindependence period, their presence was governed by a Military Bases Agreement signed in 1947. Under the Rusk-Ramos agreement of 1966, a twenty-five-year limit was set for the operation of the bases treaty. This meant that either the old treaty would expire by 16 September 1991 or a new treaty would need to be negotiated by then.[15] In approaching the negotiations the United States was conscious of the value of its bases in the Philippines but did not regard them as indispensable. As George Bush said, "If we're not wanted there, we're not going to be there."[16] On 6 July 1989, Baker had put the U.S. position as follows:

> We hope and expect to find ways to sustain our military presence in the Philippines after 1991. Such an outcome would best serve the interests of the United States, the Philippines, and stability in Southeast Asia. But whatever the outcome of the negotiations with the Philippine Government . . . we are committed to maintaining a credible deterrent in the region to honor our treaty obligations.[17]

Within the Philippines, opinion was divided. There was strong nationalist sentiment in favor of terminating the bases agreement, particularly in the Philippines Senate, where a two-thirds vote would be required to approve any new agreement.

Talks on the bases issue began in May 1990, with Foreign Minister Raul Manglapus leading the Philippines side and Richard Armitage the U.S. side. As the negotiations proceeded, a consensus developed in favor of the United States leaving Clark Field by September 1991 and phasing out the operations at Subic Bay more gradually. The points at issue were the compensation to be paid to the Philippines and the duration of the new treaty. In June 1991 the eruption of Mount Pinatubo changed the course of negotiations, by virtually closing down Clark Field and also limiting the use of Subic Bay.[18] This meant that U.S. withdrawal was likely to occur sooner than might have otherwise been the case and made it more difficult for the Philippines to argue for the level of compensation it had originally sought. The Treaty of Friendship, Cooperation and Security signed in Manila on 27 August 1991 provided that the United States could continue using Subic Bay for ten years and that the Philippines would receive U.S. $203 million annually in recompense.[19] The treaty still faced the hurdle of the Philippines Senate, and it was rejected there by a twelve to eleven vote on 16 September.[20] Aquino initially spoke of holding a referendum in an attempt to overthrow the Senate decision but soon abandoned that idea. The

United States withdrew from Clark Field in November 1991 and within another year had withdrawn from Subic Bay as well. By 1993, U.S. aid to the Philippines had fallen to U.S. $40 million.[21]

The United States accepted the decision made in the Philippines because other ASEAN states were willing to provide facilities that would make maintaining a U.S. security presence in the region feasible. Singapore was particularly eager to assist the United States, and Brunei also appeared willing to do so. While the issue of the bases was being debated, Lee Kuan Yew had expressed support for their retention, and Malaysia thought they might have value as a counterweight to the Soviet presence in Indochina. Indonesia, with its traditional stance of nonalignment and support for ASEAN's goal of a Zone of Peace, Freedom and Neutrality in Southeast Asia, was more hesitant.[22] When Singapore made public its offer to accommodate U.S. facilities on 4 August 1989, Malaysia said it would strongly oppose having U.S. troops or fighter aircraft based in Singapore, and Indonesia expressed "strong reservations."[23] Nevertheless, both Indonesia and Thailand said it was desirable to have "free-world" powers present in Southeast Asia.[24] On 13 November 1990, an agreement was signed between Lee Kuan Yew and Vice President Dan Quayle in Tokyo that enabled U.S. naval vessels to use Sembawang dockyard for repairs and U.S. aircraft to use Paya Lebar airport for training missions (meaning, in effect, a more or less permanent U.S. presence).[25]

The agreement was one of the reasons that Bush, when he visited Singapore from 3 to 5 January 1992, could say that the termination of U.S. bases in the Philippines would "not spell the end to American engagement" in Asia Pacific. It was also agreed on this occasion that U.S. naval logistic command headquarters would be moved from Subic Bay to Singapore.[26] Malaysia again expressed concern, but its opposition appeared less than vehement, and the United States was able to achieve its goal of maintaining a security presence in the region.

The Clinton Administration

Winston Lord's major initial statement of policy for the Asia Pacific region made a number of points about ASEAN.[27] Lord reflected the economic emphasis in Clinton's policies when he declared (given ASEAN's record of economic growth) the need to "intensify our efforts to promote U.S. exports and the jobs they create." In terms of security, he pointed out that ASEAN "serves regional stability as well as prosperity. The future admission of the Indochina countries would encourage them in constructive directions. The ASEAN Post-Ministerial Conference . . . is evolving into an increasingly important forum for regional security consultations." With the closure of U.S. bases in the Philippines, a "diversified pattern of security ties in Southeast Asia" was developing: "All the ASEAN countries view a continuing U.S. military presence as a stabilizing element during an uncertain period; each in its own way is helping to make it possible."

One can observe the development of U.S. policy toward ASEAN during the Clinton administration following on from Lord's initial statement.[28] Without the issue of the Philippines bases to deal with, U.S. policy toward ASEAN has become broader. Like the Bush administration, the Clinton administration has seen value in ASEAN as a factor for stability in the region. At the same time, the Clinton administration's stronger emphasis on human rights issues has caused some complications. Although Lord was reported to have won support for his "less confrontational approach" in his general dealings with ASEAN,[29] problems did arise in U.S. relations with the Philippines, Thailand, and Indonesia.

The Philippines and Thailand were traditionally the two ASEAN countries with which the United States had the closest ties. When U.S. bases in the Philippines closed, U.S. aid to that country sharply declined. In addition, there were moves in Congress to cut off U.S. support for the Multilateral Aid Initiative for the Philippines, which had commenced in 1989. According to Larry Niksch of the Congressional Research Service, this move reflected "the continuing congressional pessimism over Manila's management of the economy and over the Philippines' image of corruption, mismanagement, [and] irresponsible economic nationalism."[30]

There were moves by the United States to strengthen the security relationship with Thailand by establishing a bilateral security forum. Joint military exercises were being resumed, and U.S. forces were using the U-Tapao air base and Thai ports.[31] At the same time, there were some difficulties in the relationship, including the employment of Thai laborers in Libya and the protection of workers' rights in Thailand itself[32] and alleged connections between elements in the Thai military and the Khmer Rouge.[33]

Tensions arose with Indonesia because of a conflict between the stronger emphasis on human rights considerations in U.S. foreign policy and the traditional view of Indonesia as a major source of stability of the region. As with Thailand, there were U.S. criticisms of the failure to protect workers' rights in Indonesia. Another issue was human rights violations in East Timor, particularly the Dili massacre of November 1991.[34] In March 1993, the Clinton administration supported Portugal in voting for a UN Human Rights Commission resolution that condemned Indonesia over the situation in East Timor. Subsequently, in September 1993, the Senate Foreign Relations Committee moved to restrict U.S. arms sales to Indonesia unless there was an improvement in the human rights situation in East Timor.[35] Another irritant in Indonesian-U.S. relations concerned reports that Indonesia was proposing to sell arms to Iran.[36] In July 1993, human rights concerns had led the United States to block a request by Jordan to transfer U.S.-made Northrop F-5 aircraft to Indonesia.[37] Indonesian-U.S. relations suffered as a consequence of these developments.

In 1994 there was a shift in U.S. policy. During the first part of the year U.S. trade representative Mickey Kantor continued to put pressure on Indonesia to improve workers' rights.[38] In June there were moves in the Senate to prevent Indonesia from using U.S. military equipment in East Timor, and the House proposed banning Indonesian involvement in U.S. military training programs (even on a fee-paying basis). However, the administration was more accommodating toward Indonesia, in view of the less strident position taken on human rights issues in Asia after mid-1994.[39]

China

Historical Context

China's concerns in Southeast Asia have focused most clearly on Indochina, but the ASEAN countries (and Burma) have also been important. The establishment of ASEAN in 1967 confirmed the setback for China resulting from the demise of Sukarno in Indonesia. Under Sukarno in the 1950s and early 1960s, Indonesia was a leading nonaligned country, and it developed a close relationship with China, particularly after the Bandung Conference in 1955. Sukarno's ideology of the New Emerging Forces in the early 1960s also reinforced the relationship. When the attempted leftist coup of September 1965 failed and an anti-Communist government emerged under Suharto, China fell into disfavor. There were allegations about Chinese involvement in the coup and China was believed to be linked to the discredited PKI.

Chinese links with local Communist parties were also an issue in relation to Malaya (subsequently Malaysia), Thailand, and the Philippines. Communist-led insurgencies erupted in all three countries, the most serious of which was the Malayan Emergency of the 1950s. China was also linked to the frequently unpopular Chinese minorities in Indonesia, Malaysia, Thailand, and the Philippines. Singapore, as a predominantly Chinese city-state, had to be sensitive to the concerns of its neighbors on the issue of China. China saw the membership of Thailand and the Philippines in SEATO after 1954 as part of the Western encirclement of its territory. The role of Thailand during the Vietnam War reinforced this attitude.

As for ASEAN itself, the Chinese reaction was initially hostile,[40] and its members were seen as anti-Communist and pro-Western. Upon its formation, ASEAN was described in *Peking Review* as "an out-and-out counter-revolutionary alliance rigged up to oppose China, communism, and the people, another instrument fashioned by US imperialism and Soviet revisionism for pursuing neo-colonialist ends in Asia."[41] This was at a time when the Cultural Revolution was at its height, and U.S. involvement in the Vietnam War was reaching a peak.

Subsequently, domestic changes in China and changes in the international situation led China to reassess its view of ASEAN. Internationally, the winding down of the Vietnam War and the Sino-U.S. rapprochement contributed to improved Chinese relations with ASEAN countries. Malaysia established diplomatic relations with China in 1974, and Thailand and the Philippines followed suit in 1975. Indonesia remained more cautious; Singapore, because of the sensitivities previously referred to, declined to take action ahead of Indonesia.

In China itself, the renewed emphasis on economic modernization after Mao's death in 1976 contributed to a desire to strengthen the economic links to the ASEAN countries. The security issues of China and ASEAN coincided in Cambodia, both China and ASEAN seeking an end to Vietnamese intervention (even though China tended to be stronger in its support of the Khmer Rouge). Within ASEAN, too, there were differences of emphasis, with Thailand feeling most threatened by Vietnam. Malaysia and Indonesia supported Thailand for the sake of ASEAN unity but were more open to the possibility of rapprochement with Vietnam as a means of restraining China. China thus developed closer relations with Thailand; those with Indonesia in particular were more distant.

Post–Cold War

A major common interest of ASEAN and China during the 1980s was opposition to Vietnamese intervention in Cambodia. In the post–Cold War era, the gradual resolution of the Cambodian conflict has required China to reassess its policies toward the ASEAN countries. The expanding economies of most of these countries have been one factor favoring a closer relationship; important security considerations have also been involved. Essentially, China has sought significant influence in the ASEAN countries to counter the influence of Japan's economic power in the region, among other objectives. Concern about Japan has also led China to take a more favorable view of a continued U.S. presence in the region.[42] Although China generally did not comment on the issue, it appeared to favor the retention of the U.S. bases in the Philippines.[43] Another consideration affecting China's policies has been its opposition to attempts by Taiwan to use the country's economic power to improve its diplomatic status with other Southeast Asian governments.[44]

The issues of the overseas Chinese and Chinese support for internal Communist insurgencies have not been obstacles to Sino-ASEAN relations, as they were in the past. The overseas Chinese appear to be better integrated with their local societies; in any event, economic prosperity has reduced ethnic tensions. With the possible exception of the Philippines, Communist insurgencies no longer have the salience they once had. China has made clear that its priority is the promotion of government-to-government rela-

tions and that it will not interfere in a country's internal affairs. This atti-
tude was reciprocated at the time of the Beijing massacre, when the
ASEAN countries were restrained in their reaction.[45] China has not become
a full dialogue partner of ASEAN, but it was invited to attend the ASEAN
Ministerial Meetings in 1991.[46] China was also a participant in the ASEAN
Regional Forum, which met for the first time in Bangkok in July 1994.

Relations with Thailand and Indonesia.   The two most important
countries for China within ASEAN have been Thailand and Indonesia.
Thailand's importance derives from its strategic location in continental
Southeast Asia and from its relationship to Indochina in particular. The
coincidence between Chinese and Thai views of the situation in Indochina
has encouraged the development of a cooperative relationship between the
two countries. There has not been this coincidence of views with Indonesia,
but China has sought to improve the relationship given the fact that
Indonesia is the largest ASEAN country and therefore exerts an important
influence in the region.

Li Peng made Thailand his first destination when he took his first foreign trip as Chinese premier in November 1988. Although the Cambodian
issue was prominent at this stage in the relationship, Li also used the visit
to proclaim four principles for the development of Sino-ASEAN relations:

> First, China strictly adheres to the Five Principles of Peaceful Coexistence
> in state-to-state relations; second, China opposes hegemonism under any
> circumstances; third, in economic relations with other countries China
> upholds the principle of equality, mutual benefit and attainment of com-
> mon prosperity; and fourth, in international affairs China follows the prin-
> ciples of independence, mutual respect, cooperation and mutual support.[47]

In early 1989, there were signs of divergence between China and
Thailand over the Cambodian issue. China appeared more committed to
assigning the Khmer Rouge a role in any settlement. Thailand seemed more
willing to compromise with the Hun Sen government; in late January, Hun
Sen visited Bangkok for discussions with Thai prime minister Chatichai
Choonhavan. When Chatichai visited Beijing from 14 to 17 March 1989,
China attempted to bring Thailand back into line on the Cambodian issue.[48]
During another visit by Chatichai in October 1989, Deng Xiaoping warned:
"We should guard against . . . the occurrence of another 'Afghanistan' situ-
ation in Kampuchea."[49]

The change in Thai policy under Chatichai had been influenced by his
declared goal of turning Indochina "from a battlefield into a marketplace."
In February 1991, his government was overthrown by the military in a
bloodless coup, and Thailand reverted to its previous policy on Indochina.
High-level visits between China and Thailand continued both before and
after the coup. Li Peng visited Thailand again in August 1990 and was fol-

lowed by President Yang Shangkun in June 1991 and Foreign Minister Qian Qichen in April 1993. Thai prime ministers Anand Panyarachun and Chuan Leekpai visited China in September 1991 and August 1993, respectively. The volume of Chinese arms transfers to Thailand decreased as a result of the political instability prevailing before the military coup.[50]

China had various obstacles to overcome to promote a better relationship with Indonesia. Indonesia tended to be suspicious of China and had given support to Thailand on the Cambodian issue only for the sake of ASEAN unity. Thailand looked to improving relations with Vietnam as a way of restraining China. Thus, an important goal for China was to achieve diplomatic normalization with Indonesia. On the Indonesian side, Suharto had long held out against people such as Foreign Minister Adam Malik, who favored normalization. However, the changing world situation, Suharto's desire to play a more prominent international role, and the prospect of economic benefits appear to have tipped the balance in favor of normalization.[51] In February 1989 Suharto and Qian Qichen met in Tokyo at the funeral for Emperor Hirohito and agreed that their countries should begin talks on diplomatic normalization.[52]

Normalization was finally achieved in August 1990, when Premier Li Peng visited Djakarta. Issues that had to be dealt with included the settlement of Indonesia's debt to China and the position of stateless ethnic Chinese in Indonesia. Indonesia also sought a promise from China of non-interference in Indonesia's domestic affairs.[53] Normalization was useful to both countries in pursuing their objectives in Cambodia. Improved contact with China helped Indonesia in its role as co-chair of the Paris International Conference on Cambodia. China was in a better position to secure ASEAN support for its preferred Cambodian solution.[54] Following Li Peng's visit to Indonesia, Suharto visited China in November 1990; President Yang Shangkun visited Indonesia in June 1991.[55] In February 1994 China protested after Suharto met Taiwan's president, Lee Teng-hui, who was in Bali for "a holiday-making visit."[56]

Relations with other ASEAN states. Among the other ASEAN states, Singapore was unusual in that it had a population that was predominantly ethnic Chinese. It had thus developed close economic and political relations with China. Former Singapore prime minister Lee Kuan Yew had played a role in reunification issues,[57] and Singapore's stance on Cambodia was very close to that of Thailand. Following the diplomatic normalization between China and Indonesia, Singapore moved quickly to follow suit. The process was set in motion when Li Peng visited Singapore after his visit to Indonesia in August 1990,[58] and diplomatic normalization was achieved in October 1990. Brunei, as the last ASEAN state not to have diplomatic relations with China, subsequently achieved normalization in September 1991.[59]

Malaysia had had diplomatic relations with China since 1974. However, among the ASEAN countries, it was closest to Indonesia in its view of China and its approach to the Cambodian problem. Li Peng's visit to Malaysia in December 1990 would have been an opportunity to discuss China's view on this issue.[60] In June 1993 Malaysian prime minister Mahathir visited Beijing. President Jiang Zemin used the occasion to refute any suggestion that China sought to fill a vacuum in Asia; rather, he suggested that China and Malaysia should "seize the present opportunity to contribute to regional peace and stability and promote mutual development by actively boosting economic cooperation."[61] From Malaysia's perspective, Mahathir was able to win Chinese support for his proposal for an East Asian Economic Caucus.[62]

The protection of China's interests has been the foremost consideration for its foreign policy. Having developed a good relationship with the Marcos government in the Philippines after 1975, China subsequently moved to do the same with the Aquino government after 1986.[63] President Cory Aquino visited China in April 1988 and President Fidel Ramos in April 1993.[64] The relationship between the Philippines and Taiwan has concerned China: The Philippines' economic problems have made it vulnerable to Taiwan's economic diplomacy. China protested when Foreign Secretary Raul Manglapus made a private visit to Taiwan in October 1989.[65] The same issue arose during Li Peng's visit to the Philippines in December 1990, when he pointedly "expressed appreciation for the Philippine's [sic] 'one China' policy."[66] China also protested Ramos's meeting President Lee Teng-hui at Subic Bay when the Taiwan president was en route to Bali in February 1994.[67]

The South China Sea

One particular issue that has been important in Chinese relations with certain ASEAN countries (Malaysia, the Philippines, Brunei, Indonesia, and Vietnam) is the South China Sea. The issue has implications for Taiwan (as a claimant) as well as external powers such as the United States and Japan. Let us examine the basis of the conflict, the role played by the different claimants, and the way in which the conflict is likely to develop.

Basis of the conflict.[68] The conflict in the South China Sea relates to two groups of islands, the Paracels and the Spratlys. The Paracels (in the northern part of the sea, and known to the Chinese as the Xisha and to the Vietnamese as the Hoang Sa) are claimed by China, Taiwan, and Vietnam. The Spratlys (in the southern part of the sea, and known to the Chinese as the Nansha and to the Vietnamese as the Truong Sa) are claimed by the same three countries; Malaysia, the Philippines, and Brunei also make claims to part of this area.

Although these islands are largely uninhabited, they are important for a number of reasons. The South China Sea is a major source of fish and has potential as a source of oil and gas. One Chinese report in 1989 stated that oil and gas deposits in the Spratlys were estimated at 17.7 billion tons, compared with 13 billion tons in Kuwait.[69] The region also has a vital role in maritime navigation in the region, given its position astride the sea lanes that run north from the Straits of Melaka to China, Japan, Korea, and Pacific Russia. The South China Sea occupies an important strategic location adjoining China, Vietnam, and several other ASEAN countries. Whoever controls the South China Sea is in a position to influence developments in adjacent countries. Whatever the substantive reasons are for wanting control in the South China Sea, national prestige is also at stake in this conflict. If a particular power perceives that it has experienced a setback in the region, it could provoke a more serious conflict over the issue.

Historically, China exercised jurisdiction over the South China Sea. Since the islands were essentially uninhabited and visited mainly by fishermen, this jurisdiction was mainly uncontested and insignificant. However, when France (as the colonial power in Indochina) occupied both the Paracels and the Spratlys during the 1930s, China disputed this action. During World War II, both sets of islands were occupied by Japan. At the end of the war, Japan surrendered the islands to China, although France still maintained its claim to them. At the time of the 1951 peace treaty, Japan abandoned any claim it might have had to the islands but did not designate which state it regarded as the rightful successor. During the 1950s, North Vietnam indicated on several occasions that it accepted China's claim, but this was not South Vietnam's position. In fact, after the late 1950s, certain islands in the Paracels and Spratlys were occupied by South Vietnam. In 1974 China seized the western Paracels from South Vietnam and attempted to do likewise with the South Vietnamese–occupied islands in the Spratlys. In March 1988, a battle between China and Vietnam in the Spratlys resulted in the loss of three ships and nearly 100 men by Vietnam.[70] Most recently, conflict occurred in 1995 between China and the Philippines over the Chinese occupation of Mischief Reef.

The role of the different claimants. The situation in the South China Sea can also be examined by considering the approach adopted by the different claimants. Developments in the law of the sea are relevant to most of the claims, as are definitions of such matters as the limits of the territorial sea (twelve miles), the continental shelf, and the exclusive economic zone (EEZ). The continental shelf refers to the way in which a country's land mass extends under the sea. A gentle gradient is usually followed by a much sharper drop; the area involved can be narrow but can also be quite extensive. States do not possess sovereignty over the continental shelf, but they do have exclusive rights over its exploitation. The EEZ is an area extending 200 nautical miles from a country's shoreline within which that country has exclusive rights to the exploitation of the resources of the sea and seabed.

1. China is less concerned about law of the sea matters in making its claim than are other parties. Its claim is based on the argument that the South China Sea is its "historic waters." From this perspective, the South China Sea is seen as another issue relating to China's territorial integrity (similar to Taiwan, Hong Kong, and Tibet). In February 1992, China reiterated its claim to all the islands of the South China Sea when the National People's Congress passed a Territorial Waters Law.[71] China—which became a net oil importer in 1994—believes that the oil and gas reserves of the South China Sea may be useful to its expanding economy by reducing China's dependence on oil imports.[72]

China's stance on this issue has also been influenced by domestic politics, and it is a good example of how the Chinese leadership and other groups can use a nationalist issue to win domestic support. It has been suggested that China's perception of the national interests at stake over this issue has been influenced by bureaucratic interests.[73] In particular, China's involvement in the conflict provides a strong justification for the naval modernization supported by the People's Liberation Army. The defense of the South China Sea requires China to develop a blue-water capacity that would enhance China's ability to project its military power more generally. Hainan, a Chinese province adjoining the South China Sea, is relatively poor and stands to gain from revenues derived from the exploitation of oil and gas reserves.

2. Taiwan, in its capacity as the Republic of China, supports the "historic waters" argument put forward by China. Its presence is limited to the occupation of Itu Aba, an island in the Spratlys. It has not attempted to play a military role.

3. Vietnam does not claim the whole of the South China Sea, but it does claim both the Paracels and the Spratlys. Its claim is based partly on Vietnamese involvement on these islands during the nineteenth century but mainly on the role played by France as the former colonial power. For Vietnam, the South China Sea is important both because it is a nationalist issue and because oil and gas reserves exist in the area. As discussed in Chapter 12, the importance of the issue has varied depending on the general state of Sino-Vietnamese relations. When those relations are bad, tension over the South China Sea tends to increase; when Sino-Vietnamese relations improve, the South China Sea becomes less of an issue. The relationship has tended to improve since the armed clashes of the late 1980s.

More recently there has been tension over the granting of a concession by China in 1992 to the U.S. company Crestone. The area involved is within the territory claimed by China but is also on Vietnam's continental shelf. The Vietnamese believed that China—judging that Vietnam would not be prepared to threaten a U.S. company—was taking advantage of its efforts to improve relations with the United States. Vietnam's strategy has been to align itself as much as possible with the ASEAN countries while attempting to win support from the United States.

4. The claims of Malaysia, Brunei, and the Philippines are essentially based on their view of the continental shelf, and there has been some overlap of disputed territory. Malaysia rejects Brunei's claim, and the Philippines and China clashed over Mischief Reef in 1995. Relations between Malaysia and China over the South China Sea have generally been more cooperative.

5. China's "historic waters" claim overlaps with Indonesia's Natuna gas reserves. Indonesia has an agreement for these reserves to be developed by the U.S. Exxon Corporation, but there have been doubts because of possible conflict. Since 1990, workshops have been held under Indonesian auspices to try to promote a solution of the South China Sea conflict.

6. The United States and Japan are not claimants but have an interest in the South China Sea because of its important maritime routes and strategic stability in the region. Both countries have adopted a low profile on the issue but could become involved if the conflict were to escalate. In such circumstances, Japan would probably defer to the role the United States might play. The United States would be in a stronger position to deploy naval forces in the region.

Prospects. China's approach to discussing the South China Sea issue has been to focus on proposals for joint development and to shelve any resolution of the sovereignty issue. Thus, in Singapore on 13 August 1990, Premier Li Peng said: "China is ready to join efforts with Southeast Asian countries to develop [the Spratly] islands, while putting aside for the time being the question of sovereignty."[74] Foreign Minister Qian Qichen reinforced this view at the ASEAN meeting in July 1992.[75] A problem with this approach is that it seems to include the entire South China Sea, which involves other claimants' continental shelves. The approach also seems to suggest "foreign participation in the development of China's resources,"[76] which means that Chinese sovereignty would have to be recognized before such joint development could occur. The most likely prospect is that there will be a continuation of the status quo, with unresolved competing claims and occasional clashes.

China prefers a bilateral rather than a multilateral approach to resolve the matter because it would clearly be in a stronger position if the former approach were used.[77] However, the ASEAN countries (including Vietnam) prefer a multilateral approach because united they would be in a stronger position to deal with China. The ASEAN Regional Forum is the major multilateral context in which the issue has been discussed. However, the forum is essentially a venue for discussion, not for conducting negotiations.

Japan

The ASEAN countries have featured most prominently in Japanese policies toward Southeast Asia, though Indochina has been of some concern. Southeast Asia sits astride some of Japan's important trading routes. Some 60 percent of Japan's oil imports and 40 percent of its foreign trade passes through the Straits of Melaka and the Lombok Straits.[78] While Japan has focused primarily on its economic role in the region, it has also focused on the political context. Japan appears to assume that its interests will be best protected by an economically prosperous and politically stable Southeast Asia.

In pursuing this goal, Japan has benefited from the fact that U.S. goals in the region have been similar. The emphasis in Japanese policies has sometimes been different, but in general, Japan has been able to assume that it is working within the umbrella provided by the U.S. security presence in the region. Japan has also had to take into account China's policies in the region. In the post-Mao period, there have been many similarities in the Southeast Asian policies of the two countries. At the same time, there is also the suggestion that China and Japan are potential rivals for influence in the region, which sometimes has a bearing on the policies pursued.

Historical Context

Japan began to renew its relations with Southeast Asia in the aftermath of the 1951 peace treaty, which, among other things, provided for the payment of reparations to the Southeast Asian countries that Japan had occupied during World War II. Under Prime Minister Shigeru Yoshida, Japan began to pursue a policy known as "economic diplomacy" and looked to Southeast Asia as a source of raw materials. Japan did not follow an overtly political approach but supported policies designed to promote stability and development within the context of the U.S. containment strategy. Although it avoided direct involvement in the Vietnam War, Japan took a leading role during the 1960s in initiatives designed to promote economic development in Southeast Asia, including the Ministerial Conference on the Economic Development of Southeast Asia (MEDSEA) and the Asian Development Bank (ADB) (both of which it established in 1966), as well as the Inter-Governmental Group on Indonesia (IGGI) (which it helped found in 1966 as a channel of aid to that country).[79]

Japan was indifferent to ASEAN at the time of its establishment in 1967.[80] ASEAN did not seem particularly significant, and Japan mostly concentrated on its bilateral relations with individual Southeast Asian countries, particularly Indonesia. Mounting Southeast Asian criticism of Japanese "exploitation" came to a head when Prime Minister Kakuei Tanaka visited the region in January 1974. Anti-Japanese demonstrations occurred in Thailand, Malaysia, and Indonesia, suggesting the need for Japan to develop a cooperative approach with ASEAN.

The end of the Vietnam War in 1975 (which came in the aftermath of the Sino-U.S. rapprochement of 1972) indicated the obsolescence of regional frameworks such as SEATO, which had been based on Cold War assumptions. An organization such as ASEAN appeared more important as a basis for regionalism. ASEAN itself recognized the new situation and developed a more substantive role for itself at the Bali summit meeting in February 1976. Japan, too, looked to ASEAN as a vehicle for developing its relations with Southeast Asia. A Japanese proposal for a Japan-ASEAN Forum was accepted by ASEAN, and the first meeting took place in Djakarta in March 1977.[81]

On a visit to Manila in August 1977, Prime Minister Takeo Fukuda outlined his Fukuda Doctrine as the basis for Japanese relations with Southeast Asia.[82] Three principles were identified as particularly important. First, Japan would reject "the role of a military power." Second, Japan would "do its best for consolidating the relationship of mutual confidence and trust based on 'heart-to-heart' understanding" with the countries of Southeast Asia. Third, Japan would "be an equal partner of ASEAN and its member countries, and co-operate positively with them in their own efforts to strengthen their solidarity and resilience, together with other nations of like mind outside the region, while aiming at fostering a relationship based on mutual understanding with the nations of Indochina."[83] The Fukuda Doctrine was essentially an attempt to restate the principles underlying Japanese relations with Southeast Asia. As Alan Rix comments: "The Doctrine marked no new directions in Japanese policy: while it restated Japanese Southeast Asian diplomacy, it encapsulated twenty years of Japanese experience in the region."[84] Essentially, Japan continued its policy of giving greater attention to ASEAN while also attempting to help resolve conflicts in Indochina.

During the 1980s the principles of the Fukuda Doctrine were elaborated in visits to the ASEAN countries by successive Japanese prime ministers: Zenko Suzuki in July 1981, Yasuhiro Nakasone in April–May 1983, and Noboru Takeshita in December 1987.[85] The main focus of the visits was on schemes to assist economic development in the ASEAN countries and to facilitate Japan-ASEAN trade relations. The ASEAN countries thought that Japan had too many restrictions on ASEAN imports and that it paid more attention to the concerns of Western countries than to the issues affecting ASEAN. In the late 1980s, Japan became involved in an important aid scheme for the Philippines known as the Multilateral Aid Initiative

(MAI). At the MAI's first meeting in April 1989, Japan offered to provide U.S. $1 billion or 30 percent of the sum proposed.[86]

ASEAN remained very important as a recipient of Japanese aid. In 1989 31.5 percent of Japan's aid (U.S. $2.132 billion) went to ASEAN. Indonesia took more than half that amount (U.S. $1.145 billion), followed by Thailand (U.S. $488 million), and the Philippines (U.S. $404 million).[87] About 40 percent of the total aid to ASEAN was from Japan.[88] In 1989 ASEAN took 9.4 percent of Japan's exports and was the source of 12.2 percent of Japan's imports.[89] Indonesia stood out as a source of imports, particularly oil. In 1987 Japan was responsible for 21.7 percent of the total trade of the ASEAN countries, ranging from 39.8 percent in Indonesia to 15.1 percent in Singapore.[90] Japan was the single most important trading partner for all ASEAN countries except the Philippines and Singapore, where Japan was second to the United States.

The ASEAN countries also accounted for 6.9 percent of Japan's foreign investment in 1989.[91] In 1982 28 percent of direct foreign investment in ASEAN was from Japan, varying from 36.2 percent in Indonesia to 15.7 percent in the Philippines.[92] Whereas Indonesia had been the most important destination for Japanese investment in the past, in 1989 Singapore, Thailand, and Malaysia were all more important than Indonesia. Past investment in Indonesia had been in the extraction of raw materials; in the late 1980s, Japanese investors were attracted by the low wage rates in manufacturing industry in Thailand, Malaysia, and Indonesia.[93]

Post-Cold War

In the post–Cold War era, visits to Southeast Asia and statements by Japanese leaders have been a good indication of how Japan has viewed ASEAN. On a visit to ASEAN countries between 29 April and 7 May 1989, Prime Minister Takeshita called ASEAN "one of Japan's most important partners in economic cooperation."[94] More important, perhaps, was the visit to Southeast Asia by Prime Minister Toshiki Kaifu in May 1991. In a speech in Singapore on 3 May, Kaifu went beyond the issue of economic cooperation to the question of Japan's political role in Southeast Asia. Recognizing that a lingering suspicion of Japan remained as a result of its wartime role in the region, Kaifu went further than any previous Japanese leader by expressing "sincere contrition at Japanese past actions which inflicted unbearable suffering and sorrow on a great many people of the Asia Pacific region."[95] Although Japan had to respond to "rising expectations for Japan's international contribution today," the "appropriate role in the political sphere [was] as a nation of peace."[96] In essence, this meant Japan wished to have a role in resolving conflicts, such as the problem in Cambodia. Kaifu seemed keen to have ASEAN countries endorse a more active Japanese peacekeeping role.[97] He said that he was "well aware that the course which Japanese policy might take could well spark concerns among some of our Asian neighbors that Japan might once more be embarking on a path to military power," but that Japan had only "a moderate self-defence capability" and remained committed to its security relationship to the United States.[98] This last point seemed to reassure Southeast Asian leaders. Prime Minister Goh Chok Tong of Singapore said, "A Japan that remains firmly anchored to the US alliance system and which is trusted by its neighbours will be a positive force, not just for the Asia-Pacific, but for the whole world."[99]

The nature of Japan's political involvement in Southeast Asia was explored further when Prime Minister Kiichi Miyazawa visited the region in January 1993. One report suggested Japan was pursuing a "two-track" approach to regional security issues: Dialogue would be encouraged among the countries directly involved in particular issues, but discussions should also take place on a region-wide basis (and should include the major powers).[100] Prime Minister Tomiichi Murayama's visit to Southeast Asia in late August 1994 did not further elaborate Japan's role in the region. In fact, Murayama was urged, particularly in Malaysia and Singapore, to support a more active international role for Japan; permanent membership in the UN Security Council was seen as an important step toward this goal.[101] Prime Minister Ryutaro Hashimoto attempted to further develop Japan's role in a visit to Southeast Asia in January 1997. He proposed holding regular Japan-ASEAN summit meetings to discuss political, economic, and security issues.[102] This suggestion was in line with the more assertive Japanese role favored by Hashimoto, but its acceptance by the ASEAN countries appeared problematical.

War guilt issue. Two important issues in Japanese relations with ASEAN in the post–Cold War era have been the question of war guilt and the proposal for an East Asian Economic Caucus (EAEC). As previously mentioned, Kaifu referred to the issue of war guilt in his speech in Singapore on 3 May 1991. When Emperor Akihito visited Southeast Asia in September–October 1991, he told King Bhumibol Adulyadej of Thailand that Japan "had resolved that it would live as a nation of peace, so that it should never repeat the horrors of that most unfortunate war."[103] Prime Minister Morihiro Hosokawa's statements in August 1993 that Japan had conducted "a war of aggression" and that he "would like to sincerely express [his] feelings for all war victims and their surviving families in the neighbouring nations of Asia as well as all the world" had an impact in Southeast Asia as well as in countries such as China and the Koreas.[104] Justice Minister Shigeto Nagano's comments that the 1937 Nanjing massacre "never really happened" and that Japan had not been an aggressor in World War II because "we really believed in the Greater East Asian Co-prosperity Sphere" produced an adverse reaction in Southeast Asia and China as well as other countries.[105] When Prime Minister Murayama visited Southeast Asia in late August 1994, his expressions of regret for Japan's wartime role were accepted in countries such as Vietnam and the Philippines. In Malaysia, however, he was told by Prime Minister Mahathir that "apologising for war crimes committed 50 years ago" was no longer relevant.[106]

East Asian Economic Caucus. Mahathir, in fact, was more interested in his EAEC proposal. He had originally proposed the EAEC in December 1990 as a regional economic forum to include not only Japan and the ASEAN countries but also China, Indochina, South Korea, Hong Kong, and Taiwan.[107] Malaysia saw the EAEC as a vehicle for promoting economic integration in East Asia. Like the regional trading blocs emerging in Europe and North America (the European Union and the North American Free Trade Agreement), the EAEC would provide the basis for a similar grouping—in this case, East Asia. Malaysia also believed the EAEC would improve Malaysian access to the Japanese market.[108] From Japan's perspective, there were certain problems with the proposal: It might be seen as encouraging the development of regional trading blocs, a development to which Japan was opposed. The United States was also opposed to the proposal, which it believed would restrict its own access to Asia Pacific economies. Japanese support for the EAEC would exacerbate tensions between the United States and Japan.

Although Malaysia saw the EAEC as a group operating within the Asia-Pacific Economic Cooperation, there was also the perception that the EAEC could undermine the wider grouping. The EAEC issue was raised a number of times between Malaysia and Japan. When Malaysian trade and industry minister Rafidah Aziz visited Tokyo in April 1991, she promoted the EAEC as primarily a consultative forum.[109] When Kaifu talked with Mahathir in Malaysia the following month, the Japanese prime minister stated that Japan would not commit itself before ASEAN had reached a consensus on the proposal. Japan was also aware of the concern expressed by countries such as the United States, Canada, Australia, and New Zealand.[110] Fear of offending Washington appeared to be the reason Prime Minister Miyazawa did not endorse the proposal when he visited Malaysia in January 1993; the perceived negative effect of such an endorsement on Japanese-U.S. relations outweighed the support that existed for the EAEC proposal within Japan.[111]

By the time Prime Minister Murayama visited Kuala Lumpur in August 1994, Japan appeared to be more sympathetic to the proposal. This sentiment was confirmed when Malaysian deputy prime minister Anwar Ibrahim visited Tokyo one week later.[112] ASEAN support for the Malaysian plan since its 1992 summit was important to Japan, as was the assurance that the EAEC would operate as a grouping of Asian countries within APEC. In Kuala Lumpur, Murayama made the point that "other countries" must support the scheme, which could be an indication of continuing U.S. influence on the Japanese approach.

Indonesia.   Among all the ASEAN countries, Japan traditionally placed most emphasis on its relationship with Indonesia, a reflection of Indonesia's importance as a supplier of raw materials, particularly oil. Japan is Indonesia's major trading partner, source of foreign investment, and aid supplier,[113] and it is one of the leading recipients of Japanese aid. The importance of the relationship was confirmed when Suharto visited Tokyo in November 1990 for the enthronement of Emperor Akihito. Suharto confirmed Indonesia's role as a supplier of oil to Japan and also requested that Japan continue its aid.[114] The difficulties Indonesia faced in East Timor did not undermine the relationship. In February 1992, Japanese foreign minister Michio Watanabe informed Indonesian foreign minister Ali Alatas that the Dili massacre of November 1991 would not lead to any changes in Japanese aid to Indonesia.[115] Japan's view of Indonesia's importance was also confirmed when Miyazawa attempted to arrange a meeting between Suharto (in his capacity as chairman of the Nonaligned Movement) and the G7 leaders at the Tokyo summit of the G7 in July 1993.[116]

The Philippines and Thailand.   The Philippines and Thailand were also important ASEAN recipients of Japanese aid. As mentioned previously, Japan played a leading role in the Philippines Multilateral Aid Initiative that began in 1989. The status of Japan as the leading aid donor to the Philippines was confirmed at a February 1991 meeting of donors in Hong Kong, where Japan promised U.S. $1.3 billion in aid, compared with the U.S. offer of U.S. $160 million.[117] The Philippines has normally been on the itinerary for visits by Japanese prime ministers to Southeast Asia, and in March 1993 President Fidel Ramos visited Japan.[118]

Thailand was the second most important recipient of Japanese aid until 1987, when it subsequently fell to fourth place.[119] Unlike other Southeast Asian countries, Thailand was not occupied by Japan during World War II. This might have been a factor influencing the proposal by Thai prime minister Chatichai Choonhavan in May 1990 that the Thai and Japanese navies conduct joint exercises in the South China Sea.[120] Japan rejected the proposal on constitutional grounds, and the other ASEAN countries criticized the proposal. One factor affecting the level of Japanese aid to Thailand was the country's proximity to Indochina. Japan believed that its aid contributed to Thailand's stability and thus to the stability of Indochina. Nevertheless, Japan did not necessarily accept Chatichai's proposal during his visit to Tokyo in April 1990 that Thailand should be the "springboard" for economic involvement in Indochina.[121] Japan's relationship with Thailand was not significantly affected by the coup of February 1991, and this was confirmed when Anand Panyarachun (the new Thai prime minister) visited Japan in December 1991.[122]

The USSR and Russia

Even though relations between post-Soviet Russia and ASEAN have not been a major focus for the ASEAN countries or for Russia, historically, the relationship between those countries and the USSR was significant up through the Gorbachev era. The development of the relationship—particularly the period since the mid-1980s—will be briefly reviewed.

Historical Context

Soviet relations with the countries of Southeast Asia were slow to develop in the postwar period. As discussed in Chapter 12, the USSR did become involved in North Vietnam, but the relationship was not a priority for Soviet foreign policy. Among the non-Communist countries, Burma and Indonesia were singled out for attention during the 1950s: Their nonaligned foreign policies provided a basis for developing relations with the USSR, whereas the various pro-Western states of the region were obviously less promising. Interestingly, the USSR did not sever diplomatic relations with Indonesia in the aftermath of Sukarno's downfall in 1965 (unlike the situation with China). Nevertheless, the new direction pursued by Suharto's Indonesia did not hold out much promise for the USSR.

During the Vietnam War, the USSR's primary alignment was with North Vietnam, and the alignment colored its relationship with the rest of the region. Although ASEAN was not pro-Western as such nor formally aligned with the United States (except in the case of individual members such as the Philippines and Thailand), it did have a general interest in maintaining the existing power balance in the region. The alignment that had been evident during the Vietnam War was accentuated after the war's conclusion, when a reunified and Communist Vietnam became formally aligned with the USSR and then invaded Cambodia in late 1978. Thailand perceived the invasion as a particular threat, but all other ASEAN countries supported it. Soviet intervention in Afghanistan in late 1979 added to its negative image in Southeast Asia, particularly among Islamic-oriented states such as Indonesia and Malaysia.

The Gorbachev Era

It was clear that any change in Soviet relations with the ASEAN countries would be dependent on a resolution of the Cambodian issue. In his Vladivostok speech in July 1986, Mikhail Gorbachev signaled that he wanted to resolve the conflict, saying there were "no insurmountable obstacles to the establishment of mutually acceptable relations between the countries of Indochina and ASEAN." Gorbachev also favored a nuclear weapons free zone in Southeast Asia and wished to promote Soviet relations with individual Southeast Asian countries.[123]

Although change was not immediately forthcoming in the aftermath of the Vladivostok speech, Gorbachev's comments did seem to improve the general climate of relations between the USSR and the ASEAN countries. Soviet foreign minister Eduard Shevardnadze visited Bangkok and Djakarta in March 1987, and there were subsequent visits to Moscow by various ASEAN leaders, including Malaysian prime minister Mahathir (1987), Thai prime minister Prem Tinsulanonda (1988), Suharto (1989), and Lee Kuan Yew (1989).[124] Gorbachev himself never visited Southeast Asia, which was indicative of the priority Soviet foreign policy accorded to the region as a whole. In his Krasnoyarsk speech in September 1988, Gorbachev indicated that Soviet relations with the ASEAN countries ("primarily Indonesia," but also the Philippines, Malaysia, and Thailand) were becoming "more active." He also said that if the United States would give up its military bases in the Philippines, the USSR would leave its base at Cam Ranh Bay.[125] By the time of the Sino-Soviet summit in Beijing in May 1989, it was clear that the USSR was playing an active role in trying to facilitate a Cambodian settlement, and this in turn assisted Soviet relations with the ASEAN countries.

One feature of Gorbachev's foreign policy was his emphasis on promoting Soviet economic objectives in Southeast Asia as well as other regions. Soviet-ASEAN trade was small and biased very much in favor of the ASEAN countries. This situation did not change much during the Gorbachev period, but the USSR gave greater attention to assessing the possibilities for expansion. In 1989 Soviet exports to the ASEAN countries amounted to U.S. $107 million; Soviet imports from these countries were U.S. $916 million.[126] One indication of the new atmosphere in Soviet-ASEAN relations was that in July 1991, the Soviet Union was invited to participate in the annual ASEAN foreign ministers' meeting for the first time. The ASEAN countries also supported the admission of the USSR to PECC (Pacific Economic Cooperation Conference) in 1991.[127]

Among the ASEAN countries, Indonesia was particularly significant to the USSR. This was partly because Indonesia was the preeminent power in Southeast Asia and partly because Indonesia had never openly aligned itself with a Western country (unlike Thailand and the Philippines with the United States or Malaysia and Singapore with the United Kingdom). During the Cambodian conflict, Indonesia and Malaysia (possibly motivated by their fears of China) were the ASEAN members most inclined not to isolate Vietnam too much. From the Soviet perspective, Suharto's visit to Moscow in September 1989 was a very important development, second only to the Sino-Soviet rapprochement in its implications for the Soviet role in the region.[128]

Russia

With the demise of the USSR, the Russian Federation under Boris Yeltsin has pursued policies toward the ASEAN countries that are essentially similar to those of Gorbachev. The difference is that Russia is less significant as a power than the USSR was. As with Gorbachev, the priority accorded to Southeast Asia is far less than that given to Northeast Asia. Russia has continued to participate in the annual ASEAN foreign ministers' meetings, as well as the ASEAN Regional Forum (from 1994) and PECC. Should Russia be admitted to APEC, it would provide another context for interaction with the ASEAN countries.

Visits by the Russian foreign minister to Southeast Asia for the ASEAN foreign ministers' meeting and ASEAN Regional Forum were used to highlight Russian policy toward ASEAN. At the 1995 meeting Andrei Kozyrev's proposal for developing links between ASEAN and the Commonwealth of Independent States was favorably received.[129] Deputy Foreign Minister Alexander Panov argued in July 1996 that Russia was now seen as a "constructive partner" by Southeast Asian countries. With support from Indonesia in particular, Russia had won observer status in the Nonaligned Movement. Russian trade with ASEAN was estimated by Panov at U.S. $4.5 billion, or 30 percent of Russia's total foreign trade.[130] It is not clear how Panov arrived at this estimate; IMF figures for 1995 show Russian exports to ASEAN (including Vietnam) were U.S. $1,982 million and imports were U.S. $467 million.[131] These amounts indicate that trade with ASEAN accounts for 2.06 percent of Russia's foreign trade. Russia was interested in selling arms to Southeast Asia. Malaysia, for example, took delivery of the last of eighteen MiG-29 aircraft bought from Russia in July 1995.[132]

The ASEAN countries have been important to the regional policies of the United States, China, and Japan in the post–Cold War era. For the United States, they have provided a model for other Third World countries to follow. While there have been difficulties in particular bilateral relationships, such as that with the Philippines, this has not detracted from the overall importance of developing security and economic relations within the region.

China has hoped to promote economic relations with the ASEAN countries but also has important strategic interests of its own at stake. During the course of the Cambodian conflict, an anti-Vietnamese alignment developed between China and ASEAN. In the aftermath of that conflict, China has been attempting to develop its relations with key ASEAN countries such as Thailand and Indonesia. At the same time it has concerns that a common ASEAN position might develop in opposition to China on issues such as the South China Sea. These concerns become greater with Vietnam's adherence to ASEAN.

Japan has had important economic interests in the ASEAN countries. It has attempted to foster its political links with the region in the context of the Fukuda Doctrine, which emphasizes quiet diplomacy and the provision of aid. Although its strategy of involvement is different, Japan has generally shared the U.S. perception that the ASEAN countries play a positive role. For post-Soviet Russia, the ASEAN countries are less significant than Northeast Asia; Russia is only a minor player in Southeast Asia.

Notes

1. ASEAN is defined in this chapter in terms of its pre-1995 membership—i.e., Vietnam, Cambodia, Laos, and Burma are not included.

2. For background on ASEAN, see Sandhu, *The ASEAN Reader;* Broinowski, *ASEAN into the 1990s.*

3. Weatherbee, "Asean and Evolving Patterns of Regionalism in Southeast Asia," p. 36.

4. For an examination of the Suharto period in Indonesian foreign policy, see Suryadinata, *Indonesia's Foreign Policy Under Suharto.*

5. Hill, "The Economy," p. 57.

6. Hill, *The Indonesian Economy Since 1966,* p. 194.

7. Ibid., p. 84.

8. Lowry, "Indonesia," p. 105.

9. Simon, "The Great Powers and Southeast Asia," p. 921.

10. A theoretical analysis of the development of the U.S.-Indonesian relationship is presented in Kivimaki, "Strength of Weakness."

11. Baker, "America in Asia," pp. 13–14.

12. Ibid., p. 14.

13. For an assessment of U.S. policy in Southeast Asia in light of recent developments in the area, see Bresnan, *From Dominoes to Dynamos.*

14. The historical context of the bases is discussed in Berry, *U.S. Bases in the Philippines.* The issues that faced the Bush administration are reviewed in Greene, *The Philippine Bases.*

15. There was a difference between the United States and the Philippines as to whether termination of the treaty would require one year's notice after 16 September 1991 or whether termination would take effect from that date. The United States said the former, the Philippines the latter.

16. *Keesing's Record of World Events,* vol. 36 (1990), p. 37458.

17. James Baker, "ASEAN: Challenges and Opportunities," *Current Policy* (U.S. Department of State), no. 1190, p. 2.

18. See Pamela Fessler, "Mount Pinatubo May Reshape Debate Over Military Bases," *Congressional Quarterly Weekly Report,* 29 June 1991, pp. 1771–1772.

19. See *Keesing's Record of World Events,* vol. 37 (1991), p. 38398; *Foreign Policy Bulletin,* vol. 2 no. 2 (September–October 1991), pp. 55–56.

20. *Keesing's Record of World Events,* vol. 37 (1991), p. 38441.

21. *Asia 1994 Yearbook,* p. 194.

22. See Buszynski, "The Philippines, Asean and the Future of the American Bases," p. 84.

23. *Keesing's Record of World Events,* vol. 35 (1989), pp. 37086–37087.

24. Ibid., p. 37087.

25. Ibid., vol. 36 (1990), pp. 37860–37861, 38639.

26. Ibid., vol. 38 (1992), p. 38728.

27. Lord, "A New Pacific Community," p. 51.

28. For an overview of the prospective issues in U.S.–Southeast Asian relations during the Clinton administration, see Morrison, "U.S. Security Relations with Southeast Asia." Security issues are considered in Simon, "U.S. Strategy and Southeast Asian Security" and "The Clinton Presidency and Asian Security."

29. Michael Vatikiotis, "All Smiles for Lord," *Far Eastern Economic Review,* 27 May 1993, p. 19.

30. Quoted in Susumu Awanohara, "Down to a Trickle," *Far Eastern Economic Review,* 7 October 1993, p. 24.

31. Rodney Tasker, "Security Embrace," *Far Eastern Economic Review,* 18 February 1993, pp. 12–13.

32. Rodney Tasker, "The Libyan Connection," *Far Eastern Economic Review,* 16 September 1993, p. 27.

33. Rodney Tasker, "Plain Speaking," *Far Eastern Economic Review,* 24 March 1994, p. 28.

34. Susumu Awanohara, "Hard Labour," *Far Eastern Economic Review,* 13 May 1993, p. 13. Compare the view of the Bush administration as presented by Kenneth M. Quinn, acting assistant secretary of state for East Asian and Pacific Affairs, in the immediate aftermath of the Dili massacre that "continuing cooperative engagement [with Indonesia], not retribution, best serves the human rights goals we all seek." See "Crisis in East Timor and U.S. Policy Toward Indonesia," Hearings Before the Committee on Foreign Relations, U.S. Senate, 27 February and 6 March 1992, p. 77.

35. Susumu Awanohara, "The Right to Arm," *Far Eastern Economic Review,* 23 September 1993, p. 13.

36. Susumu Awanohara, "Weapons of Discord," *Far Eastern Economic Review,* 26 August 1993, pp. 24–25.

37. Ibid.

38. Susumu Awanohara, "Tarnished Image," *Far Eastern Economic Review,* 2 June 1994, p. 28.

39. Irene Wu, "House vs. White House," *Far Eastern Economic Review,* 30 June 1994, p. 18; Nigel Holloway, "Warts and All," *Far Eastern Economic Review,* 8 September 1994, p. 30.

40. For a good overview of China's relations with ASEAN and its members up to the late 1980s, see Kallgren, Sopiee, and Djiwandono, *ASEAN and China.*

41. *Peking Review,* 18 August 1967, as quoted in Klein, "China and ASEAN," p. 215.

42. Bert, "Chinese Policies and U.S. Interests in Southeast Asia," p. 323.

43. Ibid.

44. Julian Baum, "Looking South," *Far Eastern Economic Review,* 10 March 1994, p. 18.

45. "A Wary Eye on the Dragon," *Far Eastern Economic Review,* 22 June 1989, p. 20. Lee Kuan Yew did say the Chinese reaction was "totally disproportionate" to the resistance offered.

46. To, "ASEAN-PRC Political and Security Cooperation," p. 1096.

47. Chen Jing, "Li's Tour Strengthens Friendships," *Beijing Review,* 5–11 December 1988, p. 15.

48. Robert Delfs, "A United Front Again," *Far Eastern Economic Review,* 30 March 1989, p. 27.

49. "China, Thailand Share Views on Kampuchean Issue," *Beijing Review,* 6–12 November 1989, p. 5.

50. Gill, "China Looks to Thailand," p. 531 and *passim.*

51. See Suryadinata, "Indonesia-China Relations," pp. 686–687, 690–691; Michael Vatikiotis and Rodney Tasker, "Slow Boat to China," *Far Eastern Economic Review,* 19 May 1988, p. 42.

52. Hamish McDonald, "Breaking the Ice," *Far Eastern Economic Review,* 9 March 1989, pp. 10–11.

53. See Michael Vatikiotis and Robert Delfs, "Burying the Past," *Far Eastern Economic Review,* 12 July 1990, pp. 10–11; Michael Vatikiotis, "Red Carpets, Red Flags," *Far Eastern Economic Review,* 23 August 1990, pp. 8–9; "Memorandum on Resumption of Sino-Indonesian Diplomatic Ties," *Beijing Review,* 27 August–2 September 1990, p. 11.

54. See Liu Zhengxue, "Li Peng Speaks on Kampuchea and Gulf Crisis," *Beijing Review,* 20–26 August 1990, p. 10; Yang Mu, "A Common Understanding on Cambodia," *Beijing Review,* 27 August–2 September 1990, pp. 10–11.

55. *Keesing's Record of World Events,* vol. 36 (1990), p. 37861; vol. 37 (1991), p. 38294.

56. "China Protests Lee's Southeast Asia Tour," *Beijing Review,* 28 February–6 March 1994, p. 7.

57. N. Balakrishnan, "The Honest Broker," *Far Eastern Economic Review,* 1 February 1990, p. 23.

58. See "Li's Visit Enhances Ties with Singapore," *Beijing Review,* 20–26 August 1990, pp. 5–6; "Joint Press Statement by China and Singapore," *Beijing Review,* 27 August–2 September 1990, p. 12.

59. *Keesing's Record of World Events,* vol. 37 (1991), p. 38535.

60. "Li Peng Continues South Asian Tour," *Beijing Review,* 24–30 December 1990, pp. 4–5.

61. "Chinese and Malaysian Leaders Meet," *Beijing Review,* 28 June–4 July 1993, p. 4.

62. Michael Vatikiotis, "Mixed Motives," *Far Eastern Economic Review,* 24 June 1993, p. 13.

63. See Bert, "Chinese Policy Toward Democratization Movements," pp. 1076–1082.

64. *Keesing's Record of World Events,* vol. 35 (1989), p. 36429; "Ramos' First China Visit," *Beijing Review,* 10–16 May 1993, pp. 5–7.

65. John McBeth, "A Lesson in Diplomacy," *Far Eastern Economic Review,* 16 November 1989, p. 25.

66. "Li Peng Continues South Asian Tour," *Beijing Review,* 24–30 December 1990, p. 4. See also Frank Jiang, "China Trading," *Far Eastern Economic Review,* 27 December 1990, p. 9.

67. "China Protests Lee's Southeast Asia Tour," *Beijing Review,* 28 February–6 March 1994, p. 7.

68. For background on the South China Sea issue, see Samuels, *Contest for the South China Sea;* Lo, *China's Policy Towards Territorial Disputes;* Thomas, "The Spratly Islands Imbroglio"; "Treacherous Shoals," *Far Eastern Economic Review,* 13 August 1992, pp. 14–17; Varon, "The Spratly Islands Embroilment"; Valencia, "China and the South China Sea Disputes."

69. Leifer, "Chinese Economic Reform and Security Policy," p. 44.

70. Nayan Chanda and Tai Ming Cheung, "Reef Knots," *Far Eastern Economic Review,* 30 August 1990, p. 11. In April 1994, the Vietnamese navy surrounded a Chinese research vessel that had been working in the Spratlys and escorted it to international waters. See Nayan Chanda, "Show of Force," *Far Eastern Economic Review,* 13 October 1994, p. 29.

71. Frost, *Vietnam's Foreign Relations,* p. 39.

72. Leifer, "Chinese Economic Reform and Security Policy," p. 44.

73. See Garver, "China's Push Through the South China Sea."

74. Nayan Chanda and Tai Ming Cheung, "Reef Knots," *Far Eastern Economic Review,* 30 August 1990, p. 11.

75. *Keesing's Record of World Events,* vol. 38 (1992), p. 39006.

76. Valencia, "China and the South China Sea Disputes," p. 12.

77. Nayan Chanda, "Divide and Rule," *Far Eastern Economic Review,* 11 August 1994, p. 18.

78. Khamchoo, "Japan's Role in Southeast Asian Security," p. 7.

79. Rix, "ASEAN and Japan," pp. 173–174.

80. Japanese relations with ASEAN are examined in ibid., pp. 169–195; Elsbree and Hoong, "Japan and ASEAN"; Sudo, "Japan-ASEAN Relations"; Sudo, "From Fukuda to Takeshita"; Ping, "ASEAN and the Japanese Role in Southeast Asia"; Sudo, *The Fukuda Doctrine and ASEAN.*

81. Rix, "ASEAN and Japan," p. 186.

82. Reprinted as Appendix 1 in Sudo, *The Fukuda Doctrine and ASEAN,* pp. 241–247.

83. Ibid., p. 246.

84. Rix, "ASEAN and Japan," p. 188.

85. See Sudo, *The Fukuda Doctrine and ASEAN,* pp. 207–209.

86. Sudo, *Southeast Asia in Japanese Security Policy,* p. 44.

87. Sudo, *The Fukuda Doctrine and ASEAN,* p. 255.

88. Elsbree and Hoong, "Japan and ASEAN," p. 125.

89. Sudo, *The Fukuda Doctrine and ASEAN,* pp. 249, 251.

90. Tyabji, "The Six ASEAN Economies: 1980–88," pp. 48–49.

91. Sudo, *The Fukuda Doctrine and ASEAN,* p. 253.

92. Tyabji, "The Six ASEAN Economies: 1980–88," p. 42.

93. Sudo, *The Fukuda Doctrine and ASEAN,* p. 253; Rowley and do Rosario, "Japan's View of Asia," p. 10.

94. *Keesing's Record of World Events,* vol. 35 (1989), p. 36655.

95. Quoted, Michael Vatikiotis, "The Gentle Giant," *Far Eastern Economic Review,* 16 May 1991, p. 11.

96. Ibid.

97. Suhaini Aznam and Anthony Rowley, "Stepping Carefully," *Far Eastern Economic Review,* 9 May 1991, p. 19.

98. Quoted, Michael Richardson, "Japan Pledges Peaceful Cooperation," *Asia-Pacific Defence Reporter,* July 1991, p. 12.

99. Quoted, ibid.

100. Robert Delfs and Michael Vatikiotis, "Low Key Diplomacy," *Far Eastern Economic Review,* 14 January 1993, p. 12.

101. Charles Smith, "Forgive and Forget," *Far Eastern Economic Review,* 8 September 1994, pp. 14–15.

102. See Michael Richardson, "Japan Embraces S-E Asian Security," *Australian,* 15 January 1997, pp. 1, 7.

103. *Keesing's Record of World Events,* vol. 37 (1991), p. 38529.

104. Jonathan Friedland, "Blood Money," *Far Eastern Economic Review,* 26 August 1993, p. 21.

105. Charles Smith, "Foot in the Mouth," *Far Eastern Economic Review,* 19 May 1994, p. 30.

106. Charles Smith, "Forgive and Forget," *Far Eastern Economic Review,* 8 September 1994, p. 14.

107. Jun, "Japan and Malaysia," p. 277.

108. Tsuruoka, "Malaysia: Look East—and Up," pp. 129–130.

109. Anthony Rowley, "The Malaysian Two-Step," *Far Eastern Economic Review,* 18 April 1991, pp. 70–71.

110. Suhaini Aznam and Anthony Rowley, "Stepping Carefully," *Far Eastern Economic Review,* 9 May 1991, p. 19.

111. Michael Vatikiotis, "EAEC Fails to Appeal," *Far Eastern Economic Review,* 28 January 1993, p. 11. See also Anthony Rowley, "Cheered On by Japan," *Far Eastern Economic Review,* 20 August 1992, pp. 18–19.

112. Rodney Tasker, "Signs of Life," *Far Eastern Economic Review,* 15 September 1994, pp. 20–21.

113. See Schwarz and Vatikiotis, "Indonesia: Price of Security," pp. 95–98.

114. *Keesing's Record of World Events,* vol. 36 (1990), p. 37861.

115. Ibid., p. 38769.

116. Hisane Masaki, "Government Unsure How to Handle Suharto's G-7 Trip," *Japan Times* (Weekly International Edition), 28 June–4 July 1993, p. 3.

117. Tiglao, "The Philippines: Uncle Nippon," pp. 90–91.

118. *Keesing's Record of World Events,* vol. 39 (1993), p. 39373.

119. Tasker and Handley, "Thailand: Money Talks," p. 146.

120. Rodney Tasker, "Full Astern!" *Far Eastern Economic Review,* 24 May 1990, p. 19. See also Sudo, "Japan and the Security of Southeast Asia," pp. 337–338.

121. Tasker and Handley, "Thailand: Money Talks," p. 137.

122. *Keesing's Record of World Events,* vol. 37 (1991), pp. 38004, 38681.

123. "Text of Speech by Mikhail Gorbachev in Vladivostok, 28 July 1986," pp. 219, 223, 224.

124. Buszynski, *Gorbachev and Southeast Asia,* p. 147; Thambipillai, "Southeast Asia," p. 227.

125. "Gorbachev Offers New Bids on Asian Policy," *Current Digest of the Soviet Press,* vol. 40 no. 38 (19 October 1988), pp. 5–6.

126. Buszynski, *Gorbachev and Southeast Asia,* p. 212.

127. Chufrin, "The USSR and Asia in 1991," p. 16.

128. Williams, "New Soviet Policy Toward Southeast Asia," p. 373.

129. Official Kremlin International News Broadcast, 8 August 1995.

130. *Russian Press Digest,* 12 July 1996.

131. *Direction of Trade Statistics Yearbook 1996,* p. 375.

132. *The Military Balance 1995–1996,* p. 172.

PART V

CONCLUSION

14

EMERGING THEMES: STRATEGY, ECONOMICS, DOMESTIC POLITICS

The assumption underlying this book is that examining the role of the major powers can provide important insights into the dynamics of international politics in post–Cold War Asia Pacific. In Part I it is suggested that realism, liberalism or liberal institutionalism, and a culturalistic approach are relevant to understanding those dynamics. A preliminary assessment of what such understanding involves is presented. In this concluding chapter, we look at the main themes that have emerged in this book and see how they relate to the general perspectives that are described in Part I.

It can be argued that no one perspective holds the key to interpreting the international politics of post–Cold War Asia Pacific. Each perspective is useful depending on the particular relationship or situation one is investigating. Because this book focuses on the role of the major powers, there is a certain bias toward realism in its presentation. At the same time, the detail of the various situations discussed makes clear that domestic politics and economic considerations have a major impact even in situations that seem to be primarily influenced by strategic factors. Similar qualifications apply when one considers the relevance of liberal institutionalism or the culturalistic approach. Liberal institutionalism points to how international politics works in situations in which there is a high level of interdependence. It is particularly useful for examining the development of economic relationships and regionalism. However, again one needs to be aware of the impact of domestic politics and the way in which strategic considerations can affect situations of interdependence. The culturalistic approach analyzes what is unique about the international politics of Asia Pacific. Historical considerations and domestic politics, as well as "culture" in a broader sense, thus receive particular emphasis. The "logic" underlying realism and liberal institutionalism can highlight why certain situations develop the way they do, regardless of the more particular factors involved. Keeping these qualifications in mind, let us review briefly the major themes that have emerged in each section of the book.

A theme in Part II, which focuses on the general approaches of the

United States, China, Japan, and the USSR and Russia in post–Cold War Asia Pacific, is that there are competing perceptions about the direction of foreign policy within each power. In the United States, these different opinions concern the extent to which the country should be involved in Asia Pacific (echoing the more general debate about the U.S. role in the post–Cold War world). In China there are differences relating to the degree to which it should assert itself in the international politics of the region. There is debate in Japan about whether the country should assume a normal international role. In the USSR and Russia, beginning under Gorbachev and continuing under Yeltsin, there has been argument about the development of a new role for the country in Asia Pacific. In all cases, domestic politics has had a strong bearing on the direction taken by each country, and economic considerations have also played a very important role.

Economic factors have strongly influenced the argument about how the United States should engage itself in Asia Pacific. They have also underpinned the new role developed by the USSR and then Russia in the region. Similarly, Japan's involvement in the region is very much based on an economic rationale, and economics has also become increasingly important to China. At the same time, strategic factors (emphasized particularly by realism) should not be downplayed. Assessments of how one's state relates to the changing configuration of power in the region have been an important consideration for all four powers examined in this book. These assessments can involve military power in a more narrow sense or they can be based more broadly on the various components contributing to a state's power. A broader approach is required when one is assessing whether a power is in decline or becoming stronger.

Similar themes emerge in Part III, which examines the major power relationships in the region. While the general theories can be helpful in suggesting the underlying dynamics of various situations, there is often a need for qualification. The relationships examined have certain features in common, but they also have their own particularities. The features in common are those that derive from the underlying dynamics suggested by the different theories. The particularities, by definition, vary according to the relationship.

In the Japanese-U.S. relationship, they involve the way in which the security and economic facets of the relationship interact. The Sino-U.S. relationship is characterized by the complexity of factors involved, including strategic and economic elements, human rights issues, and domestic politics. The proximity of China and Japan means that the relationship between them is influenced by a long history and cultural orientations, although security and economic factors, as well as domestic politics, are also relevant. This relationship is also influenced by the fact that these two countries cannot retreat from the East Asian region. The relationship between Japan and the USSR and Russia is also influenced by history (but a history briefer in duration than that of China and Japan) and by a sense of cultural distance. One interesting feature of this relationship is the way in which a territorial issue has impeded the development of the more general relationship. Although the Northern Territories or southernmost Kurils might seem small and insignificant to the outsider, they have been vested with a great symbolic significance that makes it difficult to achieve any resolution of the issue. Again, this situation could serve as an illustration of the impact of domestic politics, particularly nationalism.

Part IV of the book examines three important actors in the region with which the major powers have been involved. What emerges in these chapters is the way in which local factors have combined with the objectives of the major powers to determine the direction taken by these different actors. Focusing on the role of the major powers suggests important insights about the international politics of the region, but it does not provide a complete picture. The approaches and relationships of the major powers that are discussed earlier in the book can be further illustrated in these regional situations. At the same time, one must also understand the factors that influence the various regional powers and other parties involved.

In Korea, although history and strategic factors have played an important role, economic factors have increasingly entered the equation. These factors are an important part of the changing relationship between economically dynamic South Korea and economically declining North Korea. In turn, their economic performance has influenced how the major powers relate to the two Koreas and view attempts to resolve the conflict.

Indochina, too, was viewed mainly in terms of strategic considerations by the major powers. The Cambodian conflict was approached from a strategic perspective, but, with the resolution of that conflict, there has been more emphasis on economic considerations not just in Cambodia but throughout Indochina. A good example of this shift is the new role being developed by Vietnam and the way in which that new role has affected Vietnam's relationships with the various major powers.

The number of local powers involved in ASEAN is greater than in Korea or Indochina. Although Indonesia is the key power in Southeast Asia, there are a number of local states adding to the complexity of the situation. Again, strategic considerations have affected the involvement in ASEAN of both the major powers and the local powers. However, economic considerations have become increasingly important, especially in light of the economic success achieved by a number of ASEAN states. The case of the South China Sea is a good illustration of the way in which economic and strategic considerations can interact, affecting both local powers and the major powers (particularly China in this case). Similarly, domestic politics has an important bearing on the way in which this issue and other issues affecting the ASEAN countries are played out.

The general perspectives suggested by realism, liberal institutionalism, and the culturalistic approach do suggest important insights, but they need to be modified in light of the complexities of the various situations examined. There is no one overarching theory to explain satisfactorily the dynamics of post–Cold War international politics in Asia Pacific, but there are useful perspectives available for guidance.

BIBLIOGRAPHY

Ahn, Byung-Joon. "South Korea's New Nordpolitik," *Korea and World Affairs,* vol. 12 no. 4 (Winter 1988), pp. 693–705.

Akaha, Tsuneo. "Japan's Comprehensive Security Policy: A New East Asian Environment," *Asian Survey,* vol. 31 no. 4 (April 1991), pp. 324–340.

―――. "Russia in Asia in 1994: An Emerging East Asian Power," *Asian Survey,* vol. 35 no. 1 (January 1995), pp. 100–110.

Akaha, Tsuneo, and Langdon, Frank, eds. *Japan in the Posthegemonic World.* Boulder, Colo.: Lynne Rienner Publishers, 1993.

Arase, David. "Japan in East Asia," in Tsuneo Akaha and Frank Langdon, eds., *Japan in the Posthegemonic World.* Boulder, Colo.: Lynne Rienner Publishers, 1993, pp. 113–136.

Arbatov, Alexei G. "Russia's Foreign Policy Alternatives," *International Security,* vol. 18 no. 2 (Fall 1993), pp. 5–43.

Armstrong, Charles K. "South Korea's 'Northern Policy,'" *Pacific Review,* vol. 3 no. 1 (1990), pp. 35–45.

Arnold, Walter. "Japan and China," in Robert S. Ozaki and Walter Arnold, eds., *Japan's Foreign Relations: A Global Search for Economic Security.* Boulder, Colo.: Westview Press, 1985, pp. 102–116.

―――. "Political and Economic Influences in Japan's Relations with China Since 1978," *Millennium,* vol. 18 no. 3 (Winter 1989), pp. 415–434.

Asia 1994 Yearbook. Hong Kong: Review Publishing Company, 1994.

Austin, Greg, and Callan, Tim. "Russia: A Terrier at the Feet of Asia's Great Powers," in Gary Klintworth, ed., *Asia-Pacific Security: Less Uncertainty, New Opportunities?* Melbourne: Addison Wesley Longman, 1996, pp. 79–93.

Baker, James A., III. "America in Asia: Emerging Architecture for a Pacific Community," *Foreign Affairs,* vol. 70, no. 5 (1991), pp. 1–18.

Baum, Julian, and do Rosario, Louise. "Taiwan: The Sumo Neighbour," in Nigel Holloway, ed., *Japan in Asia: The Economic Impact on the Region.* Hong Kong: Review Publishing Company, 1991, pp. 52–65.

Beresford, Melanie. "The Political Economy of Dismantling the 'Bureaucratic Centralism and Subsidy System' in Vietnam," in Kevin Hewison, Richard Robison, and Garry Rodan, eds., *Southeast Asia in the 1990s: Authoritarianism, Democracy and Capitalism.* St. Leonards, NSW: Allen and Unwin, 1993, pp. 213–236.

Berry, William E., Jr. *U.S. Bases in the Philippines: The Evolution of the Special Relationship.* Boulder, Colo.: Westview Press, 1989.

Bert, Wayne. "Chinese Policies and U.S. Interests in Southeast Asia," *Asian Survey,* vol. 33 no. 3 (March 1993), pp. 317–332.

―――. "Chinese Policy Toward Democratization Movements: Burma and the Philippines," *Asian Survey,* vol. 30 no. 11 (November 1990), pp. 1066–1083.

Berton, Peter. "Russia and Japan in the Post–Cold War Era," in James C. Hsiung, ed., *Asia Pacific in the New World Politics.* Boulder, Colo.: Lynne Rienner Publishers, 1993, pp. 21–47.

————. "Soviet-Japanese Relations: Perceptions, Goals, Interactions," *Asian Survey,* vol. 26 no. 12 (December 1986), pp. 1259–1283.

Betts, Richard K. "Vietnam's Strategic Predicament," *Survival,* vol. 37 no. 3 (Autumn 1995), pp. 61–81.

Bienen, Henry, ed. *Power, Economics, and Security: The United States and Japan in Focus.* Boulder, Colo.: Westview Press, 1992.

Bresnan, John. *From Dominoes to Dynamos: The Transformation of Southeast Asia.* New York: Council on Foreign Relations Press, 1994.

Bridges, Brian. *Japan and Korea in the 1990s: From Antagonism to Adjustment.* Aldershot, Eng.: Edward Elgar, 1993.

Brock, David. "The Theory and Practice of Japan-Bashing," *National Interest,* no. 17 (Fall 1989), pp. 29–40.

Broinowski, Alison, ed. *ASEAN into the 1990s.* London: Macmillan, 1990.

Brown, Eugene. "The Debate over Japan's Strategic Future: Bilateralism Versus Regionalism," *Asian Survey,* vol. 33 no. 6 (June 1993), pp. 543–559.

Brown, Frederick Z. *Second Chance: The United States and Indochina in the 1990s.* New York: Council on Foreign Relations Press, 1989.

Buszynski, Leszek. *Gorbachev and Southeast Asia.* London: Routledge, 1992.

————. "The Philippines, Asean and the Future of the American Bases," *World Today,* vol. 44 no. 5 (May 1988), pp. 82–85.

————. "Russia and Japan: The Unmaking of a Territorial Settlement," *World Today,* vol. 49 no. 3 (March 1993), pp. 50–54.

————. *Russian Foreign Policy After the Cold War.* Westport, Conn.: Praeger, 1996.

Chen, Qimao. "New Approaches in China's Foreign Policy: The Post–Cold War Era," *Asian Survey,* vol. 33 no. 3 (March 1993), pp. 237–251.

Chufrin, Gennady. "The USSR and Asia in 1991: Domestic Priorities Prevail," *Asian Survey,* vol. 32 no. 1 (January 1992), pp. 11–18.

————. "The USSR and Asia-Pacific in 1990," *Asian Survey,* vol. 31 no. 1 (January 1991), pp. 16–20.

Chung, Chin O. *Pyongyang Between Peking and Moscow: North Korea's Involvement in the Sino-Soviet Dispute, 1958–1975.* Tuscaloosa: University of Alabama Press, 1978.

Clough, Ralph N. *Embattled Korea: The Rivalry for International Support.* Boulder, Colo.: Westview Press, 1987.

Copper, John F. *China Diplomacy: The Washington-Taipei-Beijing Triangle.* Boulder, Colo.: Westview Press, 1992.

Crowe, William J., Jr., and Romberg, Alan D. "Rethinking Security in the Pacific," *Foreign Affairs,* vol. 70 no. 2 (Spring 1991), pp. 123–140.

Delfs, Robert, and do Rosario, Louise. "China: Sense or Sensibility," in Nigel Holloway, ed., *Japan in Asia: The Economic Impact on the Region.* Hong Kong: Review Publishing Company, 1991, pp. 37–51.

Destler, I. M., and Nacht, Michael. "U.S. Policy Toward Japan," in Robert J. Art and Seyom Brown, eds., *U.S. Foreign Policy: The Search for a New Role.* New York: Macmillan Publishing Company, 1993, pp. 289–314.

Direction of Trade Statistics Yearbook 1996. Washington, D.C.: International Monetary Fund 1996.

Dittmer, Lowell. *Sino-Soviet Normalization and Its International Implications, 1945–1990.* Seattle: University of Washington Press, 1992.

Dreyer, June Teufel, ed. *Chinese Defense and Foreign Policy.* New York: Paragon House, 1989.

Drifte, Reinhard. *Japan's Foreign Policy.* Chatham House Papers. London: Routledge, for the Royal Institute of International Affairs, 1990.

Duiker, William J. *China and Vietnam: The Roots of Conflict.* Berkeley: Institute of East Asian Studies, University of California, 1986.

Ellison, Herbert J., ed. *Japan and the Pacific Quadrille: The Major Powers in East Asia.* Boulder, Colo.: Westview Press, 1987.

Elsbree, Willard H., and Hoong, Khong Kim, "Japan and ASEAN," in Robert S. Ozaki and Walter Arnold, eds., *Japan's Foreign Relations: A Global Search for Economic Security.* Boulder, Colo.: Westview Press, 1985, pp. 119–132.

Emmott, Bill. *The Sun Also Sets: The Limits to Japan's Economic Power.* New York: Times Books, Random House, 1989.

Evans, Grant, and Rowley, Kelvin. *Red Brotherhood at War: Vietnam, Cambodia and Laos Since 1975.* London: Verso, 1990.

Faust, John R., and Kornberg, Judith F. *China in World Politics.* Boulder, Colo.: Lynne Rienner Publishers, 1995.

Frost, Frank. *Vietnam's Foreign Relations: Dynamics of Change.* Pacific Strategic Paper 6. Singapore: Institute of Southeast Asian Studies, 1993.

Garver, John W. "China's Push Through the South China Sea: The Interaction of Bureaucratic and National Interests," *China Quarterly,* no. 132 (December 1992), pp. 999–1028.

———. "The Chinese Communist Party and the Collapse of Soviet Communism," *China Quarterly,* no. 133 (March 1993), pp. 1–26.

———. "The 'New Type' of Sino-Soviet Relations," *Asian Survey,* vol. 29 no. 12 (December 1989), pp. 1136–1152.

George, Aurelia. "Japan's Participation in U.N. Peacekeeping Operations: Radical Departure or Predictable Response?" *Asian Survey,* vol. 33 no. 6 (June 1993), pp. 560–575.

Gilks, Anne. *The Breakdown of the Sino-Vietnamese Alliance, 1970–1979.* Berkeley: Institute of Asian Studies, University of California, 1992.

Gill, R. Bates. "China Looks to Thailand: Exporting Arms, Exporting Influence," *Asian Survey,* vol. 31 no. 6 (June 1991), pp. 526–539.

Glaser, Bonnie S. "China's Security Perceptions: Interests and Ambitions," *Asian Survey,* vol. 33 no. 3 (March 1993), pp. 252–271.

Godwin, Paul H. B. "Chinese Military Strategy Revised: Local and Limited War," *Annals of the American Academy of Political and Social Science,* vol. 519 (January 1992), pp. 191–201.

Goldstein, Carl, and Rowley, Anthony. "Hongkong: Shogun Wedding," in Nigel Holloway, ed., *Japan in Asia: The Economic Impact on the Region.* Hong Kong: Review Publishing Company, 1991, pp. 66–79.

Goldstein, Steven M. "Diplomacy Amid Protest: The Sino-Soviet Summit," *Problems of Communism,* vol. 38 (September–October 1989), pp. 49–71.

Goodman, Allan E. "Vietnam's Post–Cold War Diplomacy and the U.S. Response," *Asian Survey,* vol. 33 no. 8 (August 1993), pp. 832–847.

Gordon, Bernard K. "Japan: Searching Once Again," in James C. Hsiung, ed., *Asia Pacific in the New World Politics.* Boulder, Colo.: Lynne Rienner Publishers, 1993, pp. 49–70.

Greene, Fred, ed. *The Philippine Bases: Negotiating for the Future. American and Philippine Perspectives.* New York: Council on Foreign Relations, 1988.

Haas, E. B. "The Balance of Power: Prescription, Concept or Propaganda?" *World Politics,* vol. 5 no. 4 (July 1953), pp. 442–477.

Haas, Michael. *Cambodia, Pol Pot and the United States: The Faustian Pact.* New York: Praeger, 1991.

Hakjoon, Kim. "China's Korea Policy Since the Tiananmen Square Incident," in Frank J. Macchiarola and Robert B. Oxnam, eds., *The China Challenge: American Policies in East Asia, Proceedings of the Academy of Political Science,* vol. 38 no. 2 (1991), pp. 107–114.

Hao, Jia, and Qubing, Zhuang, "China's Policy Toward the Korean Peninsula," *Asian Survey,* vol. 32 no. 12 (December 1992), pp. 1137–1156.

Harding, Harry, "Asia Policy to the Brink," *Foreign Policy,* no. 96 (Fall 1994), pp. 57–74.

———. "China's American Dilemma," *Annals of the American Academy of Political and Social Science,* vol. 519 (January 1992), pp. 12–25.

———. *A Fragile Relationship: The United States and China Since 1972.* Washington, D.C.: The Brookings Institution, 1992.

Harris, Lillian Craig. "Xinjiang, Central Asia and the Implications for China's Policy in the Islamic World," *China Quarterly,* no. 133 (March 1993), pp. 111–129.

Harrison, Selig S., and Prestowitz, Clyde V., Jr. "Pacific Agenda: Defense or Economics?" *Foreign Policy,* no. 79 (Summer 1990), pp. 56–76.

Hasegawa, Tsuyoshi. "Japan," in Ramesh Thakur and Carlyle A. Thayer, eds., *Reshaping Regional Relations: Asia-Pacific and the Former Soviet Union.* Boulder, Colo.: Westview Press, 1993, pp. 101–123.

Hill, Hal. "The Economy," in Hal Hill, ed., *Indonesia's New Order: The Dynamics of Socio-economic Transformation.* St. Leonards, NSW: Allen and Unwin, 1994, pp. 54–122.

———. *The Indonesian Economy Since 1966: Southeast Asia's Emerging Giant.* Cambridge: Cambridge University Press, 1996.

Holland, Harrison M. *Japan Challenges America: Managing an Alliance in Crisis.* Boulder, Colo.: Westview Press, 1992.

Holloway, Nigel, ed. *Japan in Asia: The Economic Impact on the Region.* Hong Kong: Review Publishing Company, 1991.

Holloway, Nigel, and Rowley, Anthony. "Towards a Yen Bloc," in Nigel Holloway, ed., *Japan in Asia: The Economic Impact on the Region.* Hong Kong: Review Publishing Company, 1991, pp. 185–201.

Hoon, Shim Jae, and Clifford, Mark, "South Korea: So Near, Yet So Far," in Nigel Holloway, ed., *Japan in Asia: The Economic Impact on the Region.* Hong Kong: Review Publishing Company, 1991, pp. 21–36.

Hoong, Khong Kim. "Japan and the Problem of Kampuchea," *Contemporary Southeast Asia,* vol. 11 no. 3 (December 1989), pp. 313–331.

Hsiung, James C., ed. *Asia Pacific in the New World Politics.* Boulder, Colo.: Lynne Rienner Publishers, 1993.

———. "China in the Postnuclear World," in James C. Hsiung, ed., *Asia Pacific in the New World Politics.* Boulder, Colo.: Lynne Rienner Publishers, 1990, pp. 71–92.

Huntington, Samuel P. "America's Changing Strategic Interests," *Survival,* vol. 33 no. 1 (January/February 1991), pp. 3–17.

———. "The Clash of Civilizations," *Foreign Affairs,* vol. 72 no. 3 (Summer 1993), pp. 22–49.

———. *The Clash of Civilizations and the Remaking of World Order.* New York: Simon and Schuster, 1996.

Ijiri, Hidenori. "Sino-Japanese Controversy Since the 1972 Diplomatic Normalization," *China Quarterly,* no. 124 (December 1990), pp. 639–661.

Indochina Policy Forum. *Recommendations for the New Administration on United States Policy Toward Indochina.* Queenstown, Md.: The Aspen Institute, 1988.

Iriye, Akira. "Chinese-Japanese Relations, 1945–90," *China Quarterly,* no. 124 (December 1990), pp. 624–638.

Ishihara, Shintaro. *The Japan that Can Say No.* New York: Simon and Schuster, 1991.

Izumi, Hajime, and Kohari, Susumu. "Sino–South Korean Relations Under the Roh Administration," *China Newsletter,* no. 91 (March–April 1991), pp. 16–20.

Johnson, Chalmers. "History Restarted: Japanese-American Relations at the End of the Century," in Richard Higgott, Richard Leaver, and John Ravenhill, eds., *Pacific Economic Relations in the 1990s: Cooperation or Conflict?* St. Leonards, NSW: Allen and Unwin, 1993, pp. 39–61.

———. "Japan in Search of a 'Normal' Role," *Daedalus,* vol. 121 no. 4 (Fall 1992), pp. 1–33.

———. "Japanese-Chinese Relations, 1952–1982," in Herbert J. Ellison, ed., *Japan and the Pacific Quadrille: The Major Powers in East Asia.* Boulder, Colo.: Westview Press, 1987, pp. 107–134.

———. "Japanese-Soviet Relations in the Early Gorbachev Era," *Asian Survey,* vol. 27 no. 11 (November 1987), pp. 1145–1160.

Joo, Seung-Ho. "Russian Policy on Korean Unification in the Post–Cold War Era," *Pacific Affairs,* vol. 69 no. 1 (Spring 1996), pp. 32–48.

Jun, Onozowa. "Japan and Malaysia: The EAEC Test of Commitment," *Japan Quarterly,* vol. 40 no. 3 (July–September 1993), pp. 277–282.

Kaifu, Toshiki. "Japan's Vision," *Foreign Policy,* no. 80 (Fall 1990), pp. 28–39.

Kallgren, Joyce K., Sopiee, Noordin, and Djiwandono, Soedjati, eds. *ASEAN and China: An Evolving Relationship.* Berkeley: Institute of East Asian Studies, University of California, 1988.

Kennedy, Paul. *The Rise and Fall of the Great Powers: Economic Change and Military Conflict from 1500 to 2000.* London: Unwin Hyman, 1988.

Keohane, Robert O., and Nye, Joseph S. *Power and Interdependence,* 2d ed. Glenview, Ill.: Scott, Foresman and Company, 1989.

Kesavan, K. V. "Japan and the Tiananmen Square Incident: Aspects of the Bilateral Relationship," *Asian Survey,* vol. 30 no. 7 (July 1990), pp. 669–681.

Khamchoo, Chaiwat. "Japan's Role in Southeast Asian Security: 'Plus ça change . . . ,'" *Pacific Affairs,* vol. 64 no. 1 (Spring 1991), pp. 7–22.

Kihl, Young Whan, ed. *Korea and the World: Beyond the Cold War.* Boulder, Colo.: Westview Press, 1994.

———. "The Politics of U.S.-Korean Economic Relations," in Ilpyong J. Kim, ed., *Korean Challenges and American Policy.* New York: Paragon House, for the Washington Institute, 1991, pp. 215–231.

Kim, Hong Nack. "Japan and North Korea: Normalization Talks Between Pyongyang and Tokyo," in Young Whan Kihl, ed., *Korea and the World: Beyond the Cold War.* Boulder, Colo.: Westview Press, 1994, pp. 111–129.

———. "Japan's Policy Toward the Korean Peninsula Since 1965," in Tae-Hwan Kwak, ed., *The Two Koreas in World Politics.* Seoul: Institute for Far Eastern Studies, Kyungnam University, 1983, pp. 305–330.

———. "The Normalization of North Korean–Japanese Diplomatic Relations: Problems and Prospects," *Korea and World Affairs,* vol. 14 no. 4 (Winter 1990), pp. 649–670.

Kim, Ilpyong J. "The Soviet Union/Russia and Korea: Dynamics of 'New Thinking,'" in Young Whan Kihl, ed., *Korea and the World: Beyond the Cold War.* Boulder, Colo.: Westview Press, 1994, pp. 83–95.

Kim, Samuel S. "Peking's Foreign Policy in the Shadows of Tiananmen: The Challenge of Legitimation," in Bi-jaw Lin, ed., *The Aftermath of the 1989*

Tiananmen Crisis in Mainland China. Boulder, Colo.: Westview Press, 1992, pp. 389–416.

Kivimaki, Timo. "Strength of Weakness: American-Indonesian Hegemonic Bargaining," *Journal of Peace Research,* vol. 30 no. 4 (November 1993), pp. 391–408.

Klein, Donald. "China and ASEAN," in June Teufel Dreyer, ed., *Chinese Defense and Foreign Policy.* New York: Paragon House, 1989, pp. 215–237.

Klintworth, Gary, ed. *Asia-Pacific Security: Less Uncertainty, New Opportunities?* Melbourne: Addison Wesley Longman, 1996.

Kreisberg, Paul H. "The U.S. and Asia in 1990," *Asian Survey,* vol. 31 no. 1 (January 1991), pp. 1–13.

Langdon, Frank C., and Ross, Douglas A., eds. *Superpower Maritime Strategy in the Pacific.* London: Routledge, 1990.

Lasater, Martin L. *Policy in Evolution: The U.S. Role in China's Reunification.* Boulder, Colo.: Westview Press, 1989.

Lee, Chae-Jin. "China's Policy Toward North Korea: Changing Relations in the 1980s," in Robert A. Scalapino and Hongkoo Lee, eds., *North Korea in a Regional and Global Context.* Berkeley: Center for Korean Studies, Institute of East Asian Studies, University of California, 1986, pp. 190–225.

Lee, Chong-Sik. *Japan and Korea: The Political Dimension.* Stanford, Calif.: Hoover Institution Press, 1985.

Lee, Hong Yung. "China and the Two Koreas: New Emerging Triangle," in Young Whan Kihl, ed., *Korea and the World: Beyond the Cold War.* Boulder, Colo.: Westview Press, 1994, pp. 97–110.

Legvold, Robert. "Russia and the Strategic Quadrangle," in Michael Mandelbaum, ed., *The Strategic Quadrangle: Russia, China, Japan and the United States in East Asia.* New York: Council on Foreign Relations Press, 1994.

Leifer, Michael. "Chinese Economic Reform and Security Policy: The South China Sea Connection," *Survival,* vol. 37 no. 2 (Summer 1995), pp. 44–59.

Lepage, Françoise O. "Sino-American Relations Post-Tiananmen," *Pacific Review,* vol. 4 no. 1 (1991), pp. 63–67.

Levin, Norman D. "Evolving Chinese and Soviet Policies Toward the Korean Peninsula," in June Teufel Dreyer, ed., *Chinese Defense and Foreign Policy.* New York: Paragon House, 1989, pp. 187–213.

Liu, Hong. "The Sino–South Korean Normalization: A Triangular Explanation," *Asian Survey,* vol. 33 no. 11 (November 1993), pp. 1083–1094.

Lo, Chi-kin. *China's Policy Towards Territorial Disputes: The Case of the South China Sea Islands.* London: Routledge, 1989.

Long, Simon. "China and Kampuchea: Political Football on the Killing Fields," *Pacific Review,* vol. 2 no. 2 (1992), pp. 151–157.

Lord, Winston. "China and America: Beyond the Big Chill," *Foreign Affairs,* vol. 68 no. 4 (Fall 1989), pp. 1–26.

———. "A New Pacific Community: Ten Goals for American Policy," *Foreign Policy Bulletin,* vol. 3 no. 6 (May/June 1993), pp. 49–53.

Lowry, Bob. "Indonesia," in Gary Klintworth, ed., *Asia-Pacific Security: Less Uncertainty, New Opportunities?* Melbourne: Addison Wesley Longman, 1996, pp. 94–108.

Lukin, Alexander. "The Initial Soviet Reaction to the Events in China in 1989 and the Prospects for Sino-Soviet Relations," *China Quarterly,* no. 125 (March 1991), pp. 119–136.

Mack, Andrew, and O'Hare, Martin. "Moscow-Tokyo and the Northern Territories Dispute," *Asian Survey,* vol. 30 no. 4 (April 1990), pp. 380–394.

Malik, J. Mohan. *The Gulf War: Australia's Role and Asian-Pacific Responses.* Canberra Papers on Strategy and Defence No. 90. Canberra: Strategic and Defence Studies Centre, Research School of Pacific Studies, Australian National University, 1992.

Mandelbaum, Michael, ed. *The Strategic Quadrangle: Russia, China, Japan and the United States in East Asia.* New York: Council on Foreign Relations Press, 1994.

Manning, Robert A. "Burdens of the Past, Dilemmas of the Future: Sino-Japanese Relations in the Emerging International System," *Washington Quarterly,* vol. 17 no. 1 (Winter 1994), pp. 45–58.

Marshall, Patrick G. "The U.S. and Japan," *CQ Researcher,* 31 May 1991, pp. 327–347.

Martin, Robert. "Security Relations: A U.S. View," in Robert A. Scalapino and Hongkoo Lee, eds., *Korea-U.S. Relations: The Politics of Trade and Security.* Berkeley: Institute of East Asian Studies, University of California, 1988, pp. 185–200.

McGregor, Charles. "China, Vietnam, and the Cambodian Conflict: Beijing's End Game Strategy," *Asian Survey,* vol. 30 no. 3 (May 1990), pp. 266–283.

McLaurin, Ronald D., and Moon, Chung-in. *The United States and the Defense of the Pacific.* Boulder, Colo.: Westview Press, 1989.

Mendl, Wolf. "Stuck in a Mould: The Relationship Between Japan and the Soviet Union," *Millennium,* vol. 18 no. 3 (Winter 1989), pp. 455–478.

Menon, Rajan. "Gorbachev's Japan Policy," *Survival,* vol. 33 no. 2 (March/April 1991), pp. 158–172.

Meyer, Peggy Falkenheim. "Gorbachev and Post-Gorbachev Policy Toward the Korean Peninsula," *Asian Survey,* vol. 32 no. 8 (August 1992), pp. 759–760.

The Military Balance 1990–1991. London: Brassey's, for the International Institute for Strategic Studies, 1990.

The Military Balance 1993–1994. London: Brassey's, for the International Institute for Strategic Studies, 1993.

The Military Balance 1994–1995. London: Brassey's, for the International Institute for Strategic Studies, 1994.

The Military Balance 1996/97. London: Oxford University Press, for the International Institute for Strategic Studies, 1996.

Mochizuki, Mike M. "To Change or to Contain: Dilemmas of American Policy Toward Japan," in Kenneth A. Oye, Robert J. Lieber, and Donald Rothchild, eds., *Eagle in a New World: American Grand Strategy in the Post–Cold War Era.* New York: HarperCollins, 1992, pp. 335–359.

Morgenthau, Hans J., and Thompson, Kenneth W. *Politics Among Nations: The Struggle for Power and Peace,* 6th ed. New York: Alfred A. Knopf, 1985.

Morrison, Charles E. "US Security Relations with Southeast Asia: Possibilities and Prospects for the Clinton Administration," *Australian Journal of International Affairs,* vol. 47 no. 2 (November 1993), pp. 239–249.

Nam, Joo-Hong. *America's Commitment to South Korea: The First Decade of the Nixon Doctrine.* Cambridge: Cambridge University Press, 1986.

Nelsen, Harvey W. *Power and Insecurity: Beijing, Moscow, and Washington, 1949–1988.* Boulder, Colo.: Lynne Rienner Publishers, 1989.

Newby, Laura. *Sino-Japanese Relations: China's Perspective.* London: Routledge, for the Royal Institute of International Affairs, 1988.

Nguyen, Hung P. "Russia and China: The Genesis of an Eastern Rapallo," *Asian Survey,* vol. 33 no. 3 (March 1993), pp. 285–301.

Nimmo, William F. *Japan and Russia: A Reevaluation in the Post-Soviet Era.* Westport, Conn.: Greenwood Press, 1994.

Nish, Ian. "The United States in East Asia: Japan's Perspective," in Michael Leifer, ed., *The Balance of Power in East Asia.* Basingstoke: Macmillan, 1986, pp. 30–43.

Nye, Joseph S., Jr. "East Asian Security: The Case for Deep Engagement," *Foreign Affairs,* vol. 74 no. 4 (July/August 1995), pp. 90–102.

Olsen, Edward A. "Japan and Korea," in Robert S. Ozaki and Walter Arnold, eds., *Japan's Foreign Relations: A Global Search for Economic Security.* Boulder, Colo.: Westview Press, 1985, pp. 169–186.

———. *U.S. Policy and the Two Koreas.* San Francisco: World Affairs Council of Northern California. Boulder, Colo.: Westview Press, 1988.

Opitz, Peter J. "Changing Alliances: Chinese and Soviet Policy Toward the Korean Peninsula," *Aussenpolitik* (English edition), vol. 41 no. 3 (1990), pp. 247–257.

Ozaki, Robert S., and Arnold, Walter, eds. *Japan's Foreign Relations: A Global Search for Economic Security.* Boulder, Colo.: Westview Press, 1985.

Pacific Russia: Risks and Rewards. Canberra: East Asia Analytical Unit, Department of Foreign Affairs and Trade, 1996.

Piao, Lin. "Long Live the Victory of People's War!" in K. Fan, ed., *Mao Tse-tung and Lin Piao: Post-Revolutionary Writings.* Garden City, N.Y.: Anchor Books, 1972, pp. 357–412.

Ping, Lee Poh. "ASEAN and the Japanese Role in Southeast Asia," in Alison Broinowski, ed., *ASEAN into the 1990s.* London: Macmillan, 1990, pp. 162–183.

Pollack, Jonathan D. "The Sino-Japanese Relationship and East Asian Security: Patterns and Implications," *China Quarterly,* no. 124 (December 1990), pp. 714–729.

Polomka, Peter. "Towards a 'Pacific House,'" *Survival,* vol. 33 no. 2 (March/April 1991), pp. 173–182.

Prestowitz, Clyde V., Jr. *Trading Places: How We Allowed Japan to Take the Lead.* New York: Basic Books, 1988.

Purrington, Courtney. "Tokyo's Policy Responses During the Gulf War and the Impact of the 'Iraqi Shock' on Japan," *Pacific Affairs,* vol. 65 no. 2 (Summer 1992), pp. 161–181.

Purrington, Courtney, and A. K. "Tokyo's Policy Responses During the Gulf Crisis," *Asian Survey,* vol. 31 no. 4 (April 1991), pp. 307–323.

Pye, Lucian W. *Asian Power and Politics: The Cultural Dimensions of Politics.* Cambridge: The Belknap Press of Harvard University Press, 1985.

Quansheng, Zhao. "Domestic Factors of Chinese Foreign Policy: From Vertical to Horizontal Authoritarianism," *Annals of the American Academy of Political and Social Science,* vol. 519 (January 1992), pp. 158–175.

Richburg, Keith. "Back to Vietnam," *Foreign Affairs,* vol. 70 no. 4 (Fall 1991), pp. 111–131.

Rix, Alan. "ASEAN and Japan: More than Economics," in Alison Broinowski, ed., *Understanding ASEAN.* London: Macmillan, 1982, pp. 169–195.

Ross, Robert S. "China and Post-Cambodia Southeast Asia: Coping with Success," *Annals of the American Academy of Political and Social Science,* vol. 519 (January 1992), pp. 52–66.

———. *The Indochina Tangle: China's Vietnam Policy 1975–1979.* New York: Columbia University Press, 1988.

———. "National Security, Human Rights, and Domestic Politics: The Bush Administration and China," in Kenneth A. Oye, Robert J. Lieber, and Donald

Rothchild, eds., *Eagle in a New World: American Grand Strategy in the Post–Cold War Era*. New York: HarperCollins, 1992, pp. 281–313.

———. "Succession Politics and Post-Mao Foreign Policy," in June Teufel Dreyer, ed., *Chinese Defense and Foreign Policy*. New York: Paragon House, 1988, pp. 27–62.

———. "U.S. Policy Toward China," in Robert J. Art and Seyom Brown, eds., *U.S. Foreign Policy: The Search for a New Role*. New York: Macmillan, 1993, pp. 338–357.

Rothacher, Albrecht. "The Formulation of Japanese Foreign Policy," *Millennium*, vol. 10 no. 11 (1989), pp. 1–13.

Rowley, Anthony, and do Rosario, Louise. "Japan's View of Asia: Empire of the Sun," in Nigel Holloway, ed., *Japan in Asia: The Economic Impact on the Region*. Hong Kong: Review Publishing Company, 1991, pp. 7–20.

Rozman, Gilbert. *Japan's Response to the Gorbachev Era, 1985–1991: A Rising Superpower Views a Declining One*. Princeton, N.J.: Princeton University Press, 1992.

Rubinstein, Alvin. "Russia and North Korea: The End of an Alliance?" *Korea and World Affairs*, vol. 18 (Fall 1994), pp. 486–508.

Samuels, Marwyn S. *Contest for the South China Sea*. New York: Methuen, 1982.

Sandhu, K. S., et al., comps. *The ASEAN Reader*. Singapore: Institute of Southeast Asian Studies, 1992.

Scalapino, Robert A. "Perspectives on Modern Japanese Foreign Policy," in Robert A. Scalapino, ed., *The Foreign Policy of Modern Japan*. Berkeley: University of California Press, 1977, pp. 391–412.

Schwarz, Adam, and Vatikiotis, Michael. "Indonesia: Price of Security," in Nigel Holloway, ed., *Japan in Asia: The Economic Impact on the Region*. Hong Kong: Review Publishing Company, 1991, pp. 94–109.

Segal, Gerald. "China and the Disintegration of the Soviet Union," *Asian Survey*, vol. 32 no. 9 (September 1992), pp. 848–868.

———. "China Changes Shape: Regionalism and Foreign Policy," *Adelphi Papers*, no. 287 (1994).

———. "The Coming Confrontation Between China and Japan?" *World Policy Journal*, vol. 10 no. 2 (1993), pp. 27–32.

———. *The Fate of Hong Kong*. London: Simon and Schuster, 1993.

———. "Russia as an Asian-Pacific Power," in Ramesh Thakur and Carlyle Thayer, eds., *Reshaping Regional Relations: Asia-Pacific and the Former Soviet Union*. Boulder, Colo.: Westview Press, 1993, pp. 65–83.

———. "Sino-Soviet Relations," in Gerald Segal, ed., *Chinese Politics and Foreign Policy Reform*. London: Kegan Paul International, for the Royal Institute of International Affairs, 1990, pp. 161–179.

———. *The Soviet Union and the Pacific*. London: Unwin Hyman, 1990.

Segal, Gerald, ed. *Chinese Politics and Foreign Policy Reform*. London: Kegan Paul International, for the Royal Institute of International Affairs, 1990.

Shambaugh, David L. *Beautiful Imperialist: China Perceives America, 1972–1990*. Boulder, Colo.: Westview Press, 1992.

———. "Elite Politics and Perceptions," in Gerald Segal, ed., *Chinese Politics and Foreign Policy Reform*. London: Kegan Paul International, for the Royal Institute of International Affairs, 1990, pp. 100–114.

———. "Growing Strong: China's Challenge to Asian Security," *Survival*, vol. 36 no. 2 (Summer 1994), pp. 43–59.

Shinohara, Miyohei. "Japan as a World Economic Power," *Annals of the American Academy of Political and Social Science*, vol. 513 (January 1991), pp. 12–24.

Shiraishi, Masaya. *Japanese Relations with Vietnam: 1951–1987.* Ithaca, N.Y.: Southeast Asia Program, Cornell University, 1990.

Simon, Sheldon W. "The Clinton Presidency and Asian Security: Toward Multilateralism," *Australian Journal of International Affairs,* vol. 47 no. 2 (October 1993), pp. 250–262.

———. "The Great Powers and Southeast Asia: Cautious Minuet or Dangerous Tango?" *Asian Survey,* vol. 25 no. 9 (September 1985), pp. 918–942.

———. "U.S. Strategy and Southeast Asian Security: Issues of Compatibility," *Contemporary Southeast Asia,* vol. 14 no. 4 (March 1993), pp. 301–313.

Solomon, Richard H. "Political Culture and Diplomacy in the Twenty-first Century," in Richard J. Samuels and Myron Weiner, eds., *The Political Culture of Foreign Area and International Studies: Essays in Honor of Lucian W. Pye.* Washington, D.C.: Brassey's (U.S.), Inc., 1992, pp. 141–154.

Stephan, John J. "Japanese-Soviet Relations: Patterns and Prospects," in Herbert J. Ellison, ed., *Japan and the Pacific Quadrille: The Major Powers in East Asia.* Boulder, Colo.: Westview Press, 1987, pp. 135–159.

———. *The Kuril Islands: Russo-Japanese Frontier in the Pacific.* Oxford: Clarendon Press, 1974.

———. *The Russian Far East: A History.* Stanford, Calif.: Stanford University Press, 1994.

Stockwin, J. A. A. "Japan and the Soviet Union," in Robert S. Ozaki and Walter Arnold, eds., *Japan's Foreign Relations: A Global Search for Economic Security.* Boulder, Colo.: Westview Press, 1985, pp. 67–84.

A Strategic Framework for the Asian Pacific Rim: Report to Congress 1992. Washington, D.C.: Department of Defense, 1992.

Strategic Survey 1995–1996. London: Oxford University Press, for the International Institute for Strategic Studies, 1996.

Sudo, Sueo. "From Fukuda to Takeshita: A Decade of Japan-ASEAN Relations," *Contemporary Southeast Asia,* vol. 10 no. 2 (September 1988), pp. 119–143.

———. *The Fukuda Doctrine and ASEAN: New Dimensions in Japanese Foreign Policy.* Singapore: Institute of Southeast Asian Studies, 1992.

———. "Japan and the Security of Southeast Asia," *Pacific Review,* vol. 4 no. 4 (1991), pp. 333–344.

———. "Japan-ASEAN Relations: New Dimensions in Japanese Foreign Policy," *Asian Survey,* vol. 28 no. 5 (May 1988), pp. 509–525.

———. *Southeast Asia in Japanese Security Policy,* Pacific Strategic Paper 3. Singapore: Institute of Southeast Asian Studies, 1991.

Suryadinata, Leo. "Indonesia-China Relations: A Recent Breakthrough," *Asian Survey,* vol. 30 no. 7 (July 1990), pp. 682–696.

———. *Indonesia's Foreign Policy Under Suharto: Aspiring to International Leadership.* Singapore: Times Academic Press, 1996.

Sutter, Robert G. *East Asia and the Pacific: Challenges for U.S. Policy.* Boulder, Colo.: Westview Press, 1992.

Tamamoto, Masaru. "Japan's Search for a World Role," *World Policy Journal,* vol. 7 (1990), pp. 493–520.

Tan, Qingshan. "U.S.-China Nuclear Cooperation Agreement: China's Nonproliferation Policy," *Asian Survey,* vol. 29 no. 9 (September 1989), pp. 870–882.

Tanaka, Zen'ichiro. "The Transformation of Domestic Politics and Its Implications for Foreign Policy in Contemporary Japan," in Robert A. Scalapino et al., eds., *Asia and the Major Powers: Domestic Politics and Foreign Policy.* Berkeley: Institute of East Asian Studies, University of California, 1988, pp. 81–109.

Tasker, Rodney, and Handley, Paul. "Thailand: Money Talks," in Nigel Holloway, ed., *Japan in Asia: The Economic Impact on the Region.* Hong Kong: Review Publishing Company, 1991, pp. 136–153.

Tetsuya, Umemoto. "Comprehensive Security and the Evolution of the Japanese Security Posture," in Robert A. Scalapino, Seizaburo Sato, Jusuf Wanandi, and Sung-joo Han, eds., *Asian Security Issues: Regional and Global.* Berkeley: Institute of East Asian Studies, University of California, 1988, pp. 28–49.

"Text of Speech by Mikhail Gorbachev in Vladivostok, 28 July 1986," in Ramesh Thakur and Carlyle A. Thayer, eds., *The Soviet Union as an Asian Pacific Power: Implications of Gorbachev's 1986 Vladivostok Initiative.* Boulder, Colo.: Westview Press, 1987, pp. 201–227.

Thakur, Ramesh, and Thayer, Carlyle A., eds. *Reshaping Regional Relations: Asia-Pacific and the Former Soviet Union.* Boulder, Colo.: Westview Press, 1993.

———. *The Soviet Union as an Asian Pacific Power: Implications of Gorbachev's 1986 Vladivostok Initiative.* Boulder, Colo.: Westview Press, 1987.

Thambipillai, Pushpa. "Southeast Asia," in Ramesh Thakur and Carlyle A. Thayer, eds., *Reshaping Regional Relations: Asia-Pacific and the Former Soviet Union.* Boulder, Colo.: Westview Press, 1993, pp. 223–238.

Thayer, Carlyle A. "Beyond Indochina," *Adelphi Papers,* no. 297 (1995).

———. "Indochina," in Ramesh Thakur and Carlyle A. Thayer, eds., *Reshaping Regional Relations: Asia-Pacific and the Former Soviet Union.* Boulder, Colo.: Westview Press, 1993, pp. 201–222.

———. "Russian Policy Toward Vietnam," in Peter Shearman, ed., *Russian Foreign Policy Since 1990.* Boulder, Colo.: Westview Press, 1995, pp. 202–223.

———. "Sino-Vietnamese Relations: The Interplay of Ideology and National Interest," *Asian Survey,* vol. 34 no. 6 (June 1994), pp. 513–528.

———. "Vietnam: Coping with China," *Southeast Asian Affairs 1994,* pp. 351–367.

Thomas, Bradford L. "The Spratly Islands Imbroglio: A Tangled Web of Conflict," Working Paper No. 74. Canberra: Peace Research Centre, Australian National University, 1990.

Thurow, Lester. *Head to Head: The Coming Economic Battle Among Japan, Europe and America.* New York: William Morrow, 1992.

Tiglao, Rigoberto. "The Philippines: Uncle Nippon," in Nigel Holloway, ed., *Japan in Asia: The Economic Impact on the Region.* Hong Kong: Review Publishing Company, 1991, pp. 80–93.

To, Lee Lai. "ASEAN-PRC Political and Security Cooperation: Problems, Proposals, and Prospects," *Asian Survey,* vol. 33 no. 11 (November 1993), pp. 1095–1104.

Tomoda, Seki. "Japan's Search for a Political Role in Asia: The Cambodian Peace Settlement," *Japan Review of International Affairs,* vol. 6 no. 1 (Spring 1992), pp. 43–60.

Tow, William T. *Encountering the Dominant Player: U.S. Extended Deterrence Strategy in the Asia-Pacific.* New York: Columbia University Press, 1991.

Tsuruoka, Doug. "Malaysia: Look East—and Up," in Nigel Holloway, ed., *Japan in Asia: The Economic Impact on the Region.* Hong Kong: Review Publishing Company, 1991, pp. 119–135.

Tyabji, Amina. "The Six ASEAN Economies: 1980–88," in Alison Broinowski, ed., *ASEAN into the 1990s.* London: Macmillan, 1990, pp. 32–57.

United States Security Strategy for the East Asia-Pacific Region. Washington, D.C.: Department of Defense, 1995.

Valencia, Mark J. "China and the South China Sea Disputes," *Adelphi Papers,* no. 298 (1995).

Valencia, Mark J., ed. *The Russian Far East in Transition: Opportunities for Regional Economic Cooperation.* Boulder, Colo.: Westview Press, 1995.

Varon, Amnon. "The Spratly Islands Embroilment: A Test Case in Post–Cold War Southeast Asia," *La Trobe Politics Working Paper,* no. 3 (1994).

Walsh, J. Richard, "China and the New Geopolitics of Central Asia," *Asian Survey,* vol. 33 no. 3 (March 1993), pp. 272–284.

Waltz, Kenneth. *Theory of International Politics.* Reading, Mass.: Addison-Wesley Publishing Company, 1979.

Wang, Jianwei, and Lin, Zhimin. "Chinese Perceptions in the Post–Cold War Era: Three Images of the United States," *Asian Survey,* vol. 32 no. 10 (October 1992), pp. 902–917.

Wang, Qingxin Ken. "Toward Political Partnership: Japan's China Policy," *Pacific Review,* vol. 7 no. 2 (1994), pp. 171–182.

Weatherbee, Donald E. "Asean and Evolving Patterns of Regionalism in Southeast Asia," *Asian Journal of Political Science,* vol. 1 no. 1 (June 1993), pp. 29–54.

Whiting, Allen S. "China and Japan: Politics Versus Economics," *Annals of the American Academy of Political and Social Science,* vol. 519 (January 1992), pp. 39–51.

———. *China Eyes Japan.* Berkeley: University of California Press, 1989.

Whiting, Allen S., and Jianfei, Xin. "Sino-Japanese Relations: Pragmatism and Passion," *World Policy Journal,* vol. 8 (1990–1991), pp. 107–135.

Williams, Michael C. "New Soviet Policy Toward Southeast Asia: Reorientation and Change," *Asian Survey,* vol. 31 no. 4 (April 1991), pp. 364–377.

———. "North Korea: Tilting Towards Moscow?" *World Today,* vol. 40 no. 10 (October 1984), pp. 398–405.

Woon, Eden Y. "Chinese Arms Sales and U.S.-China Military Relations," *Asian Survey,* vol. 29 no. 6 (June 1989), pp. 601–618.

Xinghao, Ding. "Managing Sino-American Relations in a Changing World," *Asian Survey,* vol. 31 no. 12 (December 1991), pp. 1155–1169.

Yahuda, Michael. "Sino-American Relations," in Gerald Segal, ed., *Chinese Politics and Foreign Policy Reform.* London: Kegan Paul International, for the Royal Institute of International Affairs, 1990, pp. 180–194.

Yoshitaka, Sasaki. "Japan's Undue International Contribution," *Japan Quarterly,* vol. 40 no. 3 (July–September 1993), pp. 259–265.

Yu, Bin. "Sino-Russian Military Relations: Implications for Asian-Pacific Security," *Asian Survey,* vol. 33 no. 3 (March 1993), pp. 302–316.

———. "The Study of Chinese Foreign Policy: Problems and Prospects," *World Politics,* vol. 46 no. 2 (January 1994), pp. 235–261.

Zhan, Jun. *Ending the Chinese Civil War: Power, Commerce, and Conciliation Between Beijing and Taipei.* New York: St. Martin's Press, 1993.

Zhao, Quansheng. *Japanese Policymaking: The Politics Behind Politics: Informal Mechanisms and the Making of China Policy.* Westport, Conn.: Praeger, 1993.

Ziegler, Charles E. *Foreign Policy and East Asia: Learning and Adaptation in the Gorbachev Era.* Cambridge: Cambridge University Press, 1993.

———. "Russia in the Asia-Pacific: A Major Power or Minor Participant?" *Asian Survey,* vol. 34 no. 6 (June 1994), pp. 529–543.

INDEX

AFTA. *See* ASEAN Free Trade Area
Akihito, Emperor, 103, 221
Albright, Madeleine, 24
APEC. *See* Asia-Pacific Economic
  Cooperation
ASEAN. *See* Association of Southeast Asian
  Nations
ASEAN Free Trade Area (AFTA), 202
ASEAN Regional Forum, 11, 52
Asia-Pacific Economic Cooperation (APEC),
  7, 11, 23, 51; East Asian Economic
  Caucus proposal and, 222
Aspin, Les, 65
Association of Southeast Asian Nations
  (ASEAN): Cambodian invasion and,
  174–175, 176, 182, 187, 188; CIS
  (Commonwealth of Independent States)
  and, 52; economic agenda, 201, 202; for-
  mation and original member countries of,
  199–201; political coherence of,
  201–202; Russian Federation relations
  with, 52, 226; South China Sea dispute
  and, 202, 214–218; Thailand and, 188;
  U.S. foreign policy and, 205–210;
  Vietnam entry into, 180–181. *See also*
  Japanese-ASEAN relations; Sino-
  ASEAN relations; Soviet-ASEAN relations

Baker, James, 21–22, 39, 49, 87, 141–142,
  174, 175, 176, 177, 178, 206
Berger, Samuel, 24
Brezhnev, Leonid, 110, 125
Brunei, Chinese relations with, 213,
  217
Burma, Soviet relations with, 224
Bush administration, 12, 18; Asia Pacific
  policy, 21–22; Beijing massacre and,
  77–78, 79, 80–84; Cambodian invasion
  and, 174–177; FSX episode and, 60–61;
  Japanese relations and, 63, 64, 67;
  Korean policy, 141–143; Philippines
  bases issue and, 206–208

Cambodian issue: ASEAN and, 174–175,
  176, 182, 187, 188; China and, 174,
  182–186; economic reconstruction aid
  and, 189–190; Hun Sen government and,
  176, 184–186, 188, 192, 212; Japanese
  involvement in, 188–190; Khmer Rouge
  and, 174–175, 176; Paris Conference on,
  175, 176–177; Security Council settlement plan, 176–177; settlement of, 178,
  189; Sino-Soviet relations and, 111–112,
  182–183; Sino-Vietnamese relations and,
  30, 111, 182–186; Soviet involvement in,
  48, 192, 224–225; Soviet-ASEAN relations and, 224–225; Tokyo Declaration
  on, 189; UN involvement in, 174–179;
  U.S. approach to, 174–179, 183, 184,
  185, 192; U.S.-Vietnam relations and,
  177–178
Carter, Jimmy, 145; Chinese policy of, 76,
  82; Korean policy of, 140, 154
Chatichai, Choonhavan, 212, 223
Cheney, Richard, 62–63, 143
Chernomyrdin, Viktor, 131, 132
China: declining status and diplomatic isolation of, 29; domestic policies in, 30–32;
  establishment of PRC, 75; ethnic nationalism in, 29; and Thailand, cooperative
  relationship with, 212–213
Chinese foreign policy: China-U.S.-Japan tri-
  adic relationship in, 29–30; economic
  emphasis in, 30–31; good neighbor diplomacy in, 30; Indonesia and, 212, 213,
  217; military power and doctrines in, 31,
  32; multipolarity and economic
  dynamism in, 28; pragmatism in, 28, 29;
  regional and power groups' influence in,
  31–32; revolutionary phases in, 27–28;
  South China Sea issue in, 202, 214–218;
  Taiwan relations and, 29, 75, 76, 84,
  88–89, 152; Thailand and Indochina situation in, 212–213; "three worlds" doctrine in, 28. *See also* Korean-Sino relations; Sino-ASEAN relations;

ABOUT THE BOOK

A key region in contemporary international politics, Asia Pacific is a focus of interest for all of the major powers. This easily accessible book explores the regional roles and relationships of those powers in the 1990s and beyond.

McDougall first provides the context of various approaches to understanding international relations. Against this background, he considers the roles played in Asia Pacific by the United States, China, Japan, and Russia, illuminating both complex relationships and central issues. There are also chapters on the two Koreas, Indochina, and ASEAN. Although there is an emphasis on security concerns, ample attention is given to economics, domestic politics, and human rights.

A concluding chapter highlights the themes that serve as the basis of the book, further enhancing its usefulness for a range of courses.

Derek McDougall is senior lecturer in politics at the University of Melbourne. His most recent publications include *Studies in International Relations: The Asia-Pacific, the Nuclear Age, Australia* and *Soviet-American Relations Since the 1940s.*